SCOTLAND
the Movie

SCOTLAND
the Movie

■ ■ ■ ■ ■ ■ ■ ■ ■ ■

DAVID BRUCE

Polygon
Edinburgh

© David Bruce 1996

First published by
Polygon
22 George Square
Edinburgh

Designed and set in Sabon by Fionna Robson
Printed and bound in Great Britain by BPC Wheatons, Exeter

ISBN 07486 6209 X

A CIP record for this title is available

The Publisher acknowledges subsidy from

THE SCOTTISH ARTS COUNCIL

towards the publication of this title.

ILLUSTRATIONS

Every effort has been made to identify and acknowledge copyright material. Illustrations, including publicity stills, are credited to the appropriate company or agency in the captions. Film companies are also acknowledged at the end of the relevant section. Should there be any error, omission or misattribution the author and publishers apologise. All material has been included in good faith.

The sources of the illustrations are as follows:

Aberdeenshire Library and Information Service – page 240.

British Film Institute (Stills, Posters and Designs) – pages 14, 21, (top), 25, 37, 49, 58, 66, 95, 110, 115, 118, 134, 172, 201, 202, 203, 204, 213, 214, 218, (bottom), 226, 234, 235, 239.

Edinburgh Film Guild – pages 56, 71, 79, 111, 166, 169, 173, 180, 189, 190, 191, 220, 222, 223.

John Grierson Archive, University of Stirling – pages 43, 232 (top).

Post Office Film Unit – pages 32, 33.

Private Collections – pages 17, 23, 75, 77, 105, 130, 197, 216, 219, 243.

Royal Incorporation of Architects in Scotland – page 62.

Scottish Ethnological Archive (National Museums of Scotland) – page 182.

Scottish Film Council/Scottish Film Archive – frontispiece, pages 3, 8, 11, 12, 16 (top), 19, 21 (bottom), 26, 28, 29, 31, 35, 38, 46, 53, (top), 55, 60, 61, 63, 64, 68, 82, 85, 91, 100, 102, 103, 109, 113, 116, 121, 122, 123, 126, 129, 143, 144, 145, 146, 147, 148, 154, 156, 157, 158, 160, 161, 163, 165, 168, 170, 175, 176, 177, 181, 183, 185, 186, 188, 193, 194, 207, 209, 210, 218 (top), 221, 224, 227, 229, 230, 232 (bottom), 236, 238, 241, 245.

Scottish Film Production Fund – pages 69, 151, 153.

Scottish Screen Locations – pages 7, 16 (bottom), 88 (top), 120, 125, 128, 141, 198, 206.

Contents

Preface

This is a book about cinema and Scotland and the many points at which they coincide.

Since Scotland has tended to be regarded more as a film location and source of stories rather than as a film culture in its own right I have scanned the country place by place, where necessary going beyond its literal boundaries, for any signs of film activity, indigenous or imported, historical as well as contemporary.

This provides a loose framework within which the present state of affairs and the origins of individuals, trends and institutions are examined for evidence of whether film has ever been, or can be, a medium for genuine Scottish cultural expression, as opposed to merely something made elsewhere which we passively consume. Hard information is presented where it is available (with speculation to fill the gaps), and although there is much serious consideration of important issues there is also room for little-known facts and for some of the dafter aspects of our film history. The treatment reflects the fact that while it can be a very serious matter in cultural and economic terms for those directly involved, for most people film in Scotland is primarily for entertainment and enjoyment.

Structured as an informal gazetteer and companion to Scottish film, the book is a review of where we are, cinematically speaking, and where we are going in the medium whose first century has been celebrated in 1996.

David Bruce

(Please note that the dates attached to films are release dates, and not production dates.)

Acknowledgements

Scotland – The Movie could not have been written but for the help of a very large number of people and organisations. The book draws on personal and collective memory and on a wide range of documentary sources. The author is extremely grateful to the Scottish Film Council and the British Film Institute for making their extensive information resources freely available to him. In particular, data concerning feature films is largely drawn from the BFI's indispensable Film Index International on CD-Rom which proved to be a vital component in the exercise. Where a conflict of information occurred it is usually chosen as the authority. Other major sources are listed in the bibliography.

The Scottish Film Archive, and SFC's Information Service have been central to the entire exercise and it is to Janet McBain, Jamie Hall and their colleagues that most of the author's thanks are due for their patience in dealing with his endless queries. I must also thank particularly the present staff of all the Scottish film organisations and my former colleagues John Brown, Ronnie Macluskie, Graham Berry, Alan Knowles, Erika King, Kevin Cowle, Dan Macrae, and Kathleen Smith for all their encouragement and for prompting my fallible memory.

In the nature of the book it was necessary to consult very widely throughout the land and I am delighted to acknowledge the willing assistance of a very large number of local librarians and tourist officers from Shetland to the Borders.

Indeed, a great number of individuals acting in their personal or professional capacities in and around the film business have contributed to the book with information, help and encouragement. Naming them all would be impossible but I would particularly like to thank the following: Mike Alexander, Barbara Allan, Maxine Baker, Ian Bannen, Mark Cousins, Robin Clark, Robin and Trish Crichton, Eddie Dick, Ian Docherty, Douglas Eadie, Anne Fleming, Tom Fleming, Bill Forsyth, Charlie Gormley, Alex Gourlay, Lancelyn Green, Murray Grigor, Laurence Henson, Ken Ingles, Lesley Keen, Syd Kiman, Luke McKernan, Mark Maclachlan, Richard Ovenden, David Peat, Linda Pearson, Bruce Peter, Mary Picken, Jim Poole, Carolyn Rowlison, Michael Russell, Louise Scott, Tricia Shorthouse, Ronald Singleton, Kathleen Smith, Nigel Smith, Libby Stanner, Celia Stevenson, Wilf Stevenson, Ian Sutherland, Penny Thomson, David Whitton and Paul Young.

Finally, I gratefully acknowledge the enormous contributions of my editor, Glen Murray, my son, Andrew and my wife, Barbara, without whose input in time, energy, and enthusiasm there could have been no book.

PUBLISHER'S ACKNOWLEDGEMENTS
The Publishers would like to express their thanks to the Scottish Film Council for their assistance towards the costs of this book, and to the British Film Institute for providing the CD-Rom Film Index International as a principle source of film data.

Introduction

In the summer of 1959, and in the best traditions of student holiday jobs, I was working as a door-to-door encyclopaedia salesman in the Edinburgh suburb of Corstorphine. I was not having much success but had a growing awareness that most of the people who just might buy the package were the very ones least likely to be able to afford it. It was therefore a great relief to be contacted by Forsyth Hardy, Director of Films of Scotland, who had a different sort of proposition to offer.

Harry Dugan, an American film-maker, had arrived to make a travelogue of Scotland and needed an assistant to start immediately. The deal was that in return for being conducted to the 'best places' for showing off the country, he would pay £5 a week plus expenses and provide an introduction to the mysteries of film-making. For someone whose experience to date had been strictly amateur and self-taught, this seemed too good to be true.

Dugan had been a cameraman with Disney on the wildlife movies and clearly knew how to shoot pictures. His current kind of film-making, though, had its roots in the prehistory of cinema. It was, in effect, a moving magic lantern show. He would travel to an 'exotic' country, shoot a great deal of silent 16mm film, collect a few records of local music, return home, hire a big hall ('like Carnegie', he said) and then present the results with his own live commentary. Apparently there was a considerable market for this sort of thing, not least among the expatriate descendants of European tribes. He was not alone in this trade, as I found the following summer when a Canadian turned up to do exactly the same thing.

Harry Dugan had a clear idea of what he had come to Scotland to get in the can. He was not looking for surprises, though he got one or two, including Glasgow. 'Gee, if it ain't like downtown Pittsburgh!', he repeated, many times. What he did expect he told me right at the start, and there was one particular image he wanted me to lead him to straight away. It was of a thatched cottage with a heather-covered mountain behind it. Smoke was coming from the chimney; there were roses around the door. In front, there was a path with a little gate. In the garden was a dear old lady who could have been someone's long-lost grandmother.

I tried to tell him gently that although this was the kind of thing that Americans assumed was up every glen in Scotland, I personally had never seen one quite like that and that he shouldn't let his expectations be too high. There were, of course, lots of much more interesting things - the Edinburgh New Town for example or, even better, the Clyde shipyards which were much more dramatic and, besides, much truer to the Scotland of today. Unfortunately he didn't believe me and, for weeks, kept asking when I was going to show him the cottage.

The crunch came, almost literally, when we had just crossed from Skye at Kylerhea (after three cloudless days) and were driving out of Glenelg. Harry suddenly put all his weight on the brakes and slewed us into the ditch. Apart from the fact that the roof was corrugated iron, it was just as he had described it, even down to the dear old lady in the garden. His sense of triumph was difficult to live with for some time afterwards. As penance (because clearly I had been deliberately steering him away from such scenes all along and they were very common really), I had to appear in shot, walking up the path to be greeted by the old lady (who found it amusing and did indeed have relatives in the States). She pinned a rose on my jacket.

The whole expedition was a significant learning experience, at least for me. Apart from the important advance of being taught how to erect a tripod in a howling gale without losing fingers and acquiring the now long-redundant skills of reloading the 16mm Cine Kodak Special II, there were substantial and lasting lessons about place, country, representation, the moving image, the horrors of stereotyping and so on, but also a confirmation that Scotland and professional film-making were not totally incompatible. It was a conclusion which would, thankfully, be false now, but then almost invited contradiction. Even ten years later, a radio interviewer told me (on air) that his listeners would be surprised to learn there were professional film-makers based and working in Scotland.

■ ■ ■ ■ ■ ■ ■ ■ ■ ■ ■ ■

I suppose the first Scottish film my contemporaries and I saw (in the sense that it was based on a Scottish subject and was filmed in the right location) was *Whisky Galore!* (1949). Seen in Aberdeen, it was certainly very entertaining but did not relate closely to our juvenile experience of life. In fact, if anything, it confirmed our ignorant prejudices about the people who lived in the Western Isles, with their unintelligible language ('fit wey did they nae spik lik us?', as we would have said) and strange behaviour. On the other hand, there were in it actors we knew from the wireless, like Duncan Macrae and Jameson Clark. It was undeniably nearer home than the offerings of Norman Wisdom.

In the early 1950s Scotland was experiencing one of its periodic phases of being a favoured location for film-makers from London and beyond. But even then the dream of an indigenous feature film business was not new. Only a few years earlier, the attempt to set up Scottish National Film Studios had come to grief (see **Glasgow, St Vincent Street**). One of the great barriers to these ambitions had surely been psychological - the failure to believe that we had any entitlement to use the medium as a means for our own cultural expression. The other visual arts, literature, music and drama might all be legitimate vehicles for Scottish thought and experience but cinema was almost exclusively something to be imported and enjoyed, rarely if ever made here. Most of the world might, like us, be grateful consumers of the products of the American film industry but few countries or cultures other than Scotland would not have at least some domestic film production. To this day we are probably more familiar with the accents and landscapes of America than of much of our own country.

■ ■ ■ ■ ■ ■ ■ ■ ■ ■ ■ ■

Kemps Bioscope, Ayrshire c1906.

The winter and spring of 1995-96 was arguably the most dynamic period in one hundred years of Scottish film history. Certainly it was the most interesting from a public perspective. Cinema in Scotland had never been so newsworthy and, from the previous autumn, broadsheets, tabloids, radio and television carried more about film in Scotland - its production, its personalities, its successes, its ambitions, its prospects - than had appeared in most previous decades. It may also have been one of the most significant periods in terms of building for the future as new political enthusiasm for Scottish films led to the promise of new structures and new money to sustain them.

It was a time of unusual celebration. Following the award of an Oscar for Peter Capaldi's brilliant short film *Franz Kafka's It's a Wonderful Life* in 1995 two major films with a greater or lesser degree of Scottish input but both on Scottish subjects (*Braveheart* and *Rob Roy*) and two Scots (the composer Patrick Doyle and the cinematographer Michael Coulter, both for *Sense and Sensibility*) were on the list of Oscar nominees for 1996. In the event, *Braveheart* was the one that made it, winning five awards. There was rejoicing also that a very different portrayal of Scotland, the shockingly contemporary *Trainspotting*, was breaking box-office records throughout the UK with the prospect that another film from our recent history, *Small Faces*, set in sixties gangland Glasgow, would also do very well. There were others coming through, such as David Hayman's *The Near Room*, and *The Bruce*, Cromwell Films' follow-up to *Chasing the Deer*.

Opening of the 'Gothenburg Picturedrome', Cardenden, Fife, 1910.

Films shot in Scotland in the previous two years and now about to reach exhibition included *Loch Ness* and *Mary Reilly*. Location shooting by overseas companies in 1995, such as the Danish movie *Breaking the Waves* by Lars von Trier, had been at a record level and Scotland would be appearing on screen in its own right, or doubling for somewhere else, all over the world. (Someone said that had there been an 1996 Oscar for 'best supporting country' Scotland would have won.)

Moreover, there had been announcements of funding from the new National Lottery for several Scottish feature films including a new version of Neil Gunn's *The Silver Darlings* and John Byrne's *The Slab Boys*, both coming into production. Alasdair Gray's extraordinary story *Poor Things* was also in development and Ken Loach's *Carla's Song* had been shot partly in Glasgow with the actor Robert Carlyle in a principal role.

On the political front, The Scottish Office had never been so active in support of film. In April, the Secretary of State announced the replacement of the existing structure (see **Glasgow, Dowanhill**) by a new agency, Scottish Screen, which would promote and develop all aspects of film in Scotland, particularly the commercial ones. More money and a feasibility study into the prospects for creating a studio complex were promised.

Deliberately and otherwise, all of this happened to coincide with the Centenary of Cinema which, as far as Scotland was concerned, was marked by a celebration in the Edinburgh Festival Theatre on 13 April 1996, one hundred years to the day since moving pictures had first been seen in this country on that very site. The unaccustomed amount of activity, the productions, the audiences, the political movement and the general enthusiasm was very encouraging. The hope of sufficient critical mass and momentum to sustain a modest but viable domestic film industry sustained partly by work from abroad was stronger than it had ever been.

■ ■ ■ ■ ■ ■ ■ ■ ■ ■ ■ ■

There was, however, room for doubt. Indeed there had always been doubt about what sort of film should be made in Scotland, even long before there was really sufficient of it to supply the raw material for proper debate. At least now with the arrival of serious film-making in greater quantity there was something for the critics and academics to get their teeth into. The speculation about trends and aspirations could become less abstract. Moreover, quantity, though not an end in itself by any means, did greatly improve the odds on there being more than the occasional popular or critical success.

Hugh MacDiarmid once wrote that it would not have suited his book at all to be faultless. 'My job, as I see it, has never been to lay a tit's egg, but to erupt like a volcano, emitting not only flame, but a lot of rubbish.' It was a vivid metaphor for his function as a poet but could apply equally to the film industry, particularly Hollywood. Though there is nothing to be gained from accepting low production values there is a virtue in quantity if it creates the critical mass necessary to a sustainable industry in Scotland. One of the difficulties about considering 'quantity' with respect to film in Scotland, is that over the years almost all film made here has been at the behest of producers from outside the country. Even at new levels of production this will inevitably remain the case. In the worst outcome, the new situation might make the growth of commercial film such a priority, to the detriment of cultural values, that we could really be no better off in furthering indigenous film-making. It will not be an easy balance to achieve.

As to quality, assessing the general performance of Scottish film in its fragmented history is not easy. In fact, the story of film in Scotland has not been particularly well served in print. Prior to this book, only one other, *Scotland in Film* by Forsyth Hardy, published in 1990, had given broad coverage to the topic, largely on the basis of Hardy's own very important contribution to the development of the medium in this country (see **Edinburgh, Randolph Crescent**). It was not devoted to film criticism (nor is this one) and for a closer scrutiny of the issues one had to turn to two important collections of essays, *Scotch Reels* (1982) edited by Colin McArthur, and *From Limelight to Satellite* (1990) edited by Eddie Dick.

Scotch Reels was published in conjunction with a conference, an exhibition and a film, all entitled *Scotch Myths* (1982). The focus of all these was on the damaging influence of the corrupted heritage of Scotland, particularly as manifested in 'tartanry' and 'The Kailyard', on the way Scotland was portrayed in film. It was a striking message, engagingly presented, and although the Scottish film-makers of the time found it largely irrelevant to their concerns as they argued for resources to get any kind of film made at all, it was easily the most coherent attempt to stimulate debate about film in Scotland.

Indeed it has been very largely due to the persistence of the critic Colin McArthur that there has been debate, at least in the academic community and among those with an interested concern for Scottish moving image culture, and that lines of argument concerning the representation of Scotland by stereotypical images and behaviour whether 'tartan', 'kailyard', or 'hard-man Clydesidism' have been developed. In the last few years. McArthur has argued for a concentration of resources on developing exclusively low-budget indigenous film-making in Scotland, contrasting that strategy with what he perceives to be a misguided and futile ambition on the part of the Scottish film agencies to create 'Hollywood' in Scotland, complete with studios and money to match.

In fact, the polarity of the arguments is stimulating but unnecessary since the idea that anything as volatile as the film business can be constrained by logic is false. Global issues, fashion (as Hollywood's recent affection for Scotland demonstrates), domestic politics, talent, personal ambition and luck or the lack of it will determine the course of film in Scotland. The best we can ask is that the authorities ensure the infrastructure is built, the resources are adequate and the training excellent, opportunities are provided for young film makers' work to be seen, and that the system is flexible enough to deal with developments, including new technology, as they occur.

As a greater number of films are made in Scotland, there will certainly be more bad ones and, hopefully, more good ones as well. At least we will not have to invest all our expectations in (or vent our frustration on) a handful of films with Scottish connections over a twenty year period. The goal of 'critical mass' - an output of film production which enables year-round continuity of employment in high grade film making in Scotland will be very difficult to achieve - but other small countries have done it.

Paradoxically, the factor which along with talent and money makes up the trinity of cinema, namely the audience, tends to be left out of these debates. Ultimately, the question of what sort of Scottish cinema there can be will depend to a large extent on what people want to see. At present they seem keen to watch very different representations of our past and present lives; *Braveheart* and *Trainspotting* make a remarkable pair but of course they may not have exactly the same audience. The versions of late twentieth century Scotland offered by *Small Faces* and *Loch Ness* are not mutually exclusive and a sensibility that enjoys *Shallow Grave* is not debarred from appreciating anything else.

As audience numbers increased from a UK figure of 54 million attendances in 1984 to 123 million ten years later, the Scottish component was less than nine per cent of these totals, not in line with the tradition that Scots were the most avid filmgoers in Britain. On the other hand, there was a remarkable increase between 1991 and 1994 in the number of Scots who went to the cinema at least once a year (from 57 to 73 per cent). With a greater variety of Scottish films available, therefore, the possibility must be that cinema can be more closely related to our own cultural experience than previously. There will, of course, be much to suffer as well as enjoy; Hollywood (and London) will

Braveheart (1995, Twentieth Century Fox). Mel Gibson.

never get the accents right and we will undoubtedly have to sit through quaintness and toe-curling sentiment of the sort that is strangely thought of as our birthright, but so long as we can also have the chance to make our own pictures and recognise them as legitimate expressions of our experience and dreams we should not complain too much.

The hope arising from the centenary of cinema is for such a growth in indigenous film-making that in the coming century significant films based on our own culture and made by Scots in Scotland will appear to be the norm rather than the exception. Then, albeit rather late in the day, we will have acquired the medium and made it our own.

Heart of Midlothian (1914).

ABBOTSFORD:
Scotland according to Scott

As a place to start looking for 'Scotland – the Movie', Abbotsford, Sir Walter Scott's home in the heart of the Borders, has much to recommend it. It immediately confronts us with the major reason why Scotland has become a favoured location for romantic historical drama - not only on the screen. The degree to which Scott (1771-1832) shaped the perception of Scotland as a nation, heroic and quaint, is extraordinary. 'Scotland the brand-image' is as recognisable as anything on the planet but while the tourist boards and the exporters and exploiters celebrate, there are plenty of others who see the negative side. Edwin Muir's description of Scott as 'a sham bard of a sham nation' represents one of the more extreme judgements. However, it is safe to say that Scott's influence was such that even today it is impossible to avoid looking over our shoulder at him almost every time a retrospective picture of Scotland is presented, whatever the medium.

To be fair to Scott, the real sentimentalising and trivialising of Scotland was inflicted by his successors (see **The Kailyard**), but he undoubtedly provided the raw material for those who found it convenient and profitable to depict Scots and Scotland in ways that became staple on the cinema screen. Perhaps the real offence is in the way in which we ourselves became party to the process of detaching from reality when it suited us.

Just as important as Scott's effect on our view of Scotland is the monumental success he had in conveying his idea of Scotland abroad (which in turn provided validation for our own perceptions). For example, his works form the basis of over sixty operas, all of them written in the nineteenth century (mostly in the first half) and the majority in Italian. Ironically, one of the last was *Jeannie Deans* (1894) by Hamish MacCunn, one of the few Scottish composers to engage with the great man's works.

Scott's popularity had declined by the time cinema arrived but by then his version of Scotland (and corruptions of it by others) was so embedded in European and, indeed, World perception of the country that inevitably film-makers used it as their point of departure when dealing with Scottish subjects. So any film about Rob Roy (see **Aberfoyle**) was bound to owe something to the man who 'discovered' the 'Highland Rogue' whether or not the script has anything to do with Scott's novel

Ironically, most films which derive from Scott's own works draw on his English rather than his Scottish romances. *Ivanhoe* is the most popular, beginning with a version in 1913 directed by Herbert Brenon. The most famous version, achieving a nomination for Best Picture at the American Academy of Motion Pictures Arts and Sciences Awards, the 'Oscars', was the 1952 production directed by Richard Thorpe and starring Robert Taylor, Joan Fontaine and Elizabeth Taylor. (There was also an *Ivanhoe* in 1982, directed by Douglas Camfield, with James Mason, Anthony Andrews and Olivia Hussey.) Richard Thorpe again directed Robert Taylor, this time with Kay Kendall, in *Quentin Durward* in 1955.

La Rivincita d'Ivanhoe [The Revenge of Ivanhoe] (1965) was an Italian epic directed by Amerigo Anton and starring Rik van Nutter. *Young Ivanhoe* (1995), directed by R.L. Thomas, had Stacy Keach, Margot Kidder and Nick Mancuso as principals.

The first Scott story in cinema appears to have been made in America. In 1908, Vitagraph produced *The Bride of Lammermoor*, directed by J Stuart Blackton and starring Anette Kellerman and Maurice Costello. There was a *Lady of the Lake* from Vitagraph in 1912, a *Heart of Midlothian* from Hepworth in 1914, a *Lochinvar* from Gaumont in 1915 and a *Young Lochinvar* also during the silent era. This last was made in 1923 by the Stoll Film Company and was directed by W P Kellino with Owen Nares in the title role.

There appear to have been relatively few movies based on Scott's actual texts. Indeed, since the silent era, in these terms he is completely out-filmed by other Scottish authors, particularly R L Stevenson. Perhaps most of his work is now too clearly identified with set books at school. However rich and wide his output and however romantic his adventure stories, his appeal to contemporary movie-makers is relatively limited.

Films about Scott himself include *The Practical Romantic* (1969), directed by Hans Nieter for the Films of Scotland Committee and *The Caledonian Account* (1975) an imaginative short by Douglas Eadie and Brian Crumlish depicting a dialogue between Scott and his contemporary Thomas Telford sailing through the latter's great Caledonian Canal (see **Loch Ness**).

Scott was also the subject of one of the more significant 'missing' items in Scottish film history. Now lost without trace, *The Life of Sir Walter Scott* (1926) was produced by a company called the 'Scottish Film Academy' and directed by Maurice Sandground. In 1928 it was re-released, coupled with a companion piece on Robert Burns, under the title *The Immortals of Bonnie Scotland*.

● *Ivanhoe*
GB, 1952, MGM, 106 mins. Directed by Richard Thorpe. Written by Noel Langley and Aeneas Mackenzie from the novel by Sir Walter Scott. With Robert Taylor, Joan Fontaine, Elizabeth Taylor, Emlyn Williams, George Sanders, Robert Douglas, Felix Aylmer and Finlay Currie.

ABERDEEN

Cinema arrived in Britain in February 1896 with the first public performances presented by the Lumière Brothers in Regent Street in London. Among those attending these historic events were an Aberdeen bookseller and magic lanternist called William Walker and his chief technician, Paul Robello. Walker, who was already a successful showman sending teams of lanternists throughout Scotland, recognised at once the potential of the new medium and within a few months had acquired equipment from Robert Paul and J Wrench & Son to become a cinematographer in his own right.

On 16 October 1896 Walker presented his first performance of moving pictures in Marr Wood's Music Saloon at 183 Union Street, Aberdeen. Thereafter he and his colleagues toured extensively showing short films imported from the south as well as material shot by themselves. They also developed a profitable line in 'multimedia' presentations of song, recitation, lantern slides and 'moving photographs' under such titles as *A Nicht Wi' Burns*.

Walker's main fame, however, stems from his royal connection. By October 1897, he had been invited to give a presentation at Balmoral Castle and there were no fewer than eleven such screenings during the final few years of Queen Victoria's reign. More valuable, from posterity's point of view, was the fact that he was allowed to film Her Majesty on more than one occasion. His fragmentary shots of the Queen in the dog-cart at Balmoral are among the most famous early cinema images. Walker's reward was to be permitted to call his company 'Walker's Royal Cinematograph'. In 1899, Walker produced equally enduring images when he filmed the Gordon Highlanders marching along Union Terrace as they left for the Boer War.

Throughout the twentieth century, film exhibition continued to be very strong in Aberdeen. It was said at one time that Aberdeen had more cinemas in relation to population than anywhere else in Britain. In

Gordon Highlanders (1899).
Leaving Aberdeen for the Boer War.

the Capitol, opened on February 4, 1933, the city retains one of those rare classic cinemas that has kept its physical integrity and ambience while all around have been multi-plexing and compromising in an effort to stay afloat. True, the Capitol is no longer a full time cinema, but it does still very occasionally revert to its original function with great effect.

Although it was the ultimate destination of *Night Mail*, the famous Grierson documentary of 1936, provided the home port for Harry Watt's important *North Sea* (1938) about ship-to-shore radio, and has had its quota of tourist films, Aberdeen seems to have been rather under-represented on the big screen. It was also the end of the line in another *Night Mail* (1935), the not-so-famous feature by Herbert Smith about a musician with murderous intent. Television has used the city successfully for contemporary drama in, for instance, BBC's *Roughnecks*, but so far cinema has not capitalised on Aberdeen's possibilities.

However, *Ties* (1994), was made in Aberdeen by Steven Simpson (born 1970), a young Aberdonian who trained at the Concorde Studios in Los Angeles with Roger Corman. The film tells of the search by a student to find his natural parents when his adopted parents die in a car crash. Simpson received support for this enterprise from Aberdeen-based Grampian Television which itself partly grew from cinema. The consortium which won the North of Scotland franchise in 1960 was led by Caledonian Associated Cinemas whose Chairman, Sir Alexander B King, became the first Chairman of the television company. Sir Alex was also Chairman of the Films of Scotland Committee (see **Edinburgh, Randolph Crescent**).

Grampian Television went on air on September 30, 1961. In recent years, the

The Capitol Cinema, Aberdeen in the 1930s.

station has supported at least three other films with cinema aspirations - *Play Me Something* (1989, see **Barra**), *Blue Black Permanent* (1992, see **Orkney**) and *Trawler* (1994).

The impact of the oil industry, not just on Aberdeen but on the country as a whole and not just commercially but on the fabric of society, was the subject of 7:84 Theatre Company's celebrated work ('play' seems an inadequate description) *The Cheviot, the Stag, and the Black, Black Oil*, by John McGrath, which was released as a film in 1974.

Two Aberdeen singers of different eras and disciplines have had interesting movie connections. The great soprano, Mary Garden, appeared in a film version of *Thais* (1917). Although this was a silent film, she had sung the role in the opera version by Massenet. A year later, she starred in *The Splendid Sinner* (1918), a wartime melodrama of operatic proportions in which the heroine goes to France to join the Red Cross when her husband discovers her dishonourable past. There, she falls into the hands of her previous (German) lover and chooses to die by firing squad rather than to submit to his will. Garden was herself portrayed as a character (played by Mabel Albertson) in *So This is Love* (1953).

Annie Lennox (born 1955), best known as the Eurythmics' lead singer, has also appeared on the big screen, in *Revolution* (1985) directed by Hugh Hudson, and *Edward II* (1991) directed by Derek Jarman.

● *The Cheviot, the Stag, and the Black, Black Oil*

GB, 1974, 7:84, 123 mins. Directed by John Mackenzie. Produced by Graeme McDonald. From the play by John McGrath. With John Bett, David Maclennan, Dolina Maclellan, Elizabeth Maclennan, Alex Norton, Bill Paterson, Timothy Martin, Allan Ross John Byrne, John McGrath, Charles Kearney and James Cosmo.

● *Ties*

GB, 1994, INYO, 80 mins. Directed, produced and written by Steven Simpson. With Steven Duffy, Iain Agnew, Amber Murray, Sheena Dixon, Anita Gailey and Annie Ingles.

ABERFELDY: Donald Crisp

The picturesque town on the River Tay is a gift to the movie camera. Aberfeldy has made an interesting appearance in at least one historic documentary. *Freedom of Aberfeldy* (1943) was given cinema distribution as a supporting short. It was about a scheme under which troops from the Dominions spent a week with local families. In this case three young men from the Antipodes enjoyed the hospitality of the good people of Aberfeldy. The film was made by Campbell Harper of Edinburgh (see **Edinburgh, Hill Street**), directed by Alan Harper, photographed by Henry Cooper and with commentary spoken by James Mackechnie. A copy was found in the former Birks Cinema during the 1980s.

However Aberfeldy's major claim to movie fame must be as the birthplace of Donald Crisp (1880 - 1974) whose long life and career are in themselves a chronicle of the Hollywood movie. His exact origins are not clear but with the unlikely background of Eton and Oxford and service in the Boer War (in which he was wounded), Crisp found his way to America and into the movies (via theatre) where he worked in some four hundred films as an actor and director.

One of the most striking aspects of his early days in Hollywood was the company he kept. He was close to Douglas Fairbanks, for instance, and he was one of those who claimed to have given Chaplin his first break in movies (though it has to be said that he was not alone in that). His most important association, however, was with D W Griffith. He appeared as General Grant in Griffith's *Birth of a Nation* (1915) and as Lillian Gish's father in *Broken Blossoms* (1919), also for Griffith, as well as being an Assistant Director on both. When it came to battle scenes, Crisp, as a survivor of the Boer War, was well qualified to direct and his talent for handling the big scenes was put to good use by Griffith.

In 1924, Crisp co-directed a very different kind of action in *The Navigator* with Buster Keaton. According to Keaton, as recorded in Kevin Brownlow's definitive account of the silent era, *The Parade's Gone By*, the collaboration with Crisp was not entirely uneventful. Hired to ensure that the dramatic sequences were efficiently directed, Crisp turned out to be far more interested in the comedy aspect and pestered Keaton with ideas for more gags and stunts than the star could handle. 'He came to work in the morning with the goddamnedest gags you ever heard of in your life. Wild!' Keaton 'let him go'.

Crisp's directorial career continued successfully until the end of the silent era, interrupted only by what seems to have been secret intelligence work during the First World War. For whatever reason – the complexity of the new sound equipment, or perhaps more likely studio politics – he gave up directing and from that point on, that is to say for more than the next thirty years, he reverted to his original trade as an actor.

In the latter part of his life Crisp's credits are remarkable not only because they can be numbered by the score, but for several outstanding appearances including the 1935 version of *Mutiny on the Bounty* (directed by a fellow Scot, Frank Lloyd, and starring Charles Laughton). In 1941, Crisp won the Oscar for Best Supporting Actor for his portrayal of the father in John Ford's *How Green Was My Valley*. In 1955, he appeared, again in a 'senior' role, in *The Man from Laramie* directed by Anthony Mann. Not all his screen appearances were as distinguished as these or as *Broken Blossoms* (which some would argue his was his best performance), but they certainly cover a tremendous range. A number have Scottish connections: for instance, *The Bonnie Briar Bush* (1921), *The Little Minister* (1934), *What Every Woman Knows* (1934), *Mary of Scotland* (1936), *Challenge to Lassie* (1949), and *Greyfriars Bobby* (1961) (see **Edinburgh, Greyfriar's Churchyard**).

There are plenty of sentimental pictures on Crisp's filmography, including the dog-centred ones and films like *Pollyanna* (1960), but these are offset by dozens of action pictures with titles like

Johnny Get Your Gun (1919), *The Barbarian* (1921), *The Black Pirate* (1926), *Stand and Deliver* (1927), *The Viking* (1928 – in which Crisp played Leif Erikson), *Red Dust* (1932), *The Oklahoma Kid* (1939) and *The Sea Hawk* (1940).

Crisp's screen persona was very much that of the patriarch. Indeed he seems to have spent a large part of his career playing someone's father. His roles were seldom leading ones; he was mostly to be found in key supporting parts where an upright military bearing and a Scottish accent were assets.

Off-screen, Crisp was a very important figure in the development of the film industry. For many years he was Chairman of the Bank of America's Committee on Finance for the Film Industry, in which capacity he oversaw the investment of hundreds of millions of dollars in Hollywood.

Broken Blossoms (1919). Donald Crisp as 'Battling Burrows' with Lillian Gish as his daughter.

ABERFOYLE: Rob Roy

Sir Walter Scott (see **Abbotsford**) is generally credited with the 'discovery' of Rob Roy and the transformation of the awkward rebel into a folk-hero. The Clachan at Aberfoyle provided the setting for one of the key scenes in the novel and Scott's depiction of the Trossachs area was central to the development of tourism in Scotland.

In representing Rob Roy as a daring rascal who defended his clan to the last drop of blood, Scott opened a seam of drama for cinema. At least five significant productions bear the title *Rob Roy*. Easily the most important of these, in terms of the progress of Scottish film history, was the most recent (1995). Conceived by its Scottish producer, Peter Broughan, developed with assistance from the Scottish Film Production Fund, with a Scottish director of international standing, Michael Caton-Jones, and a screenplay by another Scot with an excellent Hollywood pedigree, Alan Sharp, *Rob Roy* was unique in several respects. Despite being financed by Hollywood it was essentially a home-grown product, the first ever multi-million dollar film on a Scottish subject originated and actually shot in Scotland. Most countries would regard such a proposition as commonplace. Who but ourselves should tell our own stories? For the Scots, this was something unprecedented and remarkable.

To be sure, the two principal players (Liam Neeson and Jessica Lange) were not Scots, but given the international aspirations of the film, that discrepancy did not seem particularly offensive. What is more, the film was, by any standards, a success. It even attracted an Oscar nomination, for Tim Roth as Best Supporting Actor. It presented a credible, albeit somewhat romantic, version of an episode in our history and was certainly a representation of Scotland with which most Scots could identify without embarrassment. An unusual phenomenon in itself.

It may be overstating the case to suggest that *Rob Roy* marked a turning point for film in Scotland and the way our country and

heritage were represented on the cinema screen. Such a judgement must await the perspective of many more years. But by demonstrating what could be done, given the necessary determination, it became a landmark in Scottish film-making at least as significant as that which Bill Forsyth created when *Gregory's Girl* astonished us by proving that domestic, teenage, comedy from Cumbernauld could, if done well enough, pull in large audiences around the world.

Earlier films about Rob Roy, not all as distinguished, included a 1911 version – the first Scottish three-reeler – starring John Clyde who had made the part on stage very much his own, and whose sons, Andy and David (see **Helensburgh**), achieved considerable success in Hollywood. In 1913 there was an American three-reeler *Rob Roy* and in 1922 Gaumont made a version with David Hawthorne as the hero and P Kellino directing.

Walt Disney's first Scottish foray was *Rob Roy – The Highland Rogue* (1953). This was a tale at some remove from Scott and from history but it was popular enough to encourage Disney to return to Scotland on more than one occasion. With Richard Todd (who, like Liam Neeson, the 1995 'Rob', was born in Ireland) and Glynis Johns as the main protagonists it was hardly likely to reek of authenticity but there were honourable efforts by James Robertson Justice as the Duke of Montrose, Finlay Currie as Hamish MacPherson, Jean Taylor Smith as Lady Glengyll, and Archie Duncan as Dugal MacGregor. Otherwise it was very much Rob Roy versus the Redcoats. Cedric Thorpe Davie (see **St Andrews**) wrote the music.

● *Rob Roy*
GB, 1911, United Films, 25 mins. Directed by Arthur Vivian. From the novel by Sir Walter Scott. With John Clyde, Theo Henries and Durward Lely.

● *Rob Roy - The Highland Rogue*
GB, 1953, Walt Disney Productions, 81 mins. Directed by Harold French. Produced by Perce

Rob Roy (from top left, clockwise) John Clyde (1919), Richard Todd (1953, Disney), Liam Neeson, with Jessica Lange, (1995, Talisman/United Artists).

Peirce. With Richard Todd, Glynis Johns, James Robertson Justice, Michael Gough, Finlay Currie, Jean Taylor Smith, Geoffrey Keen, Archie Duncan and Marjorie Fielding.

✓ ● *Rob Roy*
US, 1995, Talisman/United Artists, 139 mins. Directed by Michael Caton-Jones. Produced by Richard Jackson and Peter Broughan. Screenplay by Alan Sharp. With Liam Neeson, Jessica Lange, John Hurt, Tim Roth, Eric Stoltz, Andrew Keir, Brian Cox, Brian McCardie, Gilbert Martin and Vicki Masson.

AIRDRIE: Ian Bannen

Ian Bannen, one of Scotland's most distinguished actors was born in Airdrie on June 29, 1928. In addition to a very successful stage career, including *Hamlet* for The Royal Shakespeare Company in 1961, he has appeared in over forty film and television productions from *Private's Progress* in 1956 to *Braveheart* in 1995.

Bannen's credits include parts in a very wide range of films and he has shared the screen with many of the great names in the movie business. His filmography includes a Western, *Bite the Bullet* (1975); films made in Italy, including, *Il Viaggio* [The Voyage] (1973), directed by Vittorio de Sica, with Sophia Loren and Richard Burton; two films with Sean Connery, *The Hill* (1965) and *The Offence* (1972); light romantic comedy as the young king in *Carlton-Browne of the F.O.* (1987); and as Macduff in a 1960 version of *Macbeth*.

Other appearances include parts in *The Sailor from Gibraltar* (1967), *Dr Jekyll and Mr Hyde* (1980), *Gandhi* (1982), *Gorky Park* (1983), *Hope and Glory* (1987), *Damage* (1992), and as the leprous father of Robert the Bruce in *Braveheart* (1995). Inevitably, few of his roles have been played near to home with the exception of his appearance in *The Big Man* (1990) (see **Riddrie**) and, of course, his performance as Dr Cameron in the second television series based on A J Cronin's stories of *Dr. Finlay*.

Ian Bannen

Ian Bannen is one of those excellent actors who specialise in key supporting roles. It was for such a part in *The Flight of the Phoenix* (1965) that he received an Oscar nomination. In 1995 he was awarded the BAFTA Scotland Award for Lifetime Achievement.

ALLOWAY: The Bard

As Grierson said (quoted in Forsyth Hardy's *Scotland in Film*):

'The sad thing about Burns in Scotland is that so many have had a go at him and few have ever been greatly pleased with the result. Partly it is because nothing can ever quite come up to scratch when you are dealing with a national myth. Partly it is because Burns is at root a controversial figure'.

Grierson is certainly right that there is little evidence of success in the attempts to put the poet on film. In fact, perhaps surprisingly, there have been fewer of these than he suggests.

The first, *The Life of Robert Burns* was in 1926, directed by Maurice Sandground for the Scottish Film Academy. Two years later it was reissued with *The Life of Sir Walter Scott* under the joint title, *The Immortals of Bonnie Scotland.* Unfortunately, no copy of either survives. In 1930, another film biography, *The Loves of Robert Burns*, was made but by now sound had arrived and the film seems largely to have been a vehicle for the distinguished Scottish tenor, Joseph Hislop. *Auld Lang Syne* (1937) featured Andrew Cruikshank (famous, much later, as Dr Cameron, colleague of Dr Finlay). It, too, has vanished without trace. Ten years later and described as a musical, *Comin' Thro the Rye* starred Terence Alexander as the bard.

Documentaries about Burns are easier to identify. One in particular was highly regarded in its day. *The Land of Robert Burns* (1956) was one of a number of films overseen by Edgar Anstey for British Transport Films, the direct successor to the public documentary agencies of the 1930s and 1940s. The film had the virtue that it was produced by Stewart McAllister and directed by Joe Mendoza from a script by Maurice Lindsay. The music was directed by Cedric Thorpe Davie and the sound recorded by Ken Cameron. There was, therefore, substantial input from several people who understood the subject, a comparative rarity in films about Burns.

Another widely admired short film was *Tree of Liberty* (1987), devised and directed by Timothy Neat, which explored the work of the bed-ridden composer Serge Hovey who, with the help of the singer Jean Redpath, rescored Burns' songs using the original melodies. Animators have tackled 'Tam O'Shanter' from time to time but in the nature of Burns' work there are few opportunities to develop the sort of narrative best suited to film.

Among those rumoured to have unfulfilled Burns projects in mind were Gene Kelly and Bing Crosby. However, there was a much greater loss in that Bill Douglas's (see **Newcraighall**) ambition to make a Burns film was thwarted by his early death.

In the run-up to the 1996 celebrations of the bicentenary of Burns' death, an attempt was also made by David Hayman to raise the money for a major feature film on the poet. Sadly, that attempt had not met with success by the due date. Hayman (determined to persist) cited 'lack of courage' on the part of potential funders, perhaps reflecting not only the usual difficulties in obtaining money for film in a small country but something of the ambivalence felt by the nation about its bard.

● *The Loves of Robert Burns*
GB, 1930, British and Dominions Film Corporation, 96 mins. Directed by Herbert Wilcox. With Joseph Hislop, Eve Gray, Dorothy Seacombe and Jean Cadell.

● *Comin' Thro' The Rye*
GB, 1947, Advance Films, 56 mins. Directed by Walter C Mycroft. Based on a scenario by Gilbert McAllister. With Terence Alexander, Molly Weir and Olivia Barley.

APPIN: *Kidnapped*

The especially beautiful corner of Argyll between Connel and Ballachulish was the scene of 'The Appin Murder', the historical basis of the otherwise fictional adventure that is R L Stevenson's *Kidnapped*. Arguably the best Scottish adventure tale ever written, and one of the finest yarns by any standard, it is a pity that there has yet to be a film of it made by Scots (although in fact just such a project was being seriously pursued in 1996).

Most big screen versions to date have been American, beginning with the 1917 production for Edison. The 1938 edition cast Warner Baxter and Freddie Bartholomew in what seems to have been a travesty of the original story with adventure largely replaced by spurious love interest. Ten years later, William

Kidnapped (1960, Disney).
James MacArthur and Peter Finch in Appin.

Beaudine directed a now forgotten production with Roddy McDowall and Daniel O'Herlihy.

The most memorable *Kidnapped* was probably the one from Disney in 1960. Disney, whose Scottish ventures, including *Rob Roy* (1953) and *Greyfriars Bobby* (1961), were usually box office successes, was reasonably faithful to the original. At least the choice of cast and locations signalled good intent. The director was Robert Stevenson and Peter Finch was Alan Breck Stuart with the American juvenile lead, James MacArthur, as David Balfour. Among the Scots were John Laurie as Ebenezer Balfour, Finlay Currie as

Cluny MacPherson, with Duncan Macrae and several other well known faces in smaller roles.

Possibly the most memorable aspect of Delbert Mann's 1971 production of *Kidnapped* was the agreeable but incongruous performance by Michael Caine as Alan Breck Stuart. Trevor Howard, Lawrence Douglas, Jack Hawkins, Donald Pleasence and Freddie Jones took part. Gordon Jackson and Vivien Heilbron were among the token Scots.

Kidnapped has also enjoyed several television realisations in this country and abroad, for example the Tele-München production of 1978 which had a mixed-nationality cast headed by David McCallum and including Patrick Magee and Bill Simpson.

✓ The exterior of Appin's most famous landmark, Castle Stalker, had the distinction of providing the setting for the climax of *Monty Python and the Holy Grail* (1975).

✓ ● *Kidnapped*
US, 1960, Walt Disney Productions, 95 mins. Directed and written by Robert Stevenson, from the novel by Robert Louis Stevenson. Music by Cedric Thorpe Davie, directed by Muir Mathieson. With Peter Finch, James MacArthur, Bernard Lee, John Laurie, Finlay Currie, Peter O'Toole, Miles Malleson, Duncan Macrae, Andrew Cruikshank, Alex MacKenzie, Eileen Way and Abe Barker.

✔ ● *Kidnapped (David and Catriona)*
GB, 1971, Omnibus Productions, 107 mins. Directed by Delbert Mann. Written by Jack Pulman from the novels by Robert Louis Stevenson. With Michael Caine, Trevor Howard, Jack Hawkins, Donald Pleasance, Gordon Jackson, Vivien Heilbron, Lawrence Douglas, Freddie Jones, and Eric Woodburn.

APPLECROSS: *Laxdale Hall*

The remote peninsula opposite Raasay and Skye, for many years only accessible by sea or by the hazardous road over the Bealach na Ba, served as the location for two very different films separated by almost thirty years.

Laxdale Hall (1953), known in the USA as *Scotch on the Rocks*, was based on the novel by Eric Linklater. It was directed by John Eldridge (see **Edinburgh, Waverley Steps**) and was produced by John Grierson's 'Group 3'. It presented the classic confrontation between the British Establishment and wily natives, in this case represented respectively by a visiting parliamentary delegation and a band of local worthies refusing to pay their road fund licences on the reasonable grounds that they did not have a road. The basic situation was enlivened by the intervention of poachers from Glasgow and the staging of a local play. It was a genuinely funny film.

By contrast, *Ill Fares the Land* (1982), substituted Applecross for the island of St Kilda (see **St Kilda**) in the story of the evacuation of that severely isolated community in 1930. In Bill Bryden's moving film there was nothing quaintly engaging, only the realities of a community facing individual and collective death whose only hope lay in leaving their home. The conflict between the generations – the old wanting to stay, the young wanting to go – and the inevitable overlay of nostalgia for times that could not possibly have been better, but which somehow seemed so, made for a fascinating work. Great attention was given to detail and much use made of archive film of St Kilda, but there was an echo of the common complaint that films made in Scotland are too often filled with non-Scottish actors when *Ill Fares the Land* was criticised because the cast was not Hebridean enough.

The subject of the evacuation of St. Kilda was also tackled in one of the outstanding pre-war films, Michael Powell's *The Edge of the World* (1937), which also had to be relocated and was filmed on the Shetland island of Foula (see **Foula**).

● *Laxdale Hall*
GB, 1953, Group 3, 77 mins. Directed by John Eldridge. Produced by John Grierson. From the novel by Eric Linklater. With Ronald Squire, Kathleen Ryan, Raymond Huntley, Sebastian Shaw, Fulton Mackay, Jean Colin, Jameson Clark, Prunella Scales, Andrew Keir and Roddy MacMillan.

● *Ill Fares the Land*
GB, 1982, Portman Films for Scottish and Global TV Enterprises, and Channel Four, 102 mins. Written and directed by Bill Bryden. Produced by Robert Love. With Joseph Brady, James Copeland, JG Devlin, Morag Hood, Robert Stevens, Fulton Mackay and David Hayman.

(top) **Laxdale Hall** (1953, Group 3). (bottom) **Ill Fares the Land** (1982, Portman Films).

ARBROATH: rescued from drowning

Christie Johnstone (1921), shot in the area of Arbroath, was a melodrama about a laird and fisherfolk and a rescue from drowning, which, coincidentally, was an important part of the plot in a film made in the same place some fifty years later.

Arbroath and Montrose were the main locations for *Mauro the Gypsy* (1972) the third film made by Laurence Henson and Eddie McConnell for the Children's Film Foundation and whose historical significance was in continuing to develop the opportunities for Scottish film-makers to make story films on their own ground. This particular adventure concerned a young gypsy boy who gains the respect of the local community by saving a girl from drowning.

● *Christie Johnstone*
GB, 1921, Broadwest Films, 56 mins. Directed by Norman MacDonald. From the novel by Charles Reade. With Gertrude McCoy, Stewart Rome and Clive Brook.

● *Mauro the Gypsy*
GB, 1972, International Film Associates (Scotland), 58 mins. Directed and produced by Laurence Henson. Script by Patricia Latham from an original story by Ken Pople. Cinematography by Eddie McConnell. With Graeme Greenhowe. Fiona Kennedy, Andrew Byatt, Graeme Wilson, Victor Carin, Paul Kermack, Eileen McCallum, James Mackenzie, James Copeland and James Cosmo.

ARDNAMURCHAN: *Charlie & Louise*

Mainly associated, in screen terms, with wildlife documentaries, the great wilderness of Ardnamurchan (or at least the lighthouse at its western extreme) has a rather domestic movie connection. Filmed here and at Carbisdale Castle on the east coast, the German film *Charlie & Louise - Das Doppelte Lottchen* (1994) was based on a story by Erich Kastner

about identical twins saving their parents' marriage. The Disney comedy *The Parent Trap* (1961), was based on the same story.

● *Charlie & Louise*
Germany, 1994, Bavaria Film, 96 mins. Directed by Joseph Vilsmair. With Fritzi Eichhorn and Floriane Eichhorn.

ARRAN

The greatest Clyde island, referred to cosily by the tourist authorities as 'Scotland in Miniature', has been featured in travelogues and promotional films for years but its potential for fiction films has been less than fully exploited. One film which genuinely did justice to Arran as a location was *Nosey Dobson* (1976), made for the Children's Film Foundation by Pelicula films. It tells the story of a local boy-hero whose resourcefulness foils the wickedness of robbers from the mainland.

Nosey Dobson was written and directed by Mike Alexander who had a particular interest in Arran having been brought up on the island from the age of one. Aided by his brother Keith, now head of Arts Series in the BBC, Alexander began his career making short fiction films which he used to persuade established film-makers and broadcasters of his ability. After working at Campbell Harper in Edinburgh, where he first teamed up with cameraman Mark Littlewood, he joined the BBC in Glasgow. He subsequently set up Pelicula Films with Littlewood, one of a generation of excellent Scottish cinematographers including Eddie McConnell, Michael Coulter, David Peat and Martin Singleton.

Alexander's short films such as *The Bodyguard* (1969), *The Gardener* (1972) and *The Adman* (1980) were usually written by himself. A distinguished exception was *Home and Away* (1974) for which the script was by Bill Douglas, with Alexander. Like most of their contemporaries, Pelicula made several films for Films of Scotland, but much of their early experience came from educational work for Educational Films of Scotland (see **Glasgow, Dowanhill, Scottish Film Council**). Although the majority of these films were very short and didactic, *Ayrshire Lang Syne* (1972) was something of an epic with a huge cast of young people giving Alexander a first chance to direct drama on a large scale. Set in 1792, the story was an account of everyday life at a time of great social change.

A resident of Arran, the dramatist Robert McLellan (1907-85) collaborated with Alexander on two films based on his own stories, *The Donegals* (1978) and *The Daftie* (1979), the first of which was about itinerant Irish labourers who worked on the Clydeside fruit farms in the early years of the century.

Mike Alexander went on to direct many films for television and cinema including documentaries on leading sports personalities and the Gaelic feature *As an Eilean* (1993) (see **Aultbea**).

● *Nosey Dobson*
GB, 1976, Produced by Pelicula Films for the Children's Film Foundation, 59 mins. Directed by Mike Alexander. With Joe McKenna, Tom Watson, James Morrison and Gary Rankin.

● *The Donegals*
GB, 1978, Pelicula Films for the Scottish Arts Council, 30 mins. Directed by Mike Alexander. Script by Robert McLellan. With Catherine Gibson, Joe McPartland, Ian Andrew, Maureen Beattie, Willie Joss and Lennox Milne.

AUCHMITHIE: *Moon Acre*

The picturesque fishing village north of Arbroath was one of the locations for *Moon Acre* (1995), a joint Scottish, Welsh and Slovakian co-production by Edinburgh Film and Video Productions (see **Penicuik**). The story was a fantasy-adventure involving feuding families, ghosts and a legendary Moon Princess.

● *Moon Acre*
GB/Republic of Slovakia, 1995, Edinburgh Film and Video Productions, 90 mins. Directed by Robin Crichton. With Jean Anderson, Iain Cuthbertson, Philip Madoc, Miriam Margolyes, Graham Stark and Polona Vetrich.

Nosey Dobson (1976, Peculia Films). Director Mike Alexander on right.

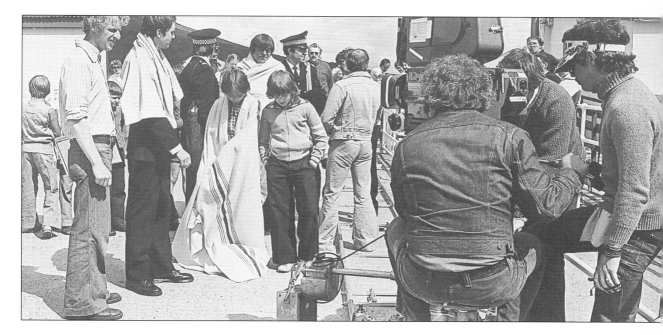

AUCHTERMUCHTY: the second Dr Finlay

The attractive village in Fife has a rather vicarious connection with the movies as the principal location for the second television manifestation of *Doctor Finlay* the series based on the stories by A J Cronin (see **Callander**). Auchtermuchty is also the home of the bespectacled pop twins, The Proclaimers, who in 1993 enjoyed massive record sales worldwide with the song 'I'm Gonna Be (500 Miles)', after its inclusion on the soundtrack to the teen movie *Benny and Joon*.

AULTBEA: *As an Eilean*

As an Eilean [From the Island] (1993) was filmed on the mainland, on the Wester Ross sea-loch of Loch Ewe, rather than in the Outer Hebrides where it was set, reflecting the universal difficulty in film-making of finding locations that look right in time and space and have the necessary facilities and access. This story of island life was based on two novels by Iain Crichton Smith concerning a young man in the process of leaving the island, a schoolmaster engaged in a photographic project to record the community, the local nurse, anxious about her forthcoming marriage and a mysterious silent stranger. The atmosphere is at once both full of light and claustrophobic.

What makes *As an Eilean* almost unique, however, is that its principal language is Gaelic. 'Almost' because one previous cinema film was made in that language. *Hero* (1982) by Barney Platts-Mills (see **The Gaidhealtachd**) required its cast, mainly of unemployed young people from Glasgow, to learn the language from scratch. Its concern was with the nature of myth and minorities. It was an extraordinary undertaking.

The idea that there could be a truly Hebridean film, let alone one in Gaelic, still seemed bizarre to many people, even after *Hero*. But attitudes to film in minority languages have been changing for some years. Since the founding of S4C (Welsh Channel Four) films in Welsh are now relatively common. The effect of boosting Gaelic language television through the support of CTG, (Comataidh Telebhisein Gaidhlig) (see **Stornoway**), one of the funders of *As an Eilean*, is bound to increase the amount of expertise in Gaelic language moving pictures. Pan-Celtic organisations like the Celtic Film and Television Association and its festival (see **Benbecula**) also help in raising the profile of languages and communities too-long neglected by the mainstream.

On a wider front, the possibilities for small but ancient cultures to express themselves on the big screen has been increased by the build-up of pan-European institutions committed to protect the interests of 'minority' cultures as well as by an increasing awareness that big countries and dominant languages do not have the monopoly of filmable stories with widespread appeal. The ultimate proof of this came from Norway with *Pathfinder* (1987) based on an ancient Sami legend and in the Sami language, which received a nomination for an Academy Award as best 'foreign language' picture.

However, it is one thing to make a film in Gaelic and another to find it an audience in Scotland. One of the ironies about *As an Eilean* was that, attractive as its story was, to say nothing of the beautiful camera work by Mark Littlewood and the music by Jim Sutherland, it could find a cinema audience for only a week in Glasgow, but for five in Berlin. It also found markets in countries as diverse as Israel and Australia, where presumably 'foreign language' was less of a problem than Gaelic is for most Scots.

● *As an Eilean*
GB, 1993, CTG, Channel Four, Pelicula Films. Directed by Mike Alexander. Written and Produced by Douglas Eadie. Based on stories by Iain Crichton Smith. Music by Jim Sutherland. With Ken Hutchison, Iain F MacLeod, DW Stiubhart, Wilma Kennedy, Tom Watson, Brian Croucher and Donna MacLeod.

B*b*

BALLACHULISH: the ferry

The phenomenon of a Hollywood icon turning up in odd corners of Scotland is nothing new. Bette Davis seen shopping in Tobermory (see **Mull**) is a good example. Another is Kirk Douglas on the old Ballachulish Ferry. He was there for a sequence in the cold war comedy thriller *Catch Me a Spy* (1971), set in Scotland and Romania. The ferryman was played by the Scots actor John Young.

● *Catch Me a Spy*
GB, 1971, Rank, 94 mins. Directed and written by Dick Clement. With Kirk Douglas, Trevor Howard and Tom Courtenay.

BALLANTRAE: Errol Flynn

Robert Louis Stevenson's classic adventure of the 1745 Jacobite Rising and fraternal strife has undergone numerous radio and television adaptations (including, allegedly, one for Italian television) but its broad canvas and promise of exotic locations from Scotland to the West Indies make it natural fodder for the big screen. In fact, there seems to have been only one version strictly for cinema (1953) although the 1983 film, produced with television in mind, by HTV and Columbia, had a particularly strong cast.

The 1953 edition diverged sharply from the original story line, but it had some fine location photography of the West Coast. Both attempts had plenty of swash and buckle, with one of

Catch Me a Spy (1971, Rank).
Kirk Douglas on the Ballachulish Ferry.

the foremost exponents of the genre, Errol Flynn, leading the earlier version.

● *The Master of Ballantrae*
US, 1953, Warner Brothers First National Productions, 88 mins. Directed by William Keighley. Cinematography, Jack Cardiff. From the novel by R L Stevenson. With Errol Flynn, Anthony Steel, Roger Livesey, Felix Aylmer, Yvonne Furneaux, Ralph Truman, Moultrie Kelsall and Archie Duncan.

● *The Master of Ballantrae*
US, 1983, Directed by Douglas Hickox. Based on R L Stevenson's novel. With Richard Thomas, Michael York, John Gielguid, Timothy Dalton, Finola Hughes, Ian Richardson and Brian Blessed.

On location for **Master Of Ballantrae** (1953, Warner Brothers).

BALMORAL: the dog cart

Some of the earliest film to be made in Scotland was shot at Balmoral Castle by William Walker of Aberdeen (see **Aberdeen**). In the last years of the nineteenth century Walker gave film performances for the Royal family and, famously, filmed the Queen in a dog cart.

The most celebrated portrayal in fiction film of Queen Victoria's ghillie, John Brown, was by Finlay Currie (see **Inveraray**), in *The Mudlark* (1950).

BANNOCKBURN: The Bruce

Since the battle of Bannockburn was the crucial event in the securing Scotland's independent nationhood, it might be expect to figure significantly in the list of great Scottish movies.

Sadly, that is not the case. Apart from a reference at the end of *Braveheart* (1995) and *The Bruce*, (1996) by Cromwell Productions, Bannockburn and indeed most of the wars and politics that surround it, remain a blank screen.

The Bruce was the second feature film from the company that made *Chasing the Deer* (1994) (see **Culloden**). Like its predecessor, it was funded by the remarkable device of inviting members of the public to pay to be extras with the added incentives of credits and attendance at premieres. The achievement in getting the film made was maybe greater than the end result but the film attracted a great deal of public attention nevertheless.

The intention was to be true to history. In that it was largely, but not totally, successful. The difficulty lay in harnessing limited resources in such a way as to create the 'epic' feeling that the subject matter deserved. The cause was both helped and hindered by the release shortly beforehand of *Braveheart* and *Rob Roy*. With their big Hollywood budgets they had generated huge interest in Scotland's violent past, creating a new market for big screen costume drama, but comparisons in script, acting and direction were bound to be made to *The Bruce's* disadvantage.

The Bruce and *Chasing the Deer* were not the first low budget attempts to tackle the broad canvas of Scotland's history. A similar approach was taken to the massacre of Glencoe in Austin Campbell's film made in 1971(see **Glencoe**).

● *The Bruce*
GB, 1996, Cromwell Films in association with Lamancha Productions, 108 mins. Directed and produced by Bob Carruthers and David McWhinnie. Screenplay by Bob Carruthers. With Oliver Reed, Brian Blessed, Sandy Welch, Hildegard Neil, Conor Chamberlain, Ronnie Browne, Michael Van Wijk, Dee Hepburn and Jake D'Arcy

BARRA: *Whisky Galore!*

There were probably more accidents and coincidences in the making of *Whisky Galore!* (1949) than befell the *S S Politician* when it came up against the island of Eriskay in the early morning of 5 February 1941. By chance, at the time the *Politician* went aground the Commander of the Home Guard on the nearby island of Barra was one Compton Mackenzie who, some years later, wrote a novel based on a partly fictional account of the wreck and the fate of a large part of its cargo. Mackenzie, unlike his creation Captain Waggett who set out to ensure that the whisky remained aboard the *S S Cabinet Minister*, saw no harm in the liberation of the otherwise doomed spirits. Fate's other major intervention took the form of a Government blunder. In a bizarre effort to ease the balance of payments deficit and capitalise on the success of American films in Britain a 75% customs duty was put on incoming movies. In response the Motion Picture Association of America suspended their film exports to Britain so that in 1948 there was such a decline in the

availability of Hollywood product that cinemas were in danger of running out of films to screen. In an effort to retrieve the situation, the Government appealed to British film-makers to increase their output.

One of the studios to respond was Ealing, a relatively small outfit already working at full capacity. Ealing's boss, Michael Balcon, decreed that any additional films would have to be made entirely on location – which was not the fashion of the times. As it happened, Monja Danischewsky, for ten years the publicity chief at Ealing, had ambitions to produce. He believed that the new Compton Mackenzie yarn was ideal for the circumstances. His choice of director was Ronald Neame, who would later make his mark on Scottish cinema with *Tunes of Glory* (1960) and *The Prime of Miss Jean Brodie* (1968), but Neame turned the offer down. However, the studio storyboard artist, Alexander Mackendrick, was desperately keen to get his first chance to direct and Balcon, who had an excellent record in encouraging new talent, agreed to let him.

Mackendrick was born in 1912 in Boston, Massachusetts, to a family from Glasgow. At the age of six, following his father's death from influenza, Mackendrick was sent to Glasgow where he was educated at Hillhead High School and Glasgow School of Art and where he picked up an indelible West of Scotland accent. His route into the film business was through advertising and wartime service in the army, where he made his first documentary. Mackendrick joined Ealing Studios in 1946, initially as a writer, and it was with them that he made five of the nine movies he directed. His Ealing films are *Whisky Galore!* (1949), *The Man in the White Suit* (1951), *Mandy* (1952), *The Maggie* (1954) (see **Islay**) and *The Ladykillers* (1955). Mackendrick subsequently returned to the United States and made *The Sweet Smell of Success* (1957). He then directed two more British films, *Sammy Going South*

Over: **Whisky Galore!** (1949, Ealing). (left) Interior shot. (right) Alexander Mackendrick, Compton Mackenzie and Monja Danischewsky: Director, Writer and Producer.

(1963) and *High Wind in Jamaica* (1965) before making his final feature, *Don't Make Waves* (1967), a Hollywood farce. From then on he devoted himself to film teaching at the California Institute of the Arts in Los Angeles, in which city he died in 1994.

So it was that a tyro producer, a first-time director and indeed as inexperienced a crew as ever set out from Ealing, descended on Barra in the truly awful summer of 1948. The full story of their tribulations, and eventual triumph, is to be found in Philip Kemp's book *Lethal Innocence: The Cinema of Alexander Mackendrick*. (see also Murray Grigor's chapter on *Whisky Galore!* in *From Limelight to Satellite*).

One of the other factors that gave the film a different feel to anything else of its period, and which set it up as a model for the future, was the essentially collaborative nature of its production. It was not that there were no disputes between director, producer, writer and studio, but that Mackendrick achieved a uniquely cooperative atmosphere around the venture. The comment is often made that the professional actors and the local 'extras' (not really the appropriate term in this instance) became indistinguishable, not through any lowering of standards but by the integration of the entire effort. The billeting of the eighty outsiders in bed-and-breakfast accommodation around the island meant that the accent and rhythms of Barra speech and the patterns of Barra life were absorbed automatically by the cast. There was a great deal more of the real Barra, Eriskay and South Uist in the fictional Great and Little Todday than would have been the case with more usual film-making practices.

In post-production, the film still had its problems. Only the unselfish (and uncredited) efforts of Charles Crichton to rescue the material from a disastrous first edit created a viable entity. There was reshooting – the final chase actually takes place not on Barra but the South Coast of England – and the initial critical response was only mildly encouraging. It was the enthusiastic reception given to export versions (*Tight Little Island* in America, and *Whisky à Gogo* in France) that convinced the producers they had something exceptional on their hands and that, in Alexander Mackendrick, they had discovered a young director of tremendous potential.

The importance of *Whisky Galore!* in the story of film in Scotland is due not only to the fact that it was probably (at least until recently) the most famous film to come from these parts. Along with Mackendrick's later work, such as *The Maggie* (1953), *Whisky Galore!* set precedents, good and bad, and taught lessons which were not properly learned for decades, particularly about the need for the maximum indigenous input, behind as well as in front of the camera, for any film aspiring to reflect Scottish culture. (We are only too familiar with the converse). The prize for getting it right, as in *Gregory's Girl*, is to discover that in being true to the particular, the chances are that the universal will follow. The imposition of the phoney, in writing, casting or cultural assumptions, will almost always be self-defeating.

Mackenzie and Mackendrick's work certainly does trade on cultural assumptions of a questionable kind. The film begins with a mock documentary about the islands, narrated by Finlay Currie, and Mackendrick is said to have been more inclined to Waggett's view of the evil effects of drink on the islanders than Mackenzie's liberal stance. But the main message is one of humanity and community. If scenes of quaint islanders with funny customs speaking a strange language sometimes approaches too close to the Kailyard for comfort, *Whisky Galore!*, like *The Maggie*, is still in a different category from such films as *The Bridal Path* or *Geordie* (see **Perthshire**). The reason is twofold. Firstly, there is a genuine intention to express a culture which provides a credible context for the narrative, rather than just exploiting it. Secondly, Mackendrick was able to manipulate or transcend stereotyping intelligently according to need, rather than merely operating within the boundaries of preconception for cheap effect.

Whisky Galore! provided a reference point for a number of subsequent films. *Rockets Galore* was an unsuccessful attempt to resuscitate the formula using many of the same ingredients. The novel was again by Compton Mackenzie. Danischewsky was the writer this time. The director was Michael Relph and the cast was largely new faces such as Jeannie Carson, Donald Sinden and Noel Purcell. Crucially, Captain Waggett was played by Roland Culver instead of the ineffable Basil Radford.

The success of *Whisky Galore!* suggested that 'comic' films about Scotland were good box office and for the next decade and more there was a steady flow of 'incomer' movies of variable quality. Intriguingly, Philip Kemp, in his book on Mackendrick, suggests that the true successor to *Whisky Galore!* is not Bill Forsyth's *Local Hero* (which in any case is closer in line and spirit to *The Maggie*) but the horror film *The Wicker Man* (1973) (see **Wigtown**) which also deals with an outsider incapable of understanding the ways of a Hebridean island.

The art of storytelling, so much a part of Celtic tradition, was explored in a novel way in Timothy Neat's *Play Me Something* (1989). Filmed in the airport building on Barra's famous beach-cum-runway, the film is about a group of passengers who pass the time by listening to the story of a romance of an Italian peasant visiting Venice. The mysterious storyteller is John Berger, and the waiting characters include Hamish Henderson, Tilda Swinton and Liz Lochhead. The contrast between the very different splendours of the Hebrides and the great Adriatic city certainly lent a curious quality to the film but the critics' reaction was varied: some saw it as a significant exercise in narrative structure, others were less enthusiastic and thought it was just pretentious.

But it was obvious that Neat's intentions were serious. Films with a clearly defined intellectual stance are vital to a film culture and with a few

Play Me Something (1989, BFI).
Hamish Henderson holds the reins.

others, particularly Murray and Barbara Grigor (see **Inverkeithing**), with whom he collaborated very successfully on, for example *Hallaig* (1984) (see **Skye**), Neat has tried to create a new dimension in Scottish film which it badly needs.

Barra also figured in *Staggered* (1994), starring Martin Clunes, a tale of an English bridegroom stranded without clothes or money with three days to find his way back to 'Civilisation' in time for his wedding.

● *Whisky Galore!*
GB, 1949, Ealing, 82 mins. Directed by Alexander Mackendrick. Produced by Monja Danischewsky. Script by Compton Mackenzie and Angus Macphail from the novel by Compton Mackenzie. With Basil Radford, Joan Greenwood, James Robertson Justice, Gordon Jackson, Duncan Macrae, Catherine Lacey, Bruce Seton, Jean Cadell, Wylie Watson, John Gregson, Jameson Clark, Morland Graham and Compton Mackenzie.

● *Play Me Something*
GB, 1989, BFI/Scottish Film Production Fund/ Grampian Television/Film Four International. Directed by Timothy Neat. Produced by Kate Swan and Timothy Neat. Written by John Berger and Timothy Neat. With John Berger, Tilda Swinton, Hamish Henderson, Margaret Bennett, Liz Lochhead, Lucia Lanzarini and Charlie Barron.

BEATTOCK: *Night Mail*

The 'steady climb' of the *Night Mail* (1936) up to Beattock Summit remains one of the most enduring images of documentary film. The sequence, including the shot in which the train crawls along the very bottom of the frame (destroyed on television), is as potent as the famous verse accompaniment by W H Auden.

This is the night mail crossing the Border,
Bringing the cheque and postal order,
Letters for the rich, letters for the poor,
The shop at the corner and the girl next door.
Pulling up Beattock, a steady climb -
The gradient's against her but she's on time...

Night Mail was arguably also the summit of Griersonian documentary (see **Cambusbarron**). Its fusion of actuality and art made something new. What set out as a humble tale of how the Post was taken overnight by rail from London to Scotland, ended up as an important essay on physical and human connections disguised as a gentle, engaging short film. It exemplified two of the great Grierson imperatives, communication, and the encouragement of talent, (another being the 'persuasion of the public authorities').

The team that made *Night Mail* was outstanding. As well as Auden's specially composed verse, there was Benjamin Britten's score, the soundtrack being crafted by Alberto Cavalcanti who had a particular interest in the experimental use of film sound. Stuart Legg spoke the commentary but the final words were uttered by Grierson himself:

And none will hear the postman's knock
Without a quickening of the heart,
For who can bear to feel himself forgotten?

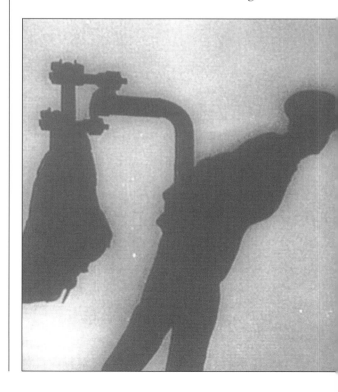

Years later, during the 1980 Edinburgh International Film Festival, at a gathering of the documentary pioneers, it emerged that the one question that would raise the temperature and cause some amusement among them was to ask who exactly directed *Night Mail*? It seems that the ultimate exercise in the creative treatment of actuality had so blurred the conventional demarcations that nobody was entirely willing to claim or attribute responsibility, perhaps for fear of causing offence. An 'official' version of the credits is set out below.

Incidentally, there was another film, a feature, called *Night Mail*, released in 1935, a year earlier than its famous namesake. Produced by British Lion and directed by Herbert Smith, it concerned an attempt to murder a judge on the overnight express to Aberdeen.

● *Night Mail*
GB, 1936, GPO Film Unit, 24 mins. Produced by John Grierson. Written and Directed by Harry Watt and Basil Wright. Edited by Richard Q McNaughton. Photography, Jonah Jones, Chick Fowle. Sound direction, Alberto Cavalcanti. Music by Benjamin Britten. Poem by W H Auden.

BENBECULA: Celtic connections

A small island in the Outer Hebrides might seem an unpromising place to initiate a significant movement in Scottish film culture but, since the movement in question was integral to Celtic as well as Scottish culture, the point of departure was entirely sensible. In the late nineteen seventies, the Scottish Film Council (SFC), not least because of its involvement in educational technology, was beginning to take an interest in video as a medium of production and distribution, particularly in the community. A Government-backed scheme, 'The Quality of Life Experiment', enabled SFC to participate in one of the first local cable television experiments, in the Vale of Leven in Dunbartonshire, in 1977.

(left and below) **Night Mail** (1936, GPO).

However, SFC, in consultation with others, decided it was in the Western Isles, where the problems of access to cinema were acute, that video technology could provide an opportunity to address both the needs of the audience (neglected since the demise of the Highlands and Islands Film Guild in 1970) and, even more importantly, of indigenous Gaelic culture. The result was the setting up of 'Cinema Sgire' (Community Cinema) in the autumn of 1977. With backing from the new bilingual local authority, the Western Isles Council, and financial help from the Calouste Gulbenkian Foundation the project ran for five years. During that time almost a hundred short community programmes were made (mostly by, with and for local people, and mostly in Gaelic) and a mobile cinema circuit operated which covered ten islands. In the end, financial constraints determined that it could not continue but the initiative had established a credibility for Gaelic-language production and for the idea of structures to promote it.

The most important spin-off from Cinema Sgire was the establishment of the Celtic Film and Television Festival which, from very modest beginnings has become a major annual gathering of programme and film-makers from all the Celtic countries. Premieres are given, awards made, seminars held and film and television concerns specific to the Celtic nations are addressed. The first festival was held at Iochar on South Uist in April 1980. The Chairman was Muiris MacGonghail who was then the Controller of RTE, the Irish broadcasting agency; there were forty delegates and a screening programme that stretched from Barra to the Butt of Lewis.

One of the main ideas behind the Festival was for those working in minority language production in Scotland to share experiences with their counterparts from Ireland, Wales and Brittany. The first event was so demonstrably successful that it was agreed to repeat it as a peripatetic festival, moving each year to a different Celtic country. The second festival attracted a hundred delegates to Harlech in North Wales. Since then it has travelled to Brittany and Ireland and has revisited all the Celtic countries year by year bringing together about three hundred programme-makers from the major television and independent film-making organisations.

In 1982, the Festival formed the Association for Film and Television in the Celtic Countries with a remit not only to organise the annual festival but to concern itself with the wider issues affecting film and television. The first full-time director of the Association was Michael Russell, who had been the original project officer of Cinema Sgire and whose tremendous enthusiasm had ensured that what began as a relatively minor project in a remote part of Scotland would grow into an important force in national and international media culture.

BERNERAY: shepherds

The tradition of semi-anthropological filming in Scotland's remoter islands, such as was pursued by Werner Kissling on Eriskay (see **Eriskay***) or Jenny Gilbertson in Shetland (see **Shetland**), had its modern equivalent in *The Shepherds of Berneray* (1981). The film, which with unusual sympathy followed the crofting year through the eyes of a shepherd and the members of a family, was partly financed by the Film Study Center at the University of Harvard, the *alma mater* of two of the film-makers, Jack Shea and Allen Moore. It also had support from the Highlands and Islands Development Board and the Scottish Arts Council.

● *The Shepherds of Berneray*
GB, 1981, 56 mins. A film by Allen Moore and Jack Shea.

THE BLACK ISLE:
Another Time, Another Place

Jessie Kesson's war-time story of the inter-relationships of the farming people of the Black Isle and Italian prisoners brought to work in their midst – with consequences ranging from the comic to the utterly tragic – provided the scenario for one of the best films to be made in Scotland in the nineteen eighties. *Another Time,*

Another Time, Another Place (1983, Channel Four). Phyllis Logan.

Another Place (1983) portrayed rural Scotland and its people without sentiment and showed it for the hard land that so much of it really is.

The central performances of Phyllis Logan as Janie and her hopelessly ill-suited lover Luigi (Giovanni Mauriello) were especially effective. With Roger Deakin's camera work in the great wide landscapes, John McLeod's music and a good script and cast, the film gave an indication of the quality of cinema that could be achieved in Scotland even with relatively modest resources. As 1983 also saw the release of *Local Hero* (see **Morar**) and *Living Apart Together* (see **Glasgow**) there was now evidence that film in Scotland had ceased to be confined to the heather stereotype and that a film culture of real variety was within our grasp.

Another Time, Another Place can be seen as an interesting reference point in the work of its director Michael Radford as well as a notable achievement in its own right. Radford, one of the first graduates of the National Film School, was not born in Scotland, but had strong family connections with the country. He had already

worked with Jessie Kesson on the screen version of *The White Bird Passes* (1980), her semi-autobiographical novel set in Elgin and produced by BBC Scotland. The Italian connection would reappear more than a decade later in Radford's marvellous Oscar-nominated and BAFTA-winning *Il Postino* (1994) in which the Italians are the host nation and the incomer is an exile, the poet Pablo Neruda, from Chile.

● *Another Time, Another Place* ✓
GB, 1983, Umbrella Films, Rediffusion Films, Channel Four, Scottish Arts Council, 102 mins. Directed by Michael Radford. Produced by Simon Perry. Script by Michael Radford from the original novel by Jessie Kesson. Cinematography, Roger Deakins. Music, John McLeod. With Phyllis Logan, Giovanni Mauriello, Denise Coffey, Tom Watson, Gian Luca Favilla, Gregor Fisher, Paul Young, Claudio Rosini and Jennifer Piercey.

BLAIRGOWRIE: John Clyde

Blairgowrie was the home of the remarkable Clyde family, famous on stage and screen in the early years of the century, before they moved to Helensburgh (see **Helensburgh**) (and some of them on to Hollywood). If Andy was the best known, because of his association with Hopalong Cassidy, his father John (1861-1920) deserves more than a passing mention.

John Clyde was the first screen *Rob Roy* (1911), having made the part his own in theatre. As the first to transfer to celluloid he was therefore at the head of a line of movie Rob Roys leading eventually to Liam Neeson and the spectacular 1995 version (see **Aberfoyle** and **Kinlochleven**).

BLANTYRE: Livingstone

The story of David Livingstone (1813-73) sounds like the stuff movies are made of. The explorer in dangerous and remote foreign parts would seem an ideal subject, yet so far it seems only one major epic has been made about him. *Stanley and Livingstone* (1939) says it all in its title. It is of course about the search for Livingstone and its hero is the journalist, not the explorer. If more evidence of its orientation were needed, the casting gives the game away. Spencer Tracy is Stanley; Cedric Hardwick is the man from Blantyre.

Given the change in attitudes to Victorian missionaries in general and Livingstone in particular, it is hard to imagine a remake of *Stanley and Livingstone*, but a serious feature film examining the good doctor from a Scottish perspective could be fascinating.

Educational and instructive films about Livingstone are easier to come by. *Livingstone* (1925) was made by the Religious Film Society and was filmed partly in Africa and partly in Scotland.

● *Stanley and Livingstone*
US, 1939, Twentieth Century Fox, 101 mins. Directed by Henry King. With Spencer Tracy,

Cedric Hardwicke, Richard Greene, Nancy Kelly, David Torrence and Walter Brennan.

BO'NESS-KINNEIL: Railway

Railway lines, particularly those with steam trains on them, seem to have a special attraction for film makers. This one appeared in the most successful ever Swedish domestic production, *The Accidental Golfer* (1991) (see **Eddleston**).

BOTHWELL: Reginald Barker

Reginald Barker (1886-1945) was born in Bothwell. If his name means little there these days that is not surprising, since he left at the age of ten. However, he deserves honour in his homeland as one of the most successful Scots in early Hollywood.

A director, specialising in action films, his credits include such resounding titles as, *The Wrath of the Gods* (1914), *The Apostle of Vengeance* (1916), *The Iced Bullet* (1917), *The Hell Cat* (1918), *The Brand* and *Flame of the Desert* (1919). He was a pioneer of the Western, directing the first cowboy hero, William S Hart, for the Thomas Ince Company.

He was also responsible for something of a minor masterpiece. *The Italian* (1915) was a drama about a Venetian gondolier who is given a year by his sweetheart's father to prove himself before he will be allowed to marry. He goes to New York and is sufficiently successful as a boot-black to be able to summon his beloved and wed her. Unfortunately, the resulting baby falls ill and dies for lack of medication, despite the father's plea to the local slum boss for the necessary cash. When the boss's own baby is similarly threatened, the ex-gondolier seeks revenge by disrupting the child's medical care but at the critical moment is overcome by conscience and retreats.

This simple tale of tragedy and revenge would be no more remarkable than hundreds of others but for the fact that it is an extremely early film of its kind (made in the same year as *Birth of a Nation*), and that, in portraying contemporary life in the New York slums in an unsentimental, almost documentary, way, Barker achieves a form of social realism well ahead of his time. *The Italian* is certainly worth reviving and suggests that there may be other films by Barker deserving modern examination. It was used by Francis Ford Coppola to help recreate New York at the turn of the century for *The Godfather – Part II* (1974).

Barker's Scottish connections may not amount to a great deal, but it is interesting that in 1921 he directed and produced a film version of *Bunty Pulls the Strings*, for Goldwyn. The play on which it was based was written by Graham Moffat from Blairgowrie and was a perennial success on the Scottish stage.

● *The Italian*
US, 1915, Paramount, 83 mins. Directed by Reginald Barker. With George Beban.

BRIGADOON

Although difficult to locate precisely, given that it only emerges from the mists once every hundred years, the Highland village of Brigadoon should be fairly easy to identify by certain unique features. For instance, the heather there grows to about six feet high and the inhabitants speak in an accent which owes more to Burbank than Burns. *Brigadoon*, the show and the Hollywood movie (1954), have come to stand for all that is awful in tartan and sentimentality – a degrading perversion of Scottish culture.

Of course it is not that simple! Dismiss *Brigadoon* as a piece of corrupt nonsense and you turn your back on a most expert work of cinema. Take it and its implications too seriously and you may find yourself in the grip of

Reginald Barker

obsession. Of its technical excellence there is no doubt; it was Oscar-nominated for design. Its energy and style are thoroughly engaging. There are good performances. It has a great title. The only trouble is that in its perverse way, it is somehow about *us*. We who live in a land constructed from myth and left in limbo while the rest of the world moved on. That is a distressing idea.

There is a genuine problem for a culture with an identity as conspicuous as ours. Too much of it for comfort is susceptible to caricature. For all that our image is of a mostly harmless people (quaint, nostalgic with much energy devoted to colourful dressing and loud music) we would rather that the world had a more serious appreciation of our nation. We are also not averse to a degree of hypocrisy in these matters. The fact that this movie cannot be defined by any means as being ours, indeed it is completely an external production, makes it easier to feel superior about it, but the truth is that it was we ourselves, mainly per Walter Scott (see **Abbotsford**), who invented the myth in the first place and we are not above exploiting it for our own purposes when it suits us.

Perhaps it is largely because its director, Vincente Minnelli, is so proficient that *Brigadoon* has a hypnotic effect on the national psyche. There are plenty of other corny tartan films about Scotland but none seems capable of attaining the same encapsulating status. At least it defines a target and gives us something to be angst-ridden about, when we need it. Alternatively, we can enjoy the movie for what it is worth and, in a mature way, move on to more pressing issues.

Forsyth Hardy's very funny account (in *Scotland in Film*) of how Brigadoon failed to be filmed in Scotland centred on his attempts to help the producer, Arthur Freed, to find locations for it. Culross, Dunkeld, Braemar and Inverary were all rejected as unsuitable. Freed returned to Hollywood having found nowhere

in Scotland that looked like Scotland. Clearly there is some satisfaction to be derived from the fact that he could find nothing sufficiently phoney to meet his purposes.

● *Brigadoon*
US, 1954, MGM, 102 mins. Directed by Vincente Minnelli. Written by Alan J Lerner. Music by Frederick Loewe. With Gene Kelly, Van Johnson, Cyd Charisse, Elaine Stewart and Barry Jones.

BRIG O'TURK

The wonderfully named Brig o' Turk, on the road from Callander to the Trossachs was the location for *Shepherd on the Rock* (1995), a tale of rural tensions between sheep farmers and property developers. Scottish films in which the environment is the hero seem to be few in number, which is a pity. The obvious major contribution to the cause is *Local Hero* (see **Morar**), but there ought surely to be more.

● *Shepherd on the Rock*
GB, 1995, String of Pearls, 90 mins. Directed by Bob Keen. Executive producer Noel Cronin. Written by Paul Adam. With Bernard Hill, Betsy Brantley, Doug Bradley and Oliver Parker.

BROXBURN: Michael Caton-Jones.

To describe the rise of the Broxburn-born director Michael Caton-Jones as phenomenal would probably be an understatement. Consider his directing credits since he reached the big time: 1988 *Scandal*; 1990 *Memphis Belle*; 1991 *Doc Hollywood* (with Michael J Fox); 1993 *This Boy's Life* (with Robert De Niro); 1995 *Rob Roy*. With the possible exception of Alexander Mackendrick no Scot has operated so consistently and successfully at this level since the Second World War. But as he himself said, 'They think they're going to meet this British person with a hyphen in his name and then it's this guy from Broxburn with this accent...'.

Brigadoon (1954, MGM).
Gene Kelly and Cyd Charisse.

Michael Caton-Jones.

for his graduation film *The Riveter* (1986). In 1987 he signalled that his was a special talent with the three-part thriller *Brond* for Channel Four. (See **Glasgow, Gibson Street**).

Only eight years later, and with the enviable record that all his movies to date had made money, he returned to Scotland to make *Rob Roy*. Caton-Jones brought together the techniques of large-scale movie-making and a character whose original was largely the creation of Sir Walter Scott and delivered a picture which was not only a very enjoyable adventure (a Western in kilts?) but showed as close an approach to a coherent and credible depiction of a particular period of Scottish history as anyone has managed so far. In doing so, he demonstrated that large-scale popular cinema could be made by Scots on Scottish subjects, including historical ones, and that such films did not necessarily have to remain the exclusive preserve of Hollywood (and therefore at the mercy of that culture's perception of ours).

Brought up on a council estate (his father was a miner), at the age of eighteen he opted to move to London when his parents emigrated to Canada. He lived in a squat in Stoke Newington and found work as a stagehand. His first experience of film production was in a similarly lowly capacity but he became completely hooked on the business and began writing, albeit only for his own benefit.

Observing what a director does and being convinced that he could do that job, in 1983 at the age of twenty five he gained a place at the National Film and Television School at Beaconsfield. There his first project *Liebe Mutter* won the Best Film prize at the European Film Students Awards and there was similar acclaim

Cc

CALLANDER: Dr Cronin and Dr Finlay

In the popular memory, Callander is commonly associated with one of the most successful small screen series, the BBC realisation of *Dr Finlay's Casebook* from the stories by A J Cronin (see **Dumbarton**). The effect of *Dr Finlay* was to create an image of rural Scotland which was rather closer to the couthiness of the Kailyard school than to the realities of the period but it was one which was immensely attractive to both domestic and foreign viewers.

Much of the success of the series was due to the acting of the three principals, Bill Simpson, Andrew Cruikshank, and Barbara Mullen who despite her Irish origins was a most convincing Scottish housekeeper (she had already starred as a Scot in *Jeannie* (1941)). Twenty years later, their successors in the Scottish Television version, filmed in Auchtermuchty, were David Rintoul, Ian Bannen (see **Airdrie**) and Annette Crosbie.

CAMBUSBARRON: John Grierson and family

Although John Grierson (1898-1972) was born in Deanston, the family moved the short distance to Cambusbarron when he was only two and it is with the latter village, where his father was the schoolmaster, that he is more usually associated.

Scots can be uncomfortable with the idea of greatness in one of their own. As Grierson's mission in life was to achieve change by

challenging accepted practices and ideas, applying his phenomenal energy and intellect to the matter in hand whatever the circumstances, some people found it difficult to accept him as a hero of the nation. A talent for disruption, subversion, fierce loyalty to individuals and causes, immense political awareness and skill allied to a permanently radical position, were key components in the make-up of one of the most influential figures in the development of cinema. Perhaps it is not surprising that modern film-makers in Scotland, particularly among the young, are inclined to seek distance between their work and the legacy of Grierson. Perhaps it is simply that he is out of fashion.

Grierson's career began with academic excellence. He won the second highest scholarship to Glasgow University in 1915 but did not take up his place until 1919; he spent the intervening time on minesweepers as a member of the Royal Naval Volunteer Reserve. The connection with the sea had been in the family for generations and he was to return to it many times in his film-making. In 1923 he graduated from Glasgow and, after a brief spell on the staff at Durham University, was awarded a Rockerfeller Research Fellowship in Social Science which enabled him to study what we would now describe as 'the media' in the United States.

During his three years in the United States Grierson's thinking on mass communication and in particular the role of the cinema as opinion former rather than as a means of artistic expression became refined to the point that when he returned to Britain he was ideally equipped to apply his conclusions to the Film Unit of The Empire Marketing Board (EMB). He joined the Film Unit in 1927 and proceeded to transform it. The recording of actuality by means of a film camera was as old as the medium itself but in Grierson's vision it was the treatment that was important. He was the first to apply the term 'documentary' to film, originally using it to describe existing films such as Flaherty's *Nanook of the North* (1922) and *Moana* (1926). *Drifters* (1929) was to be the definitive product of his principles.

Crucial to the development of the documentary was the recruitment of talent to form the nucleus of the new movement. Edgar Anstey, Basil Wright, Harry Watt, Paul Rotha, John Taylor, Stuart Legg, Arthur Elton, Alberto Cavalcanti, Humphrey Jennings and Grierson's sisters, Marion and Ruby, were to be its mainstays.

Grierson himself directed only one other film, *Granton Trawler* in 1934 (see **Granton**). By that time, the EMB Film Unit had been dissolved and reformed as the GPO Film Unit, again with Grierson as its chief. Under him, the unit produced several outstanding documentaries including *Coal Face*, *Night Mail* (both 1936) and Basil Wright's *Song of Ceylon* (1934). The first two became famous for, among other things, the collaboration between W H Auden and Benjamin Britten.

Night Mail (see **Beattock**) is probably most representative of the documentary movement at its height. It embodies most of the virtues and reveals few of the drawbacks of cinema employing reality to communicate with an audience. It is immensely attractive in its apparent simplicity. It also reminds us that the key to Grierson's approach was to manipulate 'reality' in the most creative way possible. Thus, the sorting office routine was filmed not on a train but in a studio and the 'postmen' were actors hired for the job. But all that counts is the effect, and the effect is wonderful. The marriage of visuals, music, verse and 'message' has never been matched and Grierson clearly knew the value of the work. It is he who speaks the film's last lines.

In 1937 Grierson left the GPO Film Unit, along with Arthur Elton and others, to set up a new kind of agency. Film Centre was an advisory body, a group of consultants, created to assist public bodies and others to develop documentary film projects. In that capacity, Grierson participated in the first Films of Scotland Committee which was set up to produce seven films for the Empire Exhibition at Bellahouston (see **Glasgow, Bellahouston**) in Glasgow in 1938. It was one of many occasions on which Grierson expressed his attachment to his homeland in practical ways.

His work at Film Centre also led directly to his next move, to Canada. He produced the crucial report recommending the formation of the National Film Board of Canada and, in October 1939, in an old sawmill in Ottawa, set up what was to be one of the world's great film bodies. Among those he appointed to his new organisation was Norman McLaren from Stirling, whose work Grierson had seen while McLaren was still at Glasgow School of Art (see **Glasgow**). McLaren's contribution to the art of animation was not only outstanding in its originality but provided the Film Board with a dimension that would enhance its fame world-wide .

Although he was initially on a six month contract, Grierson stayed with the Film Board of Canada until 1945. Then he moved to New York and International Film Associates, yet another new venture which, unusually for Grierson, was not a great success. Within two years he was back operating at the highest level as the Director of Mass Communications and Public Information at UNESCO. This was followed by a return to Britain as Controller of Film for the Central Office of Information. In 1951 when the National Film Finance Corporation decided to back the establishment of Group 3, a body whose brief was to encourage new talent in fiction film-making, they invited Grierson to run it.

There is something incongruous about 'The Father of the Documentary' as the boss of a feature film company and it may be significant that the most successful film he produced was close to documentary, and to his own roots. *The Brave Don't Cry* (1952) dealt with the mining disaster at Knockshinnock (see **Knockshinnock**). Group 3 was also responsible for *Laxdale Hall* (1952) (see **Applecross**) but a genuine documentary, *The Conquest of Everest* (1953), was the only one of their films that recovered its costs. Group 3 closed in 1955.

(top) The Grierson family outside Cambusbarron School. John, front left, Ruby on mother's knee.
(bottom) **The Heart of Scotland** (1965) – see page 101.

Grierson's Canadian reputation and experience were responsible for his last, rather unexpected, move. Roy Thomson (later Lord Thomson), owner of Scottish Television and a Canadian newspaper empire, wished to extend his Canadian interests into the new field of commercial television. He believed, correctly, that Grierson could provide him with 'class' in his output. The result was *This Wonderful World*, a series of factual film compilations which in other hands would have been off the air in a month. With Grierson selecting the material and fronting it, it ran for eight years. It also made him famous on the streets. He even developed a catchphrase. Signing off, he invariably wished us 'In the Highlands and the Lowlands, and over the Border, a very good night.'

The facts about Grierson, his opinions, theories, writings, speeches and virtually his whole life were meticulously gathered and chronicled by Forsyth Hardy. Hardy's books, *Grierson on Documentary* (1946), *John Grierson – a Documentary Biography*, *John Grierson's Scotland* (both 1979), and *Grierson on the Movies* (1981), which contain a great deal of Grierson's own writings, resonant and provocative like the man himself, ensure that Grierson and his work will not be lost from view. In addition, the University of Stirling hosts the John Grierson Archive in collaboration with McGill University in Montreal, an institution with which Grierson was closely associated. In 1990 the Archive published *Eyes of Democracy* edited by Ian Lockerbie, evidently the draft of a book Grierson had been commissioned to write in 1939 but had never completed.

There is therefore no difficulty in finding information about Grierson; what is somewhat problematic is seeing how he fits into the map of Scottish film culture. It is certainly the case that much of his most important work had a strong Scottish reference: *Drifters* and *Granton Trawler* in the early years, and later at Group 3 *The Brave Don't Cry* and *Laxdale Hall*. As a member of the second Films of Scotland Committee he had an immediate and practical impact on several films, providing the outline treatments for *The Heart of Scotland* (about his native Stirlingshire) and the Oscar-winning *Seawards the Great Ships*. Just as important, he was a tremendous encourager of talent, as much in Scotland as anywhere. Jenny Gilbertson in Shetland in the thirties and Laurence Henson and Eddie McConnel in the late fifties are prime examples.

Henson, who worked as Grierson's assistant on Scottish Television's *This Wonderful World* was given his first opportunity to direct *(The Heart of Scotland)* through no formal means but because Grierson simply said, 'Go on, do it!', with the sort of fierce encouragement, brooking no possibility of failure whatever, that had launched dozens, perhaps hundreds of Grierson-inspired careers. Yet even Henson, for all his proximity to Grierson over many years, finds it impossible to pin the man down. The truth, probably, is that genius is beyond category and that the fierce little man who could make cabinet ministers quake (someone said that he could be ferocious with you before you had even met) had such a sense of mission to communicate that it was the rest of us who were at fault for not being up to his speed.

Leaving aside the personality, his work as a theoretician and proselytiser (for the preacher in the pulpit was never far away) was greater than the films he made. His success lay in being influential to a degree that very few Scots in the media (or anywhere else) could aspire to. Lord Reith at the BBC is perhaps the only other contender. It was not simply Grierson's belief (as noted in William Stott's *Documentary Expression and Thirties America*) that the factual film was the means of conveying 'the information necessary to organised and harmonious living' but his recognition that emotion counted more than fact that made him such a notable film-maker, producer of films and encourager of film-makers .

John Grierson's sisters, Ruby and Marion, were members of the original team at the EMB. Inevitably, their contributions have been almost wholly overshadowed by that of their illustrious brother but both became significant film-makers in their own right. Ruby, especially, was regarded by the rest of the group as having played a very distinctive role in the early progress of the documentary movement.

In contrast to John, she was always very amiable and was particularly good at dealing with camera-shy ordinary people. She is credited with the first straight-to-camera appearances of working class folk, in *Housing Problems* (1935), the first tentative step towards giving people some control over how they were represented on screen. This more sociological approach, informed by an inclination to take the part of the underprivileged was, in effect, a change in direction for documentary film even in these formative years.

Ruby's radicalism (her mother had been a suffragette) was most clearly expressed in the anti-war *People of Britain – the Peace Film* (1936), directed by Paul Rotha. In the gender neutral form 'R I Grierson' Ruby was credited as Assistant Producer which may not entirely do her justice. *The Peace Film* caused tremendous problems with the censor but was eventually shown to the public.

Her film about life on the island of Islay, *Cargo for Ardrossan* (1939), took her back, in the best Grierson tradition, to the sea and, tragically, it was at sea, a victim of U-boat action, that she died in September 1940. She was on her way to Canada on the *City of Benares*, whose four hundred passengers included the ninety children about whose evacuation she was making a film. Her loss deeply affected not only John Grierson and the entire documentary community, but possibly the direction of the movement itself.

CAMPBELTOWN: The New Picture House

On Monday May 26 1913 'an enterprise of a kind hitherto unknown in this district' was reported by the *Campbeltown Courier*. It was the grand opening of The New Picture House. At the time, said the Courier, picture theatres were springing up 'with mushroom-like rapidity and in astonishing numbers'. The house was, 'in the

matter of comfort, a marked advance on anything the community has ever known in connection with public entertainment. The building is lit by electricity'. *The Argyllshire Herald* reported the presence of local dignitaries, including the Town Council. 'A selection of pictures was shown, and afternoon tea was handed round'.

The relatively sophisticated ambience and equipment – accommodation for 640 patrons, fireproof projection box, internal telephones – was offset by the fact that there was no screen, only the back wall painted white.

What makes The New Picture House very special is that more than eighty years later it is still operating and has done so continuously for longer than any other cinema in Scotland. Its history is a fascinating tale of survival against the odds. Because of its remoteness at the end of the Mull of Kintyre it often had difficulty with film supply. On the other hand, it paid less for its newsreels than other cinemas – they were liable to be a week out of date.

In recent times, small town cinemas have had a high mortality rate, but where one has unusually strong ties with its locality (the New Picture House was run by three generations of the Armour family), the chances of keeping going are obviously greater. Today, The New Picture House is a community business.

CAWDOR: *Macbeth*

The film connections between Scotland and Shakespeare's 'Scottish Play' are so tenuous it is hard to believe that any of the many screen versions of *Macbeth* have had an impact on Scottish film culture or indeed owe anything to Scotland beyond the setting of the play.

There are certainly plenty of film versions of *Macbeth*, beginning with a Vitagraph production in 1908. Other silent era contributions were from Italy in 1909, France (Pathé) in 1910, the UK in 1911, Germany in 1914 and two from America in 1916, one of which was from D W Griffith's company, directed by John Emerson and starring Herbert Beerbohm Tree and Constance Collier. In 1922, Russell and Sybil

Thorndyke appeared as the hapless couple in one of a series of shorts engagingly entitled, *Tense Moments from Great Plays*.

Among the many foreign-language adaptations, which include films of the Verdi opera, the most memorable, and arguably the best production in any medium, was Kurosawa's *Kumonosu-Jo [Throne of Blood]* (1957). Paradoxically, there are perhaps more clues in Kurosawa's vision as to how a Scottish *Macbeth* might work, than in any of the others.

Of the three major English language productions since the war only the one directed by George Schaefer (1960) and made primarily for American television, used any Scottish locations. It did, however, cast Ian Bannen as MacDuff. The two others are rather more famous, or notorious.

Orson Welles attempt (1948) to make a studio version in three weeks was generally regarded as a disaster and the passage of time has done little to revise that view, although it remains an interesting record of a great actor at full blast. Alarmingly from our point of view, the dialogue was said to be delivered in authentic Scottish accents.

What remains in the mind about Polanski's *Macbeth* (1972) is not the acting or the settings (it was filmed in Northumbria and Wales) but the violence. As Pauline Kael said, 'Slaughter is the star'. Much was made at the time of the fact that Polanski's own wife had been brutally murdered only the previous year, but the style and the excesses were typical of the director in any case.

A plan for a Scottish Macbeth was anounced in early 1996 by Cromwell Films whose previous films were *Chasing the Deer* (see **Culloden**) and *The Bruce* (see **Bannockburn**). Such proposals deserve to be taken seriously. Shakespeare can be filmed successfully in Scotland (*vide* Zeffirelli's *Hamlet*) and the talent exists to do what Finland, Denmark, Japan and plenty of other countries have done in putting Shakespeare's vision of part of our history on screen.

Orson Welles' **Macbeth** (1948, Republic).

● *Macbeth*
US, 1948, Republic/Mercury, 89 mins. Directed by Orson Welles. With Orson Welles, Jeanette Nolan, Dan O'Herlihy, Roddy McDowall and Edgar Barrier.

● *Macbeth*
US/GB, 1960, Grand Prize Productions, 108 mins. Directed by George Schaefer. With Maurice Evans, Judith Anderson, Michael Hordern, Ian Bannen, Jeremy Brett, and Malcolm Keen.

● *Macbeth*
GB, 1972, Playboy/Caliban, 140 mins. Directed by Roman Polanski. Screenplay by Roman Polanski and Kenneth Tynan. With Jon Finch, Francesca Annis, Martin Shaw, Nicholas Selby, Stephen Chase and Terence Bayler.

CLYDEBANK: shipbuilders

Two sets of moving images from Clydebank stick firmly in the mind. The first dates from the Second World War and is of the devastation caused by the blitz. The second comes from a more recent period in the life of the shipyards which were the target of the bombing raids. One particular sequence from the latter, a ship slipping down the ways seen from beneath the stern, was so powerful that it came to symbolise not only the work of the shipbuilders but of cinema documentary at its most imaginative.

The sequence was created in an extraordinary way. A platform supporting an unmanned camera was mounted at the stern of a ship as it waited on the slipway to be launched. It was fixed at the level of the rudder so that the camera saw it end-on with the propeller beyond. As the ship was launched, the idea was that the whole assembly would float and therefore move up the stern of the vessel as it entered the water. In practice, what happened was that the force of the water caused the rig to break up and instead of floating free, the camera ended up at the bottom of the Clyde. Amazingly, it was retrieved by a diver. The film was rescued and processed and the result was the most remarkable record of how a ship meets the water. It provides the stunning opening moment of *Seawards the Great Ships* (1961).

Seawards was the most important and famous short film of its time. It was made by Templar Films of Glasgow for the Films of Scotland Committee and was based on a treatment by John Grierson, the doyen and 'father' of the documentary. There is a certain symmetry in Grierson being the creative force behind this Scottish film to do with the sea. His very first film, *Drifters*, (1929) also on a Scottish sea subject, effectively marked the beginning of the documentary movement; *Seawards the Great Ships* virtually marked the end.

Grierson's approach to *Seawards* was characteristic. He saw it as a broad, big (a favourite Grierson word), celebration not only of the skills of the Clyde in making a huge percentage of the world's shipping over many years, but also the triumph of the human intellect in creating mighty vessels to reach the far corners of the world. In the words of Cliff Hanley's commentary, 'The biggest ship ever built takes its first shape in the small chamber of a human brain'.

It was also entirely characteristic of Grierson that the director he found to make the picture was a young man whose work he had spotted at a festival and who he knew by instinct had something out of the ordinary to bring to the project. Hilary Harris was a New Yorker whose previous films had been quite some way from the mainstream of industrial documentary. His output had been largely experimental but Grierson recognised that in his feeling for shapes and structures he would bring a new vision to the story of Clyde shipbuilding. If objective proof were required of that judgement it came afterwards in the award of the Hollywood Oscar to Harris and *Seawards* for 'Best Short Subject (Live Action)' in 1961.

There are several ironies associated with *Seawards*. Despite involving just about every film-maker in Scotland (dozens of launches had to be covered) it was an American who directed. More significant was the historical coincidence

that a film which came at the end of a line of great cinema documentaries was about an industry which was itself just about to suffer a catastrophic decline. Perhaps most ironically of all *Seawards* proved that Scottish film-making, relying only on sponsorship, could win an Academy Award, the highest accolade. If the Government required evidence to support its belief that there was no need to subsidise Films of Scotland from the public purse, this was it. Maybe if Films of Scotland had won the Oscar and gone bust at the same time, something might have been done, but it was not to be.

Quite apart from shipbuilding documentaries (John Brown's and the other Clyde yards figured in industrial and educational films other than *Seawards*), the Clyde yards had their place in feature film making. Michael Powell's first film with a Scottish connection, *Red Ensign* (1934), was a tale of rival boatbuilders, one determined to reinvigorate shipbuilding with new designs and the other bent on stopping him.

To modern eyes *Red Ensign* is a strange work; its message is 'patriotism before business'. Although it is very much a studio affair with stilted dialogue and awkward, stagy set pieces, it also contains brilliantly creative documentary shipbuilding sequences. Powell, who was most definitely not a documentarist, mischievously named one of the characters, a riveter, 'Grierson'. The hero, Barr (Leslie Banks), introduces him thus: 'Grierson taught me to rivet when I first came to the Clyde'. There is also the strong suspicion of a sub-text that this is a film as much about the British film industry as about shipbuilding.

Floodtide (1949) contained only a few sequences shot on location but it did have the virtue of a strong Scottish dimension in the writing by George Blake and in the casting of a number of Scots actors. The story concerns the rise of a country boy who works his way up to become the shipyard's best designer and falls in love with the boss' daughter. The melodramatic climax occurs when the ship he has designed is threatened by a gale.

An earlier film scripted by George Blake was

also concerned with shipbuilding, and had patriotism and wartime morale very much in mind. Set in the thirties *The Shipbuilders* (1943) was about the wartime need to sustain the country's sea power whatever the odds.

In the field of film exhibition, Clydebank had the distinction of being the location for the first 'multiplex' cinema in Scotland when what is now the UCI opened the doors on its ten screens in August 1988.

The town also boasts film connections through a former pupil at the High School, Fulton Mackay (1922-87). Mackay had a distinguished stage career and was himself a dramatist. His screen appearances covered the best part of forty years, and were often in films with Scottish subjects, such as *The Brave Don't Cry* (1952) (see **Knockshinnoch**), *Laxdale Hall* (1953) and *Ill Fares the Land* (1983)(see **Applecross**). Perhaps his most memorable role was as Ben Knox, the beach-dweller in Bill Forsyth's *Local Hero* (1983) (see **Morar**). He appeared in *Gumshoe* (1971) and *Britannia Hospital* (1982) and in 1979 played his famous television persona, Mr Mackay, the prison warder, in the big screen version of *Porridge* with Ronnie Barker.

Clydebank's famous musical sons, Wet Wet Wet, sustained the number one spot in the charts for a record breaking fifteen weeks in 1995 with their version of 'Love is All Around' from *Four Weddings and a Funeral*.

Floodtide (1949, Aquila). Gordon Jackson and Jimmy Logan.

● *Red Ensign*
GB, 1934, Gaumont, 69 mins. Written and directed by Michael Powell. With Leslie Banks, Carol Goodner, Frank Vosper and John Laurie.

● *The Shipbuilders*
GB, 1943, British National, 89 mins. Directed by John Baxter. With Clive Brook, Morland Graham and Finlay Currie.

● *Floodtide*
GB, 1949, Aquila, 90 mins. Directed by Frederick Wilson. Written by George Blake. With Gordon Jackson, Elizabeth Sellars, John Laurie, Jack Lambert, Jimmy Logan and Archie Duncan.

● *Seawards the Great Ships*
GB, 1961, Templar Film Studios, 29 mins. Directed by Hilary Harris. Treatment by John Grierson. Commentary by Clifford Hanley. Music by Iain Hamilton.

COATBRIDGE: a film museum

On the face of it, Coatbridge is in much the same situation as any medium-sized Scottish town that has lost all its cinemas. Anyone wanting to see a movie has to travel. There can be little or no sense of film belonging to the community. That could change radically in a few years. Coatbridge has ambitions to have a central role in Scottish film affairs.

For several years, the Summerlee Heritage Trust has been collecting materials related to the history of film in Scotland. These range from production equipment from Templar Films (see **Glasgow, Lynedoch Street**) and artefacts on loan from the Scottish Film Council, to a full-scale cinema organ.

With these collections as its base, a Scottish Film Museum is proposed near the town centre. Part of the project will be to create a *cinema dynamique*, with a high definition projection system and seats that move in synchronisation with the images. There will also be a conventional cinema where the people of Coatbridge, Airdrie and many miles around can once more enjoy the movies.

Scottish cinema history has tended to look more closely at social rather than technical or economic aspects. Whereas film museums in other places (The Museum of the Moving Image, in London, or the National Film and Television Museum, in Bradford) have the technology of the medium well to the fore, in Scotland it seems that there is an insatiable interest in the story of cinema-going itself. No doubt nostalgia has something to do with it. Debates about paying with a 'jeely-jar' to get into the pictures recur frequently and inconclusively. The importance of divan, 'chummy', seats and their role in increasing the population; the use of mass disinfectants during performances; the definition of a 'flea pit'; the idiosyncrasies of staff, particularly managers and usherettes, seem to take precedence over the films themselves. What seemed to matter, for at least the first half of cinema's history, was the communal experience.

Scotland owes the survival of much of the tangible evidence of its cinema history to the fact that one or two individuals, such Ronald B Macluskie, the Director of SFC (1968-86)(see **Glasgow, Dowanhill**), had a clear sense of its importance and ensured that, as far as possible, nothing to do with cinema in Scotland, however ephemeral, was thrown away. It would be good to think that a part of the past that touched virtually everybody was finally to be secured for posterity.

COLONSAY: a destination

As is clear from the map we are shown in the film, and the reference to 'Pig's Paradise', Colonsay was the island of 'Kiloran', the heroine's intended destination, in the Powell and Pressburger film *I Know Where I'm Going* (1945). The famous whirlpool in the Gulf of Corrievreckan, to the north-east, provides the climax of the romance. Most of the location work, however was carried out on Mull (see **Mull**).

CRIEFF: Neil Paterson

Crieff and its environs, notably the Sma' Glen (see **Sma' Glen**), have been the scene of film and television-making for many years, but the town's main claim to movie fame is as the home of the Oscar-winning screenwriter Neil Paterson. Although he was born in Greenock in 1915, Paterson was most firmly identified with Crieff. He remained there, despite the opportunity to move to Hollywood that his success earned him, until his death in 1995.

Paterson was one of that extremely rare species, a Scot who makes it big in the movies without leaving home. Grierson even quoted him as an example of why it was not really necessary to have an indigenous film industry; the argument was that if you had the talent you could become part of the international film scene wherever you were – a thesis that might apply to writers but not to many others.

Paterson began his professional life as a journalist in Dundee and it was there he achieved what he regarded as his greatest success in life. Despite being an amateur he became captain of Dundee United Football Club. But there is strong evidence that his literary accomplishments overshadowed his football achievements. His first novel *The China Run*, published in 1948, is a minor masterpiece and really ought to have been filmed by now.

Paterson's *Man on a Tightrope* (1953) and *The Kidnappers* (also 1953) did make it to the screen (see **Glen Affric**) and, in 1959, his screenplay adaptation of the John Braine novel *Room at the Top* (1958) won an Academy Award.

Paterson also involved himself in the promotion of film. He was a governor of the British Film Institute and was a key figure in the establishment of the National Film School. For a short time he also acted as Director of the Films of Scotland Committee.

The actor Denis Lawson was born (1947) and brought up in Crieff. Best known in a Scottish context for his role as the multi-talented Gordon Urquhart in *Local Hero* (1983) (see **Morar, Pennan**), his other big screen credits include 'Wedge', the Red Two pilot in the *Star Wars* trilogy.

CRINAN: puffers

The area around Crinan and its famous Canal is particularly associated with puffers, the stout little steam freighters which for many years carried general cargoes all over the west coast of Scotland. Parts of the *Para Handy* series and the poaching sequence in *The Maggie* (1953) (see **Islay**) were filmed here. The area has also been used for its 'wilderness' qualities as in, for example, *From Russia with Love* (1963) (see **Rannoch Moor**).

CRUACHAN: *The Hollow Mountain*

The splendid Ben Cruachan is unique among Scottish mountains by being hollow. Deep within it there is a power station which operates on the 'pump-storage' system, generating electricity from water descending from a dam above it and using surplus power to send the water back up again as the demand allows. A rather less simplistic explanation, and the record of the building of this curiosity, was contained in *The Hollow Mountain* (1966) produced by Templar Films for Films of Scotland. The commentary was spoken by Joseph Macleod who, twenty years previously, had made an abortive attempt to launch a full-scale Scottish film industry under the banner of 'Scottish National Film Studios' (see **Glasgow, St Vincent Street**).

● *The Hollow Mountain*
GB, 1966, Templar Film Studios, 15 mins. Directed by Robert Riddell Black. Camera, David Low. Commentary by Joseph Macleod.

CRUDEN BAY: Dracula

If, as some people fondly believe, Bram Stoker found the inspiration for 'Dracula' in the Aberdeenshire fishing village and the nearby Castle of Slains, then Scotland is responsible for an extraordinary number of bad films (and a few funny ones). However there seems to be evidence that Stoker had at least begun his famous novel before he first visited Cruden Bay and although there may be a case for saying that he was influenced by local customs and scenery, which is certainly dramatic (though in a very un-Transylvanian way), it may be safer not to claim that the Dracula film industry was invented here.

CULLODEN

On 16 April 1746 the Duke of Cumberland defeated the army of Charles Edward Stuart, The Young Pretender, on Culloden Moor. Culloden was a dreadful turning point in the history of the Highlands.

The story of *Bonnie Prince Charlie* has often found its way to the screen, but never satisfactorily. A silent version from Gaumont in 1923 starred Ivor Novello and Gladys Cooper. David Niven was the Prince in the tartan drenched (and very expensive) 1948 effort directed by Anthony Kimmins. This one had a screenplay by Clemence Dane, a good supporting cast and music by Ian Whyte, best known as the conductor of the BBC Scottish Orchestra, but it was generally considered a disaster.

The battle of Culloden was the focus of Peter Watkins' remarkable film *Culloden*, produced in 1963 for the BBC. The quasi-documentary style involved the use of a hand-held camera, 'interviews' with the protagonists and highly dynamic editing to place the viewer uncomfortably in the middle of the action. The audience is left in no doubt about, for example, the effect of grapeshot on the human frame. In *The War Game* (1966) Watkins used the same techniques so powerfully that the film was deemed unshowable on television.

The bitter account of the history of the battle, which attributed defeat to incompetence as much as to the overwhelming strength of one side, was controversial but the audiovisual impact of *Culloden* was unforgettable. There could be nothing but admiration for the ingenuity with which microscopic resources were deployed to convince the viewer that a real battle was in progress. The crew had only one field gun at their disposal to represent the

whole artillery and it was said that extras were re-made up several times to appear as different individuals on both sides.

Although it was widely shown at film festivals and in film theatres all over the world it was its contribution to the development of television and its techniques that made *Culloden* famous. Seen more thirty years after its production and in the context of the two hundred and fiftieth anniversary of the battle it still had the power and freshness to overshadow any of the other TV accounts. Unfortunately, little attention was paid (especially in television) to Watkins' experimentation with ways in which the moving image might meaningfully handle history and contemporary issues. After *The War Game* Watkins retreated from TV film-making entirely.

It is axiomatic (or certainly should be) that anyone who achieves the near impossibility of making a feature film deserves to be treated with respect, whatever the quality of the outcome. Ingenuity, not just in the making but in the financing, was at a premium for *Chasing the Deer* (1994). In an almost unprecedented procedure, members of the public were invited to invest in the film of the Jacobite adventure of 1745-46 in return for the opportunity to take part as extras, to be listed on the credits as associate producers and to attend gala presentations of the completed work. Contrary to the expectations of most film professionals, the film was made and premiered to enthusiastic audiences throughout Scotland. It even made a creditable ninth place in the list of British films on cinema release in 1994. Further films financed on this basis were planned. *The Bruce* (see **Bannockburn**) was released in 1996 and a *Macbeth* is expected.

The critics acknowledged the achievement but were, at best, charitable about the movie. Just as there are no awards for bringing a film in on budget, audiences are only mildly interested in the circumstances of a production and, however strong the appeal to their patriotism, judge the worth of a film by what they see on the unforgiving screen. It is production values, particularly script and acting, that they notice, especially when there are similar films with which to make comparisons.

A healthy film culture needs diversity of production and in pioneering a new way of making movies *Chasing the Deer* represents a form of progress for film in Scotland. Any new funding method that delivers satisfaction to investors as well as to the hired participants deserves applause. Low-budget and virtually-no-budget films can just occasionally surprise and delight and even break through into the mainstream with happy results for all concerned. The key, however, is that old commodity, talent.

Donald of the Colours (1975) took Culloden as the starting point for an adventure story of fleeing clansmen, Redcoats and loyalty in the aftermath of the battle. It was a 16mm amateur production, but one out of the ordinary. It was typical of the work of Ron Millar and the Aberdeen-based Group Five (formed in 1962), which fearlessly

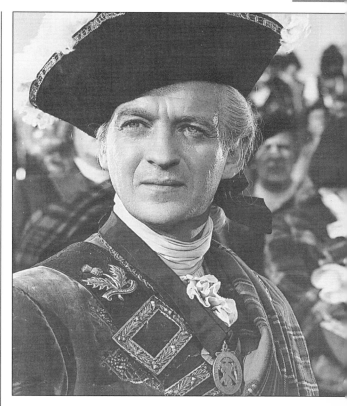

(right) **Bonnie Prince Charlie** (1948). David Niven.
(below) **Culloden** (1964, BBC).

tackled epic subjects with titles such as *Race to Nowhere* and *Time Bomb* and took in their stride the filming of blazing cars going over cliffs and submarines diving with actors standing on the outside. Not normally the stuff of amateur films!

● *Bonnie Prince Charlie*
GB, 1948, London Films, 118 mins. Directed by Anthony Kimmins. Screenplay, Clemence Dane. Music by Ian Whyte. With David Niven, Margaret Leighton, Jack Hawkins, Judy Campbell, Finlay Currie, Ronald Adam and John Laurie.

● *Culloden*
GB, 1964, BBC, 71 mins. Directed and written by Peter Watkins. Historical adviser, John Prebble. Cinematography, Dick Bush. With George McBean and Alan Pope.

● *Chasing the Deer*
GB, 1994, Cromwell Films in association with Lamancha Productions, 105 mins. Directed by Graham Holloway. Produced by Bob Carruthers. With Brian Blessed, Iain Cuthbertson, Matthew Zajac, Fish, Brian Donald, Dominique Carrara and Jake D'Arcy.

CUMBERNAULD: *Gregory's Girl*

Scotland's new towns all had promotional films made about them, mostly during the sixties through Films of Scotland, but it was a feature film that gave Cumbernauld a very special place in the story of Scottish film.

Gregory's Girl (1980) was conceived by Bill Forsyth before *That Sinking Feeling* (see **Glasgow**) but the money for it, little as it was, could not be raised until after the success of the even more shoestring Glasgow film which was received with surprise and delight at the Edinburgh Film Festival in 1979. With proof that Forsyth was a genuine feature film-maker, funds from Scottish Television and the National Film Finance Corporation were at last forthcoming. Even so, the total budget was less than £300,000.

The story of Bill Forsyth and *Gregory's Girl*'s contribution to his progress from tea boy at Stanley Russell's Thames and Clyde Films to director of some of Hollywood's finest, is one of the few parts of Scottish cinema history to have been thoroughly documented and dissected. Despite that attention, and the passage of time, it is still possible to look again at the movie, enjoy its freshness, its style, its fun and marvel at the fact that a film about adolescents in a Scottish new town could turn out to be so universal in its appeal as to generate cinema queues from Tollcross to Toronto and Tokyo.

The apparent innocence of *Gregory's Girl* (and some of his other films) hid the serious Forsyth, but one's chief recollection of it is delight and the sense, for the first time, that truly indigenous Scottish film-making to a world standard was a possibility. A Scotland represented by tartan-free teenage romance was not to everyone's taste but for most people associated with film in Scotland this was an occasion for celebration, for a new confidence in the future. It was maybe a reflection on our national psyche, however, that the cheering only really began when the film's London and overseas success became fully apparent. As ever, it required external verification that something good had happened in Scotland before we really believed it.

There were several notable acting performances in *Gregory's Girl* not least those of John Gordon Sinclair, Dee Hepburn, Clare Grogan, Jake D'Arcy and Chic Murray but it is to collective effort and to the special human insight of Forsyth that the credit mainly belongs. A key contribution, however, was made by the camera-work of Michael Coulter, one of a family of contributors to film in Scotland, who has worked with Forsyth on all but one of his feature films. Coulter's own film career to date has been one of the most successful of all the contemporary Scots. His credits for cinematography, in addition to the Forsyth films, include *The Dressmaker* (1988), *The Long Day Closes* (1992), *Four Weddings and a Funeral* (1994) and *Sense and Sensibility*

(1996) for which he received an Oscar nomination in 1996.

Chic Murray (1921-85) whose brilliant cameo as the piano-playing headmaster was one of the joys of *Gregory's Girl*, appeared in a small number of films, mostly sex comedies and farces such as *Secrets of a Door to Door Salesman* (1973), *What's Up Nurse* (1977) *Can I Come Too* (1979). He also appeared in the James Bond send-up, *Casino Royale* (1979). The only serious attempts to use his talents on the big screen, other than in *Gregory's Girl*, were in *The Boat* (1976) directed by Laurence Henson and in Murray Grigor's *Scotch Myths* (1982).

In early 1996, Bill Forsyth announced his intention to make a follow-up to *Gregory's Girl* in which the adult Gregory, still confused about life, was a teacher at the same school he had attended as a pupil sixteen years previously.

● *Gregory's Girl*
GB, 1980, Lake Films/NFFC/Scottish Television, 91 mins. Written and Directed by Bill Forsyth. Produced by Clive Parsons and Davina Belling. Photography Michael Coulter. With John Gordon Sinclair, Dee Hepburn, Clare Grogan, Jake D'Arcy and Chic Murray.

D*d*

DIRLETON: Bardot

Dirleton Castle, twenty miles or so east of Edinburgh, was chosen by Serge Bourguignon as the principal location for his 1967 production *A Coeur Joie* [*Two Weeks in September*]. His star was Brigitte Bardot, who caused something of a stir in East Lothian.

The Ghost Goes West (1935). Robert Donat with packaged castle.

Sadly, the film, which was premiered at the Edinburgh Film Festival, was not one of her, or Bourguignon's, best. The story of a French model in London who, on a whim, goes off to Scotland with a handsome man she has just met, was just silly. James Robertson Justice as 'Mclintock', provided local colour.

● *A Coeur Joie*
France/GB, 1967, Francos Films, 100 mins. Directed by Serge Bourguignon. With Brigitte Bardot, Laurent Terzieff, Jean Rochefort and James Robertson Justice.

DOUNE: castles

Scottish castles appeal not only to those who want to depict the dramatic and the romantic but also to those who trade in the surreal. Nobody fits the latter category quite like the Monty Python team and Doune Castle is only one ancient Scottish site that has been honoured with their presence. Sheriffmuir, Killin, Castle Stalker and Doune all feature in *Monty Python and the Holy Grail* (1975).

Perhaps the oddest use of an imaginary Scottish castle occurs in *The Ghost Goes West* (1935). René Clair (director of *The Italian Straw Hat, Le Million, Sous Les Toits de Paris* and many films of great charm and wit) was imported by Alexander Korda to make a film about an American who buys a Scottish castle and transports it home, stone by stone, only to find that the resident ghost has come along as part of the package. Apart from tartan, the Scottish connection is minimal. The characters have names like Glourie and McNiff and Robert Donat appears in full highland dress. Muir Mathieson directed the music.

● *The Ghost Goes West*
GB, 1935, London Film Productions, 90 mins. Directed by René Clair. Produced by Alexander Korda. Music by Mischa Spoliansky, directed by Muir Mathieson. With Robert Donat, Jean Parker and Elsa Lanchester.

DRUMMOND CASTLE

In *Rob Roy* (1995)(see **Aberfoyle**) Drummond Castle near Perth spectacularly represented the Duke of Montrose's seat of power. One of the castle's greatest assets was its formal garden which gave a strong sense of contrast with the poverty of the living conditions in the MacGregors' clachan.

DUMBARTON: A J Cronin

A J Cronin (1896-1981), most famous as the originator of Dr Finlay, (see **Callander**) was born in Cardross and brought up in Dumbarton where he attended the Academy before going to Glasgow University and the study of medicine, which in due course led him Harley Street. His own childhood provided the raw material for the novel filmed as *The Green Years* (1946). One of his grandfathers was a hatter who had a shop in Dumbarton High Street so Cronin was writing from immediate knowledge when he produced, in 1931, *Hatter's Castle*, the novel which effectively launched his new career.

Hatter's Castle was set in 'Levenford', a thin disguise for Cronin's home town. It tells the tale of a family dominated by a tyrannical father, and is usually described as grim and melodramatic. Nonetheless it was a popular success and in 1941 it was filmed with a strong cast, at least one of whom, Deborah Kerr, had a connection with the area. Her original home was in Helensburgh (see **Helensburgh**).

A J Cronin was the author of at least four other works which found their way to the big screen. Each was distinguished by a strong director and cast. The first, *The Citadel* (1938) directed by King Vidor, starred Robert Donat, Ralph Richardson and Rosalind Russell. It received an Oscar nomination for its tale of a young doctor's struggles in a mining village. The following year RKO released *Vigil in the Night* a hospital drama directed by George Stevens. *The Spanish Gardener* (1956), directed by Philip Leacock, starred Dirk Bogarde with Michael Hordern and with Jon Whiteley who had partnered Bogarde in *Hunted* (1952) (see **Portpatrick**). *Beyond this Place* (1959) was the story of a son's fight to win his father's freedom from wrongful conviction. The director was Jack Cardiff and the cast included two Scots well known as character actors, Moultrie Kelsall and Jameson Clark.

Dumbarton was the birthplace of a leading New York rock musician with a interesting film connection. David Byrne (born 1952) formed the band Talking Heads who achieved international success in the nineteen eighties and led to him being described in *Baseline's Encyclopaedia of Film* as 'one of the most celebrated popular musicians in the world'. Byrne's movie credits include providing music for, amongst others, Bertollucci's *The Last Emperor* (1987) for which he shared an Oscar with Ryuichi Sakamoto and Cong Su. One of his first critically acclaimed successes was for his collaboration with Jonathan Demme in *Stop Making Sense* (1984). Byrne directed *Once in a Lifetime* (1980), *True Stories* (1986) and *Between the Teeth* (1993) as well as making various screen appearances.

James Cosmo, a familiar face on Scottish screens, often in the role of a 'heavy', was also born in Dumbarton. He followed in the footsteps of his father, James Copeland, by becoming an actor. His first screen appearance was at the age of eighteen in *Battle of Britain* (1969). His most recent credits include *Braveheart* (1995) and *Trainspotting* (1996).

Dumbarton itself appears in some remarkable colour footage of the town's V E Day celebrations in 1945, now preserved in the Scottish Film Archive. Colour stock was extremely hard to come by at that time, particularly for amateurs, but the celebrations to mark the end of the war in Europe were successfully recorded for posterity.

● *The Citadel*
GB, 1938, MGM, 110 mins. Directed by King Vidor. Based on the novel by AJ Cronin. With Robert Donat, Ralph Richardson, Rosalind Russell, Rex Harrison, Emlyn Williams and Felix Aylmer.

Hatter's Castle (1941, Paramount). Deborah Kerr and Emlyn Williams.

● *Vigil in the Night*
US, 1939, RKO, 96 mins. Directed by George Stevens. Based on the novel by AJ Cronin, adapted by Fred Guiol, PJ Wolfson and Rowland Leigh. With Carole Lombard, Brian Aherne, Anne Shirley, Julien Mitchell and Peter Cushing.

● *Hatter's Castle*
GB, 1941, Paramount, 102 mins. Directed by Lance Comfort. Based on the novel by AJ Cronin. With Robert Newton, Deborah Kerr, James Mason, Emlyn Williams and Beatrice Varley.

● *The Green Years*
US, 1946, MGM, 125 mins. Directed by Victor Saville. Based on the novel by AJ Cronin. With Charles Coburn, Tom Drake, Dean Stockwell, Gladys Cooper, Jessica Tandy and Andy Clyde.

● *The Spanish Gardner*

GB, 1956, Rank Film Productions, 97 mins. Directed by Philip Leacock. From the novel by AJ Cronin. With Dirk Bogarde, Michael Hordern, Jon Whiteley, Cyril Cusack, Geoffrey Keen, Bernard Lee and Rosalie Crutchley.

● *Beyond This Place*

GB, 1959, Georgefield Productions, 90 mins. Directed by Jack Cardiff. From the novel by AJ Cronin. With Van Johnson, Vera Miles, Emlyn Williams, Bernard Lee, Moultrie Kelsall, Leo McKern and Jameson Clark.

DUMFRIES

Despite the valiant efforts of David Hayman in the bicentennial year of the poet's death (see **Alloway**), a serious contemporary film on the life of Robert Burns has yet to get off the ground. Among the list of great unmade Scottish films, a Burns film figures large. However, the town of Dumfries makes a useful connection between the bard and the movies by housing the local regional film theatre in the Robert Burns Centre beside the River Nith.

Some of the country to the west of Dumfries, the more pastoral bits, look surprisingly unlike Scotland. This can occasionally be an advantage for the South West Scotland Screen Commission, promoting the area's suitability for location filming. A classic case of 'second unit' work occurred with Brian De Palma's *Mission Impossible* (1996), the high-tec, big screen adaptation of the television series. Requiring a stretch of railway line, free of overhead wires and bridges, the Tom Cruise, Jon Voight action spectacular chose the Dumfries-Stranraer line to double for the approach to the Channel Tunnel in Kent.

William Shea (1862-1918) was a native of Dumfries who acted in American films from as early as 1905. He was described as the first comedian of the Vitagraph company. His huge credits list includes *Julius Ceasar* and *Romeo and Juliet* (both 1908) for the director William V Ranous and numerous short silent films for George Baker, Wally Van, Herbert Brenon, Edmund F Stratton, Ralph Ince and many others.

John Laurie, one of Scotland's most accomplished actors, was born in Dumfries in 1897. His London debut was in 1922. A distinguished stage career in which he played all the great Shakespeare roles at The Old Vic and Stratford and which took him all over the world (he played Lear in Australia in 1959) was complemented by no less than sixty film appearances, beginning in 1930 with *Juno and the Paycock*.

In cinema, Laurie tended to get the dour and crusty roles, though not invariably. He could be threatening, as the crofter in Hitchcock's *The Thirty Nine Steps* (1935) (see **Forth Bridge**) or patrician in *The Edge of the World* (1937) (see **Foula**) but, whatever the part, his was a genuine screen presence. His other Scottish films (of which there were very few) included *The Brothers* (1947) (see **Skye**), *Floodtide* (1949) (see **Clydebank**) and the 1960 Disney version of *Kidnapped* (see **Appin**) in which he was splendidly cast as Ebenezer Balfour. He was John Knox in *Tudor Rose* (1936). In his later years he became very famous for his television role as Private Frazer in *Dad's Army* which was released in a big screen version in 1971. John Laurie died in 1980.

DUNBEATH: Neil Gunn

Neil Gunn (1891-1974), was born in Dunbeath on the Caithness coast where his father was the skipper of a fishing boat. Gunn's identification with that part of the world, with its people and their history, was total. Almost all his writing was informed by the communal experience of displacement and resettlement in the Clearances, by the crossover of Gaelic and Norse cultures and by the impact of landscape and sea on the people who made their hard livings from them.

With their sense of humanity in a hostile environment and the dramas they contain, Gunn's novels should be strong candidates for translation to cinema. In fact, with the exception of a largely forgotten production of

The Silver Darlings (premiered at the first Edinburgh Film Festival in 1947) and so-far unrealised proposals for *Morning Tide* and *Butcher's Broom*, little has been accomplished.

In February 1996, however, it was announced that with the help of a grant from the National Lottery a new production of *The Silver Darlings* was to be produced and scripted by John McGrath. McGrath, with a distinguished track record as writer, adapter and producer (for example *Billion Dollar Brain* (1967), *Bofors Gun* (1968), *The Dressmaker* (1988), *Robin Hood* (1991)) had already made a significant contribution to Scottish screen culture through the filming of his plays, *The Cheviot, the Stag, and the Black Black Oil* (1974) and *Blood Red Roses* (1986) and as the writer and producer of *Mairi Mhor* (1994) (see **Skye**). Within these lie themes of cultural conflict and change in Scotland which are promisingly close to Gunn's concerns.

The Silver Darlings (1947).

● *The Silver Darlings*
GB, 1947, Holyrood Film Productions, 85 mins. Directed by Clarence Elder. With Clifford Evans, Helen Shingler and Carl Bernard.

DUNDEE

Dundee's initial experience of film was the result of enthusiasm on the part of one local individual, Peter Feathers, who gave the city's first showing of moving pictures at his shop in Castle Street in 1896.

With one notable exception, Dundee's film fame is mostly of the vicarious kind. The exception is a dramatised documentary made in 1944. *Children of the City* was about the unglamorous subject of juvenile delinquency, a problem that had been exacerbated during the war through the absence of male parents. It was produced by Paul Rotha for the Scottish Home Department and directed by Budge Cooper (whose husband, Donald Alexander, directed *Wealth of a Nation* (1938)). It was a model of its kind.

It told very simply the story of three boys caught by the police breaking into a shop and the procedures used to deal with them. The setting was Dundee (although some footage was shot in Aberdeen) and the sense of time and place was remarkably strong, thanks in no small part to exceptional camera-work by Wolfgang Suschitsky. (Suschitsky was also the cinematographer for *Ring of Bright Water* (1969) (see **Loch Hourn**)). It was a rather brave film in its candour about the problems but also humane and instructive in presenting an essentially enlightened system's attempts to deal with them.

Otherwise, the city of jute, jam and journalism has seldom been called on to be itself in movies (television has been slightly more generous with the thriller *Jute City* in 1991). In 1943, Dundee doubled for Holland in a powerful war story *The Silver Fleet* in which a Dutch submarine builder sabotaged his own boats to deny the Nazis their use, sacrificing his own life in the process. There was a distinguished cast, led by Ralph Richardson, Googie Withers and Esmund Knight. There was little of Dundee to recognise in the film other than a few shots of the docks and a glimpse of the Fife coast across the Firth, but years later stories were told of the shock caused to Dundonians by the sight of people in Gestapo uniforms having tea in Reform Street. The producers of *The Silver Fleet* were Michael Powell and Emeric Pressburger whose professional interest in Scotland manifested itself in several important films (see **Foula** and **Orkney, Scapa Flow**).

A more recent role for Dundee was as Moscow in *An Englishman Abroad* (1983), a part it shared with Glasgow (see **Glasgow**). It may seem a backhanded compliment to be thought compatible with the outward appearance of the Soviet Union.

A positive and significant contribution to the progress of moving images is to be found in the work of Duncan of Jordanstone College,

Children of the City (1944).

The Super Sound Cinema, Dundee, in the 1930s.

now a faculty of the University of Dundee. Within the college, the School of Television and Imaging offers undergraduate courses in computer animation design and time-based art and a postgraduate diploma in electronic imaging. The school has built a reputation as one of the finest centres for the teaching of electronic graphics for television and its graduates are regarded as among the UK's best in the discipline.

The actor Brian Cox was born in Dundee in 1946. Best known for his distinguished stage and television work, his big screen credits include both the 1995 historical epics *Braveheart* and *Rob Roy*.

Dundee's most famous citizen, the poet and tragedian William McGonagall, received rough treatment in *The Great McGonagall* (1974). The combination of Spike Milligan as the great man and Peter Sellers as Queen Victoria should have been irresistible, but it wasn't.

● *The Silver Fleet*
GB, 1943, Archers Film Productions, 88 mins. Directed by Gordon Wellesley and Vernon Sewell. Produced by Michael Powell and Emeric Pressburger. With Ralph Richardson, Googie Withers, Esmond Knight, Beresford Egan and Valentine Dyall.

● *Children of the City*
GB, 1944, Paul Rotha Productions for The Ministry of Information and The Scottish Home Department. 20 mins. Written and Directed by Budge Cooper. Cinematography by Wolfgang Suschitsky.

● *The Great McGonagall*
GB, 1974, Darlton, 89 mins. Directed by Joe McGrath. With Spike Milligan, Peter Sellers, Julia Foster, Julian Chagrin, John Bluthal and Valentine Dyall.

DUNFERMLINE: Moira Shearer

Moira Shearer was born in Dunfermline in 1926. An outstanding young ballerina, she joined Sadler's Wells Ballet at the age of sixteen and later extended her activities to film and stage. Her film debut, as Victoria Page, the central character in Powell and Pressburger's *The Red Shoes* (1948), could hardly have been more propitious. The role needed (and got) an entirely credible performance as both a top flight dancer and actress. Unlike most 'behind the scenes' movies, this one required that the heroine sustain a complete short ballet embedded in the plot. The dance, the music (for which Brian Easdale received an Oscar nomination) and some

Moira Shearer in Powell and Pressburger's
Red Shoes (1948).

extraordinary cinematic imagination blended exceptionally well, though the melodramatic nature of the story now seems a little dated.

Subsequently, Moira Shearer, appeared in another Powell and Pressburger film, *The Tales of Hoffman* (1951), as well as in Powell's *Peeping Tom* (1948).

● *The Red Shoes*
GB, 1948, Rank/Archers Film Productions, 136 mins. Directed, Produced and Scripted by Emeric Pressburger and Michael Powell. Cinematography by Jack Cardiff. Music by Brian Easdale, directed by Thomas Beecham. Choreography by Robert Helpman. With Anton Walbrook, Marius Goring, Moira Shearer, Léonide Massine, Robert Helpman and Ludmilla Tcherina.

Hamlet (1990, Warner Bros). Mel Gibson.

DUNNOTTAR CASTLE: *Hamlet*

Dunnottar, on its rocky outcrop above curved beaches just south of Stonehaven, is one of Scotland's most spectacularly located castles, even by the standards of such as Tantallon and Slains. Its history is equally dramatic and it is perhaps surprising that its movie potential took so long to be recognised. It finally was, and for an appropriately glamorous production, Zeffirelli's 1990 version of *Hamlet*, starring Mel Gibson as the unhappy Prince. The film also used parts of Blackness Castle on the Firth of Forth but those who were doubtful about the setting or the casting were satisfactorily confounded by a thoughtful and thoroughly textured film, which if not the greatest ever screen realisation of the play was certainly one of the best performed and most convincingly set.

The cast had considerable strength in depth. There were three former theatrical Hamlets in other roles – Alan Bates (Claudius), Paul Scofield (The Ghost) and Ian Holm (Polonius). With Glenn Close as Gertrude and Helena Bonham-Carter as Ophelia this was clearly going to be one of the most significant films to choose Scotland for its location work.

In advancing the general cause of film in Scotland the film took on even greater significance. At the time of its shooting, moves were being made to set up a film commission for Scotland to attract foreign companies to shoot here. Local authorities and others were being canvassed for their support and a brochure was being prepared advocating the establishment of what became Scottish Screen Locations (see **Glasgow, Dowanhill**). Capitalising on the publicity surrounding the shooting of *Hamlet*, and the growing realisation of the economic impact such a shoot had on the local economy, The Scottish Film Council asked Signor Zeffirelli to provide the preface to the publication, which he kindly did, and his film and Dunnottar became part of Scottish film history.

● *Hamlet*
US, 1990, Warner/Nelson, 135 mins. Directed by Franco Zeffirelli. Produced by Dante Ferretti. Cinematography, David Watkins. Music, Ennio Morricone. With Mel Gibson, Glenn Close, Alan Bates, Helena Bonham-Carter, Paul Scofield and Ian Holm.

DUNOON AND THE HOLY LOCH: Polaris and Eric Campbell

The paradox that for many years one of the most beautiful corners of the Clyde should host the most appalling weapons of mass destruction in the form of the United States Polaris submarine base has not been lost on Scottish film-makers. In particular, Paul Murton and his colleague David Halliday returned to the place and the theme on more than one occasion.

Tin Fish (1990) was Murton's graduation film from the National Film and Television School. It concentrated on the local community's fears of the nuclear submarine base, as expressed by a local taxi driver. The cast included Jon Morrison, Matt Costello and Emma Thompson. The producer was Andrea Calderwood, later head of drama at BBC Scotland. Some years later, Emma Thompson, by now an international star, returned to work with Murton in the same area of Dunoon's hinterland on *The Blue Boy* (1994), a film primarily for television (though it had successful film festival showings) about a couple whose marital problems are exacerbated by a ghostly encounter.

Eric Campbell, who was born in Dunoon, was the first, and maybe the ultimate, film 'heavy'. There was no-one quite like him. His fame comes from his time with Chaplin who recognised him as the ideal foil for his 'little man'. Campbell is unforgettable as the villain in *The Count, The Cure, The Floorwalker, The Rink* and, most memorably of all, *Easy Street* (1917). Following the death of his wife, Campbell took to drink and his life came to a tragically premature end when he overturned his car in a high speed crash in Hollywood on 20 December 1917. Chaplin, despite his best efforts, was unable to find anyone quite the same to replace him. The oration at Campbell's funeral was delivered by his friend, Stan Laurel.

Although there is uncertainty about many of the details of Eric Campbell's life, even some doubts about his name and date of birth, it is known that he was born in Dunoon, in 1878 or 1882. His early stage experience was in the Glasgow music halls before he joined up with Fred Karno and he is reputed to have partnered Syd, Charlie Chaplin's brother. He also appeared with D'Oyly Carte as 'The Mikado', which must have been a wonderful piece of casting given that Campbell was six foot five and weighed about twenty stone.

In America, he appeared in some minor roles before joining Chaplin's Mutual Company for the two short years that made him one of the greatest screen villains.

Charlie Chaplin and Eric Campbell in **Easy Street** (1917).

● *Tin Fish*
GB, 1990, National Film and Television
School, 45 mins. Directed and written by Paul
Murton. Produced by Andrea Calderwood.
With Jon Morrison, Mat Costello and Emma
Thompson.

● *The Blue Boy*
GB, 1994, BBC Scotland, 64 mins. Directed by
Paul Murton. Produced by Kate Swan. With
Emma Thompson, Adrian Dunbar, Eleanor
Bron, David Horovitch, Joanna Roth and
Phyllida Law.

E*e*

The Accidental Golfer

The Scottish Borders might seem an unlikely setting for what is reputed to be the most successful home-grown Swedish film in cinema history, but *Den Ofrivillige Golfaren* [*The Accidental Golfer*](1991) was just that. Directed by, and starring, Lasse Aberg, it was one of a series whose nearest British equivalent would be the 'Carry On' films. The formula was to take a group of comic Swedes abroad on holiday and the plot centred on a bet between two of them that one can learn to play golf in a week.

The film was originally to have been made in Ireland but the newly formed Scottish Screen Locations attracted the company to Scotland. A beneficiary of the move was Jimmy Logan, an actor more associated with stage than screen, who played the key local character. Logan, who has been central to entertainment in Scotland since the nineteen forties, has been a comic, a great pantomime dame, an impresario, and on stage a straight actor of distinction (as Archie Rice in John Osborne's *The Entertainer*, for example). His cinema appearances have been relatively rare and have mostly done less than justice to his ability. His previous film credits included *Floodtide* (1949) (see **Clydebank**), *Wild Affair* (1963), *Carry On Abroad* (1972), *Carry On Girls* (1973) and Charlie Gormley's Glasgow film, *Living Apart Together* (1983).

Den Ofrivillige Golfaren [*The Accidental Golfer*]
Sweden, 1991, Viking Film, 100 mins. Written, directed by and starring Lasse Aberg. With Jon Skolmen, Hege Schoyen, Jimmy Logan, Mats Bergman and Margo Gunn.

EDINBURGH

There are few cities as blessed by geography and geology as Edinburgh. It has great vistas and poky corners and is ideal territory for movie-making. It can provide the setting for most human activity, and the light is frequently wonderful.

Edinburgh's history, real or imagined, has provided the raw material for dozens of films and in Robert Louis Stevenson (see **Howard Place**) and Sir Arthur Conan Doyle (see **Picardy Place**) the city produced two of the most filmed authors on the planet.

The connection between Edinburgh and the movies extends beyond the making to the celebrating. The city hosts the longest running film festival in the world and the Edinburgh Film Guild is probably the oldest extant film society (see **Lothian Road**). Moreover, the first commercial cinema show in Scotland was presented in Nicolson Street (see **Nicolson Street**).

There are many films about Edinburgh. Lots of short films, mostly of the tourist sort, such as *Waverley Steps* (1947), *Festival in Edinburgh* (1955), *The Edinburgh Festival* (1965), *Walkabout Edinburgh* with Richard Demarco (1970), *Sean Connery's Edinburgh* (1982) (see **Fountainbridge**), celebrate Edinburgh's cityscape and its Festival. There are feature films which go no further than representing the city with a cardboard castle and a superimposed caption, 'Edinburgh - Capital of Scotland'. Then there are films which show a bit of the place incidentally to the main action.

However, there is a small group of movies in which the character of the city is intended to be integral to the shape and feel of the film. *The Battle of the Sexes* (1959), for example, is an unlikely Edinburgh film in that it originates in 'The Cat-bird Seat', a James Thurber short story whose title refers to baseball. The translation to the Capital of Scotland is remarkably successful. The American commercial efficiency expert (played by Constance Cummings) is at odds with all the traditional values of Edinburgh, specifically of the old-established tweed firm owned by the besotted and hopelessly anglicised Macpherson (Robert Morley). Her main opposition is provided by Martin (Peter Sellers in one of his best roles) and there is a collection of worthies portrayed by some of the best-known Scottish actors of the time including Jameson Clark, Moultrie Kesall, Alex Mackenzie, Roddy McMillan, Abe Barker and James Gibson.

The director was Charles Crichton and the writer/producer was Monja Danischewsky who had worked with Alexander Mackendrick on *Whisky Galore!* (see **Barra**). The film was largely carried by Sellers who kept up an impeccable Edinburgh accent throughout. Of course, the movie takes liberties with the city; George Street

Peter Sellers affects surprise in **The Battle of the Sexes** (1959, Prometheus).

appears at right angles to Princes Street; Waverley Station exits at the back of the Royal Scottish Academy; Arthur's Seat doubles as the Highlands. But none of this matters. The image of Edinburgh as cold, hide-bound, reactionary, and harbouring homicidal accountants, may not be entirely fair, but it is certainly very funny.

A not entirely unrelated Edinburgh appeared in *The Prime of Miss Jean Brodie* (1968), directed by Ronald Neame (see **Stirling**). Muriel Spark's novel became a play and film in quick succession, both written by Jay Presson Allen. Although some of the location shooting was done in Glasgow, in every other regard this was an Edinburgh film with sequences shot in various parts of the city.

Maggie Smith won the 1969 Oscar for Best Actress for her performance as Jean Brodie, the eccentrically liberal teacher at the Marcia Blane School for Young Ladies. Her ambition for her selected brood of impressionable 'gels' leads to disaster in the Spanish Civil War for one of them and to no better fate for Miss Brodie herself.

Jean Brodie had the perfect Edinburgh name for someone with dangerously schizophrenic

tendencies and was proud of being descended from that other Brodie, the infamous deacon, whom Stevenson transfigured into Jekyll and Hyde. Perhaps not all the accents in the film were perfect and it was suggested that something of the original had been lost from book to play, and a little more from play to film. Nonetheless, it managed to evoke Edinburgh as well as any movie has done.

The Edinburgh Festival provided the context for *Happy Go Lovely* (1950) a semi-musical about a millionaire and a chorus girl. It starred David Niven and Vera-Ellen. Confusingly, Vera Ellen also led in the similar *Let's Be Happy* (1957), a remake of *Jeannie* (1941) in which the Scots girl was played by Barbara Mullen (see **Callander**).

The dark side of historic Edinburgh has had plenty of airing in films, from Rizzio's murder to Victorian body snatching. The realisation that this tradition of sinister deeds is being maintained is almost comforting but it still came as a shock to discover that in *Shallow Grave* (1994), directed by Danny Boyle, Scotland, let alone Edinburgh,

was capable of producing the smartest piece of 'film noir' to be seen in a long time. It confirmed the suspicion that behind the elegant facade of the New Town there were things going on that were better left untold. A tale of murder and greed in a yuppie flat to the north of Charlotte Square, told with tremendous panache, was a major addition to Edinburgh films. In truth, it was a story which might have been set anywhere young professionals on the make are thrown together, but somehow Edinburgh seemed just right. There is something in John Hodge's script that places it perfectly in the Capital. Ironically, the interiors were shot in a warehouse in Glasgow and the few Edinburgh exteriors are largely confined to the cobbled streets of the opening sequence.

Within two years, the team that made *Shallow Grave*, writer John Hodge, director Danny Boyle and producer Andrew Macdonald, had presented Edinburgh and Leith even more starkly as the setting for *Trainspotting* (1996) (see **Leith**).

Shallow Grave (1994, Figment Films). Kerry Fox, Ewan McGregor and Christopher Eccleston discover the corpse.

A similar kind of contemporary darkness was explored in *Tickets to the Zoo* (1994). The predicament of the young homeless and unemployed is as much a problem in Edinburgh as anywhere else and the fact that, as in *Trainspotting*, such human conditions exist in a city seen as glamorous by the outsider adds to the poignancy. The film by the late Brian Crumlish, and Christeen Winford was one of the first to show a very different Edinburgh from the rest, but with it a sympathetic understanding not often seen in Scottish film.

Edinburgh is the birthplace of one indisputable superstar, Sean Connery (see **Edinburgh, Fountainbridge**), and of another very distinguished actor, the marvellous Alastair Sim (1900–1976).

Although he tends to be remembered for his droll and sardonic appearances, Sim had in fact a considerable range, as a glance at his credits in over fifty films shows. Many of his parts were detective films of the thirties and forties, including the *Inspector Hornleigh* series, and had titles such as *Riverside Murder* (1935) and *Murder on Diamond Row* (1937). He was Scrooge in *A Christmas Carol* (1951) and the Laird in *Geordie* (1955). His Edinburgh accent does not seem to have been to his disadvantage but it is surprising he did not play in more Scottish films.

However, there is no point in denying that it is as the headmistress of hell's boarding school (and her brother), in *The Belles of St. Trinian's* (1955) and *Blue Murder at St. Trinian's* (1957), that he sticks in the public memory. Curiously, there is a further Edinburgh connection here. St Trinian's (actually St Trinnean's) was a private school in Palmerston Place and later at St Leonard's, Edinburgh, run by a Miss Catherine Lee from 1922 to 1946, when it closed. Miss Lee wrote a book called *The Real St Trinnean's*. Ronald Searle, on whose cartoon characters the films were based, met two of the pupils on holiday in Kirkcudbright in 1940. The rest is history.

Edinburgh's contribution to early American cinema included the work of two lesser known movie actors. The brothers David and Ernest Torrence were born in the city in the 1860s and they, like Connery, made their way to Hollywood and success. Ernest's credits include appearing in several classics including *The Covered Wagon* (1923), often regarded as the first true western and, the same year, the Lon Chaney version of *The Hunchback of Notre Dame*. He was also in *The Pony Express* (1924), *King of Kings* (1927) and Buster Keaton's *Steamboat Bill Jnr* (1928). He died in 1933.

David Torrence (1864-1951) was a Broadway actor and sometime rancher in Mexico who first appeared in Hollywood in 1913 in *The Prisoner of Zenda*, left, and then returned in 1921 in *Tess of the D'Urbervilles*. The following year he played in *Sherlock Holmes* with John Barrymore. Like Donald Crisp (see **Aberfeldy**), he played patriarchal roles including that of Lillian Gish's father in *Annie Laurie* (1927). (Crisp was Gish's father in *Broken Blossoms*.) Torrence's last two films (both 1939) were *Stanley and Livingstone* (see **Blantyre**) and *Rulers of the Sea* (see **Greenock**), the latter directed by the Glasgow-born Frank Lloyd.

An early Hollywood director, Colin T Campbell (1859-1928), was also born in Edinburgh. For about ten years from 1912 he directed silent films such as *The Fisherboy's Faith, Alas! Poor Yorick!, Carpet from Bagdad, Her Sacrifice, The Romance of the Rio Grande, The Smouldering Spark, Monte Cristo, When Men Forget, Unto Those who Sin* and dozens more. *The Spoilers* (1914), an eight reeler, was arguably the first American film epic, prompted several remakes, including one by Frank Lloyd, and had a contemporary status only matched by the work of D W Griffith.

● *The Battle of the Sexes* ✓

GB, 1960, Prometheus, 84 mins. Directed by Charles Crichton. From the story, 'The Catbird Seat' by James Thurber. Written and Produced by Monja Danischewsky. With Peter Sellers, Constance Cummings, Robert Morley, Jameson Clark, Moultrie Kelsall, Roddy McMillan and Donald Pleasance.

The Prime Of Miss Jean Brodie (1969, Twentieth Century Fox).
Maggie Smith with Jane Carr, Pamela Franklin, Diane Grayson and Shirley Steedman.

● *The Prime of Miss Jean Brodie* ✓
GB, 1969, Twentieth Century Fox, 116 mins. Directed by Ronald Neame. Written by Jay Presson Allen from the novel by Muriel Spark. With Maggie Smith, Roberts Stephens, Pamela Franklin, Celia Johnson and Gordon Jackson.

● *Shallow Grave* ✓
GB, 1994, Figment Films, 91 mins. Directed by Danny Boyle. Produced by Andrew Macdonald. Written by John Hodge. With Kerry Fox, Christopher Eccleston and Ewan McGregor.

● *Tickets for the Zoo*
GB, 1991, Cormorant Films, 90 mins. Directed by Brian Crumlish. Produced by Christeen Winford. With Alice Broe, Fiona Chalmers and Micky McPherson.

Albany Street: workshops.

Edinburgh Film Workshop Trust (EFWT), which is based in Albany Street, was founded in 1977. Since 1983 it has produced television programmes (often very successfully) for BBC, Channel Four and ITV, depending for the bulk of its income on commissions. It has also provided training, access, distribution and consultancy.

Measured in terms of the number of productions on cinema screens, the impact of the 'Workshop Sector' on film in Scotland has been relatively modest, though since the workshops' concerns have primarily been in other areas that is not a criticism. There is some difficulty in discussing their collective role, not least because of the disparate nature of the organisations which make up the sector and, indeed, in defining the exact meaning of the term 'workshop'. A major commissioned report on the sector dealt with the seven organisations usually thought to comprise the group (EFWT, Aberdeen Video Access, Castlemilk Video Workshop, Glasgow Film and Video Workshop, Film and Video Access, Video in Pilton (see **Edinburgh, Pilton**), and Young People Speak Out), but in 1995 the industry directory *Film Bang* listed eleven which claimed workshop status.

At one end of the spectrum, workshops are organisations geared to community activity, dealing with immediate issues, offering extremely useful access to video technology and providing training for whoever is interested in becoming involved. At the other, they are self-contained production companies whose principal distinction from the rest of the independent producers is that they are not profit distributing. Their one common feature is that they are essentially local in nature, although that has not prevented EFWT, for example, from making programmes about a wide range of Scottish subjects, including defence issues (*Northern Front*) and Gaelic culture (*Uamh an Oir*).

The history of the workshop sector in Scotland is as uneven as any other part of the scene. When the workshop movement began in England and Wales it benefited from a unique collaboration between the Union (then the Association of Cinema and Television Technicians, ACTT), the English regional arts associations, the Welsh Arts Council, the BFI and Channel Four. Known as the 'Workshop Declaration', published in June 1984, it allowed pay and conditions to be applied at lower rates than was normal in film and television in recognition of the essentially co-operative nature of their work. In Scotland, the relevant funder should have been the Scottish Film Council (SFC), but it did not provide the nascent workshops with revenue because, despite being sympathetic to the cause, at that time it had no money for new enterprises. To do so, it would have had to cut grants to established clients, particularly the regional film theatres, which it was not prepared to contemplate.

This meant that Scottish workshops were even more heavily dependent on local authority funding than their equivalents in the South. It also meant that although the SFC and the other agencies might produce occasional funding for specific projects, there was little possibility of the development of a national strategy for access to video production. As it happened, the central funding of English and Welsh workshops as envisaged under the original 'Workshop Declaration' did not last and they too had to become more self-sufficient or seek increased local funding to survive.

The role of the workshops in Scottish film culture continues to be uncertain in some ways. There appear to be large numbers of people interested in producing video material – the growth of the 'camcorder' is sufficient proof of that – many of whom would like to improve their skills. The workshops have also demonstrated an important role in educating children and adults in media matters and there is no doubt that workshop productions at their best can stand alongside those from any other sector. The problem remains that without an increased sense of homogeneity and coherence within the sector itself, and a clear overview by SFC and the other agencies of their role, it is difficult to see how the workshops as a group can fulfil their full potential as major contributors to Scottish film culture, although individual workshops may continue to do very well as production houses and as a significant breeding ground for new talent.

Alva Street: the European connection

The Commission of the European Community has its Scottish office at 9 Alva Street, in the West End of Edinburgh. For most of the century, Scotland's film connections with Europe were confined to the showing of 'continental' movies in one or two art-houses, among the film societies and at the Edinburgh Film Festival. 'Film' in Scotland, as in most of the world, mainly meant American movies.

As to production, Scotland provided the occasional location for European film-makers, but that was about it. However, even before the coming of the European Community, there were a few Scottish film-makers who had established European links. In the late 1960s, Charlie Gormley met the Dutch film-makers Pim de la Parra and Wim Verstappen at the Edinburgh Film Festival with the result that he became the writer for a number of their films and subsequently for other Dutch film-makers. Gormley found a very different and much more relaxed attitude to film in the small country of the Netherlands than he was used to in the small country of Scotland and was introduced to the strength of film culture in Europe. Another Scot early into Europe was Robin Crichton of Edinburgh Film Productions who has worked in partnership with European companies throughout his career (see **Penicuik**).

With the European Community's decision to set up a major programme of assistance to the 'audio-visual' industry, under the title MEDIA, in the late 1980s there was suddenly a potential for change affecting film-makers wherever they were in the Community. It was clear that for Scotland to achieve a true and complete film culture of its own it was going to have to define itself in European terms; for many purposes

relating to film, Scotland needed to be an identifiable entity rather than just part of a larger political or cultural whole. The Scottish Film Council's officers had experience of attending educational film events in Europe, where Scotland's status, stemming from its recognised separate education system, allowed them to deal as equals with other countries. At any rate, it seemed that if we needed models and examples of how film, particularly the institutions of film, might develop, we were quite likely to find them among the small countries like Norway and Denmark or regions, such as Catalonia. Therefore the more contact we could have with Europeans and their film institutions the better.

MEDIA I was established in 1991 to run to 1995 although there had been a number of Europe-wide projects in place for some time previously. The MEDIA programmes covered: training for film professionals through schemes such as EAVE (European Audio-Visual Entrepreneurs) and the MEDIA Business School known as ACE (Ateliers du Cinéma Européan); schemes to improve production conditions (but not production itself, since that would have been regarded as intervention in the market place), including the European Script Fund and organisations concerned with specialised areas such as animation (CARTOON) and documentary; and assistance in the distribution of films (EFDO – the European Film Distribution Office). There were also schemes to help cinema exhibition.

More than thirty Scots have benefited from participation in a number of these projects, notably EAVE, the Script Fund (Peter Broughan for *Rob Roy*, Mike Alexander for *As an Eilan)* and cinema exhibition assistance (the Cameo, The Filmhouse and Glasgow Film Theatre) and in a recent survey of Scottish film-makers more than half were engaged in, or were considering, joint European projects. In the spring of 1996, four of the ten attendees at a session of ACE were Scots – Christopher Young, Penny Thomson, Ian Brown and Peter Broughan, indicating an unusually high number of

Scottish feature film projects in development.

In addition to the European Community (latterly Union) audio-visual projects, The Council of Europe with nearly thirty member states also encourages the growth of the media in Europe. One of its most successful schemes has been 'Eurimages' supporting a total of 56 British films. Inexplicably, the British Government withdrew from it in 1995. Ironically, the agency is run by a British director, Barrie Ellis-Jones, formerly of the BFI and at one time the assistant director at Films of Scotland (see **Edinburgh, Randolph Crescent**).

In engaging enthusiastically with European institutions, part of the Scottish strategy has been to ensure a steady supply of European events staged in Scotland thereby bringing top European film-makers on to our own ground. The most spectacular of these, brought about by a huge combined effort on the part of the BFI and SFC under the remarkable leadership of Sir Richard (now Lord) Attenborough, was the hosting of the European Film Awards in Glasgow when it was European City of Culture in 1990. It was attended by, among many others, Ingmar Bergman, Deborah Kerr, Jeanne Moreau, Nastassia Kinski, Andrzej Wajda and Max von Sydow.

There have regularly been other meetings, conferences, courses and seminars (less glamorous but equally important) dealing with specific aspects of film in Europe. The annual convention of all Europe's animators CARTOON FORUM took place in Inverness in 1993, and there have been sessions of EAVE. In November 1992, the Scottish Film Council established a MEDIA 'Antenna' providing a permanent representative of the MEDIA programme in Scotland to improve access to its information and activities.

All this Euro-friendliness certainly provided benefits, including financial ones, to the Scottish film community. It also produced moments of deep frustration. In the late 1980s three of the smaller European countries, Scotland, Ireland and Portugal got together to propose a MEDIA project that would examine, and try to do

something about, the particular difficulties experienced by the small nations and regions in a European audio-visual industry that was inevitably dominated by the larger countries. The idea was generally supported and a project known as SCALE set up. The only slight drawback from a Scottish point of view was that, not being a small member state but a part of a large one, we were firmly excluded from it.

In other areas of European activity, there was not the same daftness. The discovery that European film institutions, from Scandinavia to the Mediterranean, had a great deal in common (not least in their struggles with their Governments), led to the formation of the Association of European Film Institutes with the author of this book, then Director of The Scottish Film Council, as the first Chairman.

MEDIA I came to an end and MEDIA 2 was in process of formation in 1996. Most of the previous schemes were terminated – the passing of some caused little mourning – and a new deal was promised to see Europe's audio-visual industry through to the Millennium. Europe, faced with the might of American competition in film, television and the new media technologies certainly needs a coherent strategy for growth, or perhaps survival, not least for the sake of small countries like Scotland.

Arthur's Seat

Edinburgh's domestic mountain, once the centre of mighty volcanic activity but now rather less volatile, dominates the Queen's Park and provides splendid opportunities for all sorts of film-makers (once they have acquired the requisite permits for filming in a Royal Park). Over the years, countless reels have been shot and it might be hard to find a documentary travelogue of Edinburgh that does not show the Park, Salisbury Crags, Arthur's Seat and the views across the City.

Among the more significant feature films to have had a sequence shot here is *Chariots of Fire* (1981) (see **St Andrews**). The most unlikely use of the area was as a substitute for the West Highlands in *The Battle of the Sexes* (1960).

Café Royal

One of the most famous Edinburgh locations used in *Chariots of Fire* (1981) (there were others including the stadiums at Goldenacre and Inverleith), the Café Royal just off the east end of Princes Street has a curious connection with the prehistory of cinema. Depicted in the splendid tiling above the table seen in *Chariots of Fire* is Jacques Louis Mandé Daguerre, one of the inventors of photography. Ironically, a few hundred yards to the east of the Café Royal is Rock House, Calton Hill, where from 1843 to 1848 David Octavius Hill and Robert Adamson brought the new medium of photography to its earliest pinnacle as an art form, using the system devised by Daguerre's rival, William Henry Fox Talbot.

Calton Hill

This splendid vantage point at the east end of Princes Street was the site of the invention of the Panorama, one of the precursors of cinema. In 1787 an Irish portrait-painter, Robert Barker (1739-1806), patented this new entertainment for the public, and a new way of seeing. His first 360-degree panoramic painting was the 'View of Edinburgh' from the Calton Hill, the predecessor of all the other panoramas, dioramas, cycloramas, and myrioramas that enthralled the public in the late eighteenth and nineteenth centuries and which, with their eternal striving for spectacle and novelty were truly the ancestors of the movies.

There may also be a case to be made for the Calton Hill as the birthplace of documentary. Rock House, just below the Observatory was the home and studio of the pioneer photographers, David Octavius Hill and Robert Adamson. Their series of calotypes on 'The Fishermen and Women of the Firth of Forth', announced in 1844, was probably the first instance of photography used systematically to explore a community's way of life.

Bill Forsyth in the Film Bang poster, 1976.

Calton Studios: independents

Calton Studios, at one time Grampian Television's Edinburgh base , was set up in the mid 1970s by Bill Landale and Steve Clark-Hall (also the originators of Sidhartha Films) as a studio, cinema and conference centre. In December 1977 it was the venue for a conference called 'Cinema in a Small Country' (the title was Bill Forsyth's idea). It marked an important stage in the development of the film production community in Scotland as it began to define itself and to address the problems inherent in film-making in Scotland.

This was not quite the first gathering of its sort. A year earlier, at the Glasgow Film Theatre, there had been what one participant described as 'a cross between a union meeting and a demo' when for the first time the

At the Glasgow Film Theatre
Thursday 22nd January 2–5pm
Friday 23rd January 10–5pm

FILM BANG

– 75 –

independent sector, in the guise of the Union (ACTT) membership in Scotland, had expressed its concerns loudly, particularly concerning the dominance of the film scene by Films of Scotland, virtually the only source of work in Scotland for those who wanted to make films for the big screen. That event was called 'Film Bang' (the title was the idea of Murray Grigor) and the expression lives on to this day in the name of the vital annual directory of film people and services in Scotland.

'Cinema in a Small Country' was more than a cry for help. It was funded by the Association of Independent Producers (Scotland) and by the Scottish Arts Council (see **Manor Place**), which at this stage was, paradoxically, in a more powerful position to intervene in film production than the Scottish Film Council. What was particularly innovative about the event was the presence of film-makers from other parts of the world to offer their experience in the context of discussion on the future of film in Scotland. Thus, Hans van Taalingen, president of the Dutch Cinema Association, Claude Degand from Paris (talking about European Cinema and the Common Market) and Maurice Bulbulian from Quebec brought a new perspective to bear on film-making in this small country.

As an expression of increasing self confidence and, at the very least, as a way of giving articulate voice to hopes and fears, the conference was something of a milestone. It ended by passing two resolutions. One condemned the Interim Action Committee on the Film Industry (Chairman, Sir Harold Wilson) for failing to send a representative to the event. The other, more constructively, was to submit to the Secretary of State for Scotland that a working party should be set up to inquire into and report on 'the means of ensuring that Scottish film-makers make the fullest possible contribution to the cultural life of Scotland'.

Those who made up the Scottish workforce were very conscious that they represented the largest group of film (and television programme) makers outside London. Many of them, thanks to Films of Scotland, had developed a high level of practical skills and were anxious to progress from documentary to fiction. Some, such as Laurence Henson and Mike Alexander, had done that anyway, either courtesy of the Children's Film Foundation or by virtue of self-help and determination. The politics of the situation were partly helped and partly confused by the fact that most Scottish film-making was undertaken by companies of one or two people. The same people were both workers and bosses (a not uncommon phenomenon throughout the industry). However there was a real need to find a collective voice to help deal with the peculiarities of film-making in Scotland and particularly to negotiate with television companies and the public institutions.

A perennial political and psychological difficulty lay in fielding endless questions about 'a Scottish Film Industry'. Was there, or even could there be, such a thing? Most film-makers were inclined to ignore theoretical issues and get on with whatever work was to hand, but there were moments when the matter of cultural identity impinged on everyone's thinking (see **Brigadoon**).

Even at a purely practical level it was sometimes necessary to take a position. For example, at one point the SFC considered trying to secure for Scottish productions a portion of the BFI's production funding, calculated according to national population and other factors. Consultation with the independent producers resulted in a one vote decision not to back the SFC's proposed initiative on the grounds that individual Scottish film-makers might get a bigger slice of the action by bidding to London than they could expect from a purely Scottish fund.

The constitutional evolution of the independent sector (like that of Scottish film culture as a whole) has not been smooth. The emergence of IPPA (the Independent Programme Producers' Association) provided a new strong voice in dealing with television, particularly the new and crucially important Channel Four, and the merging of IPPA and the Producers' Association (never very strong north of the

Poole's Synod Hall, Christmas 1906 and 31 October 1965 (the last day).

Border) brought a new player, PACT (the Producers' Alliance for Cinema and Television), onto the scene, with a permanent office in Glasgow.

In the 1990s, the issues facing Scottish independents, at any rate the majority who make their living by producing programmes for television, are essentially the same as they have been for some time. In some ways they are more acute, despite the introduction of 25% independent production quotas on independent television. Some companies, the larger ones with London connections, undoubtedly do very well, but complaints continue that the proportion of Channel Four commissions coming to Scottish independents is nothing like pro rata for the UK as a whole and that the other television organisations are squeezing budgets to a life-threatening degree.

Nevertheless, the small independent companies remain vital to film in Scotland. The quality of their output may vary but they represent the core and soul of indigenous film-making in Scotland.

Castle Terrace: Poole's Synod Hall

The terrace at Edinburgh's West End has an important place in the Capital's film history. When the Edinburgh Film Festival was staged at the Caley Cinema, just round the corner in Lothian Road, it provided a most useful view of the Castle as backdrop to photographs of visiting celebrities. It was also the site of a truly unique cinema, Poole's Synod Hall.

Even the name 'Poole's Synod Hall' signalled something out of the ordinary and hinted at the splendid contradictions which were central to its character. This was a building with ecclesiastical, show-business and horror film connections. Even the mention of its post-mortem existence, as Edinburgh's shameful hole in the ground wherein it was intended an opera-house worthy of a great European City should be built, can still ring a mournful bell in the Capital. The site, now devoted unequivocally to Mammon, is occupied by 'Saltire Court', home of the Edinburgh Stock Exchange.

Opened as the New Edinburgh Theatre on 20 December 1875, the Hall, ironically, had aspirations to be an opera house. That first venture went bust and by 1877 the building had acquired its famous name of 'Synod Hall' from its new owners, the United Presbyterian Church. Subsequently, the Town Council bought it but the name stuck. In due course it became the venue for various activities and entertainments including those purveyed by Charles W Poole who had first arrived in Edinburgh in 1906 with a travelling diorama show.

Two succeeding generations of the Poole family were to present the latest in visual entertainment to the Edinburgh public in the Synod Hall. John R Poole effected the transition from myriorama to movie and, by the mid 1930s, it was epics such as *The Four Horsemen of the Apocalypse* that filled the place. The Pooles also acquired other cinemas and in one of these, The Regent (now The Odeon), in Aberdeen, J K S (Jim) Poole began his career in management.

The Synod Hall's heyday was in the fifties, by which time it was specialising in horror movies (in contrast to the douce continental fare at the Cameo, the other Poole venture up the road at Home Street (see **Edinburgh, Home Street**)). It was niche marketing of a high order. One knew exactly what to expect within the imposing portals on Castle Terrace. Not that there was sleaze in the Synod; only the classiest horror. Fittingly, it was with the most stylish and chilling film of the genre, Polanski's *Repulsion*, that it closed in 1965 when the local authority wanted the site for the never-to-be-built opera house.

The enduring memory of Poole's Synod Hall is of a most enjoyable but unconventional cinema. Its echoing corridors were complemented by a peculiar interior in which balcony seats were so arranged that many were almost at right angles to the screen. Adjacent seats cost either one shilling and sixpence or three shillings and sixpence depending on the viewing position. Jim Poole reckons that this was unique in Britain. Since so much else about the establishment was unique, that is not surprising.

Cowgate: *Mary Reilly*

Of Edinburgh's urban glens, the Cowgate, at the bottom of the steep slope on the south side of the High Street, is not the most glamorous. Overshadowed by George IV Bridge and the South Bridge, it encourages thoughts of dark deeds. So it was an entirely suitable location for *Mary Reilly* (1996), the latest in the long line of screen adaptations of Stevenson's classic, *Dr Jekyll and Mr Hyde*, this one told from a maidservant's point of view. (see **Edinburgh, Howard Place**).

Cramond: *Marigold*

Cramond, the picturesque village on the Forth to the west of Edinburgh, was the setting for a highly romantic work, *Marigold* (1938), advertised as 'The Sweetest Love Story Ever Told'. Set in 1842, it starred Sophie Stewart and Patrick Barr. Jean Clyde, sister of Andy (see **Helensburgh**), who had starred in over a thousand performances of the stage version of *Marigold* and had been successful throughout the world in *Bunty Pulls the Strings*, also featured.

● *Marigold*
GB, 1938, Associated British Picture Corporation, 74 mins. Directed by Thomas Bentley. From the play by Charles Garvice. With Sophie Stewart, Patrick Barr, Nicholas Hannen, Phyllis Dare and Jean Clyde.

Marigold (1938). Sophie Stewart.

Easter Road: the pianny wumman

The street most readily identified as home to Hibernian Football Club also supported a cinema now only preserved in a writer's recollection of childhood. The Picturedrome was perhaps not a great deal different from others of its ilk but it deserves to be remembered for its association with the Edinburgh poet Robert Garioch (1909-1981).

Garioch, himself one of the last picture-house pianists (at the Lyric in Nicolson Square), recalled in Maurice Lindsay's anthology *As I Remember* how his mother...

...had given up most of her professional piano playing, but kept on her Saturday afternoon job as 'pianny wumman' at the children's matinees of The Picturedrome near the top of Easter Road. A supermarket now occupies the site of that picture-house that I knew so well. The piano was in a curtained corner to the right of the screen, and there were chairs and stands for the fiddler and cello-player who played in the evening along with another pianist.

My mother and I sat in the darkness, with the hooded light of the music stand and the screen flickering above, or I could look for a seat in the front of the house if I liked. The children got in for a penny each, infants-in-arms for nothing. You would see a boy staggering past the box-office, carrying his wee sister, nearly as big as himself.

They read the printed bits of the picture out loud in unison, as if they were in school, and shouted all the time. When the baddie was creeping up behind Pearl White, they all cried 'Shoat!', and when she got the better of him in the last episode of the serial, after I don't know how many Saturdays, they cheered with all their might. But my mother gave them a good pennyworth of music, mostly from memory. Sometimes she put a novel on the stand and read that, while she kept playing just the same.

Garioch goes on to recall how he once sat in the balcony next to Houdini when a film featuring the great escapologist was presented, and how he shook his hand. Extraordinary times in Easter Road!

Edinburgh Castle: cardboard cut-outs and giant screens

The Castle's status as the instantly recognisable symbol of all things Edinburgh, even all things Scottish, has meant that it is difficult to make a film in the Capital without showing it. Films purporting to show Edinburgh, such as, *Challenge to Lassie* (1949) (see **Edinburgh, Greyfriars**), even invented a studio version of the Castle in an attempt at verisimilitude. Mostly its presence has been as backdrop rather than at the centre of the action but in one extraordinary film, *This is Cinerama* (1952), the Castle and the Esplanade appear to the best possible advantage.

Films projected onto multiple screens have been around since the beginning of the medium. Usually no more than a gimmick, they have occasionally been used to great effect, most notably by Abel Gance for the three-screen climactic moments of *Napoleon* (1927), presented with a live orchestra in The Playhouse at the 1981 Edinburgh International Film Festival when a audience of more than two thousand stood to applaud at the end of the five-hour performance (see **Leith Walk**).

For the World's Fair in New York in 1939, Fred Waller (1886-1954) of the Paramount special effects team built an eleven projector system which reappeared some years later in simplified form as 'Cinerama'. This three-projector version used a huge screen, curved to 165 degrees, film shot at 26 frames per second and the projectors positioned so that the left and right ones projected across each other while the centre one shone straight ahead.

The unimaginatively titled *This is Cinerama* which launched the system was an epic adventure-travelogue on a scale consistent with the technological achievement. In its two-and-a-half-hour tour of the globe, it offered the inevitable rollercoaster ride, and the flight over the Grand Canyon, but also extended sequences of a less predictable nature such as a scene from *Aida* at La Scala, Milan, and an excerpt from the Edinburgh Military Tattoo.

Edinburgh Castle has never looked better than on that gigantic screen. *This is Cinerama* can still be seen. It is regularly available at the National Museum of Photography, Film and Television in Bradford where Cinerama has been fully reconstructed in its 1950s form.

Cinerama lasted not much more than ten years. Its first real feature movie was *How the West was Won* (1962) but the inherent limitations in the system (the join between the screens was the most irritating) were against it. 70mm film from anamorphic lenses on a single camera took over big screen presentation in cinemas, but special spectacular systems have continued to flourish.

The most successful of these are the Imax and Omnimax systems (the former also to be found in Bradford) and it is a matter of continuing frustration that Scotland with its tremendous wealth of the visually spectacular has yet to produce a film in these formats, let alone a purpose-built hall in which to show them.

● *This is Cinerama*
US, 1952, Cinerama, 150 mins. Produced, Directed and Supervised by Fred Waller, Merian Cooper, Robert Bendick, Michael Todd, Michael Todd Jnr and Walter Thompson. Cameraman, Harry Squire.

Fountainbridge: a superstar

As anyone sufficiently interested in Scottish cinema to get this far in this book is almost bound to know, Sean Connery was born in Fountainbridge. The exact date was 25 August 1930. Connery may well be the most famous Scotsman in the latter half of the twentieth century (at least).

His status in the world of cinema is neatly summed up in the first sentence of the entry in

Baseline's Encyclopaedia of Film: 'Dashing, charismatic, and effortlessly masculine Scottish leading man who successfully escaped the profitable straitjacket of James Bond to become one of the most beloved and respected stars of contemporary Hollywood'. There is perhaps a tendency (as in the above) to undervalue Connery's achievement in making Bond compulsively watchable but there is no doubt that the range and quality of his subsequent work is extraordinary and his position in world cinema quite unique. In 1987 he received the Oscar for Best Supporting Actor for his performance as the tough Chicago cop, Jimmy Malone, in Brian De Palma's *The Untouchables*.

Thomas Sean Connery's career has the good old-fashioned rags-to-riches quality about it that is part of Hollywood's standard romantic kit. However, in Connery's case it happens to be true. The boy who left school at thirteen to be a milkman and whose subsequent stint with the Royal Navy came to a premature end through illness, certainly made something of himself by exploiting his physique as model and body-builder (a bronze medal in the Mr Universe contest in London in 1950) before graduating to the chorus in a stage production of *South Pacific*.

If the look of him was the passport to movies, beginning in minor roles with *No Road Back*, *Action of the Tiger* and *Time Lock* in 1957, it was the style and presence of the man that gave him the part of James Bond in *Dr No* (1962), *From Russia with Love* (1963), *Goldfinger* (1964), *Thunderball* (1965), *You Only Live Twice* (1967), *Diamonds Are Forever* (1971) and *Never Say Never Again* (1983). In most of the writings about Connery, the standard line on the subject of his acting talent seems to be that all he has to do is be himself. The commonest comparison is with Clark Gable - someone who needs merely to be on screen to do the job. No commentator fails to mention the accent ('soft Scottish burr' is the favourite description) and to marvel at how this obvious impediment has miraculously failed to halt the great man's progress, as though speech which identifies the speaker's

Never Say Never Again (1983, Warner).
Kim Bassinger and Sean Connery.

geographic or ethnic origins as other than American or English is bound to mark them out as less able as a screen actor.

In his fifty or so movies it is true that with Connery you get what you see. His honesty almost seems at variance with an actor's obligation to dissemble and convincing characterisations are achieved by intelligence rather than gimmicks. Consider the later and non-Bond roles. They are not all great parts. In fact, some are moderate roles in pretty awful films, such as *Highlander*, though even there he manages to make something from virtually nothing. But in the Sidney Lumet Films, *The Hill* (1965), *The Anderson Tapes* (1972) and *The Offence* (1973) we are looking at superior screen acting.

There may be fewer surprises in Connery's more recent performances, but in films such as *The Name of the Rose* (1986), *The Hunt For Red October* (1990) and *The Russia House* (also 1990) the old magic still comes through.

Who knows what is to come?

One of the most remarkable things about Connery is his strong attachment to his roots. Despite world acclaim, he has no difficulty in continuing to identify himself with his origins. For example, he is Patron of the Drambuie Edinburgh Film Festival and anyone who was fortunate enough to see him receive the Freedom of his native City of Edinburgh in 1991 could be in no doubt about the tremendous pleasure the occasion gave him. His generosity in donating his share of the profits of *Diamonds Are Forever* towards the setting up of the Scottish International Education Trust to further the progress of young people of special ability, is indicative of his feelings.

In 1967 he expressed his solidarity in a remarkable film for television, *The Bowler and the Bunnet*, an account of the attempt to save Fairfields' shipyard on the Clyde from extinction. He directed the film himself and appeared explaining the deal between workers and mangement on which the new plan was based.

His affection for his origins is also delightfully illustrated in Murray Grigor's film *Sean Connery's Edinburgh* (1982) which tours the great man through the city, revisiting his milk-round and reflecting on his early life.

● *The Bowler and the Bunnet*

GB, 1967, STV/Sean Connery Productions, 47 mins. Directed by Sean Connery. Produced by Brian Izzard. Researched and written by Cliff Hanley. Camera, Mario Ford. With Sean Connery.

● *Sean Connery's Edinburgh*

GB, 1982, Viz, 30 mins. Written and Directed by Murray Grigor. Produced by Lynda Myles. Camera, Mark Littlewood. With Sean Connery.

Granton: Grierson as director

The village of Granton on the Firth of Forth, long since incorporated in the mass of Edinburgh, was once as important a fishing port as any on the east coast. In the 1930s it was home to the trawler *Isabella Greig*, which played a significant role in the progress of the documentary movement.

It is one of the remarkable aspects of John Grierson's contribution to film history (see **Cambusbarron**) that for all his influence as the 'Father of the Documentary', he himself made very few films. However, in the case of *Granton Trawler* (1934), he was both director and cameraman.

The trip to the Viking Bank, east of Shetland, was extremely rough and filming was nearly impossible. The results, when examined back at The Empire Marketing Board, were far from encouraging. Grierson handed the material over to the young Edgar Anstey (a fellow pioneer, later head of British Transport Films) to see if he could make anything of it. Fortunately, he did, and produced one of the documentary classics, only eleven minutes in length but full of the hard life of the boat and the fishermen, a creative treatment of actuality that is the essence of documentary. Sadly, the *Isabella Greig* was bombed and sunk in September 1941.

● *Granton Trawler*

GB, 1934, Empire Marketing Board, 11 mins. Director and Cinematographer, John Grierson. Editor, Edgar Anstey. Sound, Alberto Cavalcanti.

Greyfriars Churchyard: a small dog

The story of Greyfriars Bobby is a gift for cinema with its sentimental mix of Victorian Edinburgh, morality and mortality and, as hero, a very attractive dog. The real dog, whose policeman master John Gray died in 1858, remained in the vicinity of the grave until its own death in 1872. Every day, except Sunday, at the sound of the One-o'clock Gun, and watched by crowds who came to witness the ritual, he would leave the churchyard to lunch at Traill's restaurant. It was good material for Disney who made *Greyfriars Bobby* in 1961.

Greyfriars Bobby (1961) was, strictly speaking, a re-make of *Challenge to Lassie* (1949) which was based on the novel *Greyfriars Bobby* by Eleanor Atkinson (1912). Atkinson's central character was a Skye terrier, which became a more glamorous collie in the film. Lassie, incidentally, was male, and there was more than one.

Although the *Challenge to Lassie* version is thoroughly Hollywood (for the facts, see *Greyfriars Bobby - The real Story* by Forbes Macgregor), the 1961 remake, directed by Don Chaffey (with a Skye terrier restored to the central role), did at least try to use Edinburgh locations and employed a number of well-known Scottish actors including Alexander Mackenzie, Andrew Cruikshank (as the Lord Provost), Moultrie Kelsall, Gordon Jackson, Duncan Macrae and Jameson Clark.

There is one striking piece of continuity between the two films. In 1949, Auld Jock Gray, the unfortunate owner of the dog, was played by Donald Crisp (see **Aberfeldy**). Twelve years later, Crisp played the part of Brown, the cemetery keeper. That apart, the *Challenge to Lassie* credit list is fairly unremarkable other than that the music was by a twenty-year-old called André Previn.

Crisp also played along with Edmund Gwenn in the first 'Lassie' film, *Lassie Come Home* (1943)(directed by Fred M Wilcox and featuring the young Elizabeth Taylor). He later appeared in *Son of Lassie* (1945) and *Hills of Home* (1948) in which a hydrophobic (merely in the sense of being afraid of water) Lassie rescues her Scottish doctor master from drowning.

● *Challenge to Lassie*
US, 1949, MGM, 76 mins. Directed by Richard Thorpe. Based on a novel by Eleanor Atkinson. With Edmund Gwenn, Donald Crisp, Geraldine Brooks, Reginald Owen and Lassie.

● *Greyfriars Bobby*
US, 1961, Disney, 91 mins. Directed by Don Chaffey. Based on the novel by Eleanor Atkinson. With Donald Crisp, Alexander Mackenzie, Duncan Macrae, Laurence Naismith, Kay Walsh and Gordon Jackson.

Hill Street: Campbell Harper Films and Film House.

In 1946, the Edinburgh Film Guild and Campbell Harper Films bought adjoining properties in Hill Street (between George and Queen Streets) with a view to sharing facilities which included a fifty seat 35mm cinema. This development stemmed from the Guild's success as the largest film society in Britain and turned out to be crucial in the progress of film in Scotland.

The existence of this base allowed the Guild to establish the Edinburgh Film Festival in 1949. For the next twelve years, until the Guild moved to Randolph Crescent (see **Edinburgh, Randolph Crescent**), 'Film House' provided the focus of Edinburgh's film scene.

Campbell Harper Films was founded in the nineteen thirties by Alan Harper as an offshoot of his father's photography business which had been established in 1892. Like several of his generation, Alan Harper was an amateur who turned professional as the demand for Government-sponsored information films grew,

particularly during the war. *The Freedom of Aberfeldy* (1943) and *Caller Herrin'* (1947) were documentaries for cinema release. Among the Scottish companies, Campbell Harper was one of the most technically adept and, as a result, sustained a steady flow of commissions.

Postwar customers included the Scottish Office, the Central Office of Information, Educational Films of Scotland (the Scottish Educational Film Association and the Scottish Film Council) and television. In 1954, the second Films of Scotland Committee was formed. Campbell Harper produced more than twenty films for it. Many of these had Edinburgh subjects (*The Edinburgh Tattoo* (1959) and *The Edinburgh Festival* (1965)) and there were also films on agriculture, Scottish country dancing, and The National Trust for Scotland.

One of the most important *de facto* functions of the original Scottish film production companies was to provide training for young film makers. The closure of Campbell Harper Films and Templar Film Studios prompted the need for the film-making community to devise its own systems for recruiting and training new talent. The 'Technician Training Scheme' (see **Glasgow, Park Gardens**) was the direct result. Its emphasis on practical experience was a continuation of the work ethic that had prevailed in the companies. As well as documentaries, Campbell Harper produced inserts for television programmes, news items and coverage of football matches. This basic kind of film-making was vital in building up experience. The effect was that a steady flow of people acquired the skills and moved on, usually to BBC television.

Alan Harper retired from the business in 1972 and died the same year.

Home Street, Tollcross: The Cameo

The Cameo Cinema, just down the road from the King's Theatre, began life as the King's Cinema. It was opened on 8 January 1914 and boasted musical accompaniment by Madame Egger's Ladies Costume Orchestra. The Talkies duly arrived in 1930 (presumably Madame Egger and her colleagues joining the thousands of suddenly redundant musicians) and after a change of ownership in the thirties became part of the Poole family business (see **Edinburgh, Castle Terrace, Poole's Synod Hall**).

The crucial date for the cinema was 25 March, 1949 when it was reopened as the Cameo, a 'continental' cinema showing foreign language films. There generations of Edinburgh film enthusiasts were able to see the latest in world cinema. This provision was reinforced by a long-standing link with the Edinburgh Film Festival and many distinguished films and their makers first met the public in the Cameo's comfortable auditorium.

The cinema's owner, J K S Poole, continued to be an innovator – the Cameo was, for instance, the first Edinburgh cinema to acquire a licensed bar - but with changes in taste and an increase in alternative venues showing 'minority' interest films, such as the Film House, the University Film Society, and, for a time Calton Studios, the Cameo showed progressively less foreign language material. It closed in September 1982.

Happily, this was not the final curtain. In 1986 it was refurbished and once again opened its doors, under new ownership. By the end of 1991 it had grown to a three screen operation, the links with the Film Festival had been re-established and the Cameo, once more a key component in Edinburgh's film scene, continues to this day.

Greyfriars Bobby (1961, Disney). With Donald Crisp.

Howard Place: R L Stevenson

It is an unlikely fact that two of the most filmed authors in cinema history were born only a mile apart in Edinburgh: Robert Louis Balfour Stevenson (1850-94) at 8 Howard Place; Arthur Conan Doyle (1859-1930) at Picardy Place (see **Edinburgh, Picardy Place**). (A third contender for the category, Walter Scott (see **Abbotsford**), was born a mile further south at College Wynd).

Unlike Conan Doyle, whose screen credits are almost wholly dependent on the celebrity of one outstanding character, Stevenson supplied cinema with the raw material for a wide variety of films, the common feature being plenty of dramatic action, often with a sinister element. He was, it could be argued, the greatest screenwriter who never wrote for the screen.

Also unlike Conan Doyle, much of Stevenson's work that was filmed, for example *Kidnapped* (see **Appin**), *Catriona* and *The Master of Ballantrae* (see **Ballantrae**) related to his native land. Moreover, Edinburgh's claim on the origins of *Dr Jekyll and Mr Hyde* are well known. Not many subjects have been so regularly reinvented in such a range of disguises and derivations, but since few make any reference to Edinburgh, they need not concern us here. An interesting exception is *Mary Reilly* (1996), partly filmed in Edinburgh and purporting to tell the tale from the perspective of Dr Jekyll's maid.

Still with the Edinburgh connection, there is at least one remarkable rendering of a Stevenson short story, *The Body Snatcher* (1945), in which Boris Karloff and Bela Lugosi made their last appearance together. It was directed by Robert Wise and produced by Val Lewton for RKO. Like Jekyll and Hyde, the body snatchers provided a theme capable of endless variations which cinema has gratefully exploited.

The enduring appeal to film-makers and their audiences of Stevenson's foreign adventure stories is most obvious in the popularity of *Treasure Island*. There are more than a dozen examples listed by the British Film Institute (but there may well be many more). They include a Japanese animated film, French, Russian, Italian, Czech and Spanish versions and several British and American productions, even including a musical (1982), based on the Bernard Miles stage production at the Mermaid Theatre.

Probably the most celebrated version of *Treasure Island*, certainly the one most quoted and sent up, is Disney's of 1950. It was Disney's first all live-action film and one of the most expensive. Robert Newton's *tour-de-force* performance as Long John Silver provided the benchmark for the part and in effect took over his career. He later made a television series based on it and in 1954 appeared in *Long John Silver*, an attempt at a sequel, directed by Byron Haskin (who also made the original). By then, it seems, contact with Stevenson's intentions had been left well behind.

The 1950 version also included the Edinburgh-born Finlay Currie as Captain Bones and John Laurie as Pew (twenty three years after they had appeared together in a very different island story *The Edge of the World* (see **Foula**)). The musical director was also a Scot, Muir Matheson.

As Silver, Robert Newton was in good company. Other occupants of the role included Wallace Beery (1934), Charlton Heston (1990) and (can it be true?) Orson Welles in a British/French/German/Spanish co-production in 1971.

Other Stevenson adventure stories have made it to the screen. Among them are four versions of *Ebb Tide*. The first two were in 1915 and 1922. A 1937 production starred Ray Milland and, in 1947, there was a re-make under the title *Adventure Island*. Stevenson stories also provided the basis for *The Strange Door* (1951), *The Testament of Doctor Cordelier* (1961) and *The Secret of St. Ives* (1949).

The Wrong Box was surely Stevenson's funniest and blackest book but despite a remarkable cast (which included Ralph Richardson, John Mills, Michael Caine, Wilfred Lawson, Nanette Newman, Peter Cook, Dudley Moore, Peter Sellers and Tony Hancock), the mildly amusing 1966 film version, directed by Bryan Forbes, did not live up to its original.

Leith: *Trainspotting*

Of the films commanding attention in the early months of 1996 on account of their release, their awards or their planned production, *Trainspotting*(1996) was the most phenomenal. Even the Oscar-hype of *Braveheart* and *Rob Roy* could only temporarily overshadow the fact that a film about heroin addicts set mainly in Leith was breaking box-office records all over the place. The stark contrast between the subjects was extraordinary. The *Braveheart* version of Scottish history mediated by Hollywood and the contemporary human experience in *Trainspotting* could scarcely have been more at odds. Yet the very fact that they were simultaneously on offer, and indeed that there were other accounts of Scotland on film around, was immensely encouraging.

Whatever the authenticity of the historical epics, there was no doubting that *Trainspotting* was genuinely of our culture, whether we liked it or not. Irvine Welsh's novel may have had to wear the label 'cult' but there was no question that the film derived from it extended its appeal to a wide audience, not least because it was essentially a comic film, albeit as black and bleak as they come.

The story of Renton, Spud, Sick Boy, Tommy, Begbie, Diane and company living their various but related forms of hell was scarcely a celebration of Scotland in the nineties. Politicians and tourist bosses must have been distressed by the image of the country it projected. But what *Trainspotting* proved beyond reasonable doubt was the Scottish capacity to make films of tremendous intelligence and impact about contemporary issues. That could only be a matter for great celebration.

That *Trainspotting* was so sharp and powerful was no surprise given the success director Danny Boyle, producer Andrew Macdonald and screenwriter John Hodge had had the previous year with *Shallow Grave*. The new work, however, took a major step forward from the comedy thriller. The fantasy of the basic premise in the earlier work had become the graphic horror of the addict in the grip of heroin. *Shallow Grave's* success led to the inevitable Hollywood offers (rumoured or real). It says a great deal for the film-maker's awareness of the potential of *Trainspotting*, and the importance of a subject close to home, that such possibilities were put aside, at least for the time being.

Leith was also the base for an earlier film dealing with the desperate problems of youth. *Conquest of the South Pole* (1989) was a film version of the stage play by Manfred Karge in which a group of unemployed young men attempt to restrain one of their number from suicide by re-enacting Amundsen's polar journey of 1911. The director was Gillies MacKinnon whose *Small Faces* (1996) (see **Glasgow**) was released a few weeks after *Trainspotting* and recognised as another genuine (and outstanding) account of young lives in urban Scotland.

MacKinnon graduated from the National Film and Television School with his first film *Passing Glory* (1968). Prior to *Small Faces,* he made *The Grass Arena* (1991), the Irish-American *The Playboys* (1992) with Albert Finney and Aidan Quinn, and *A Simple Twist of Fate* (1994) with Steve Martin. His brother is the screenwriter Billy Mackinnon, with whom he collaborated on both *Conquest of the South Pole* and *Small Faces*.

The back greens of Leith were the setting for *The Singing Street* (1951), described by John Grierson as, 'the best amateur film I ever saw... in some ways technically terrible but ...wonderful. Somebody loved something and conveyed it'. What was conveyed so effectively was children's singing games in their natural environment. The film was made by the Norton Park Group led by Nigel McIsaac, James T R Ritchie and Raymond Townsend.

● *Conquest of the South Pole*
GB, 1989, Jam Jar/Film Four International, 95 mins. Directed by Gillies Mackinnon. Produced by Gareth Wardell. From the play by Manfred Karge. With Ewen Bremner, Steven Rimkus,

Trainspotting (1996, Figment Films).

Leonard O'Malley, Laura Girling, Gordon Cameron and Alastair Galbraith.

● *Trainspotting*

GB, 1996, Figment Films/Channel Four, 93 mins. Directed by Danny Boyle. Produced by Andrew Macdonald. Screenplay by John Hodge based on the novel by Irvine Welsh. With Ewan McGregor, Ewen Bremner, Johnny Lee Miller, Kevin McKidd, Robert Carlyle, Kelly Macdonald, Peter Mullan, James Cosmo and Eileen Nicholas.

Leith Walk: The Playhouse

With just over three thousand seats, The Playhouse, at the top of Leith Walk, was the second biggest cinema in Scotland after Green's Playhouse in Glasgow. Built by Maguire and Lumley, its completion coincided with the advent of talking pictures and it opened on 12 August 1929 with *The Doctor's Secret* (1929), a screen adaptation of J M Barrie's *Half an Hour*, starring Ruth Chatterton and directed by William C de Mille.

Despite its capacity to show movies with sound, The Playhouse had not only an orchestra but a rising organ as well. It was a spectacular cinema to rank with the great movie palaces. Its ancillary accommodation included fifty dressing rooms and a large tea-room. Archive film shows it being run by an army of uniformed staff marshalled in a quasi-military manner with regimented lines of attendants being smartly drilled in preparation for the public's arrival.

Perhaps the most remarkable film record of The Playhouse was made by Alan Harper (see **Edinburgh, Hill Street**) and covers the visit of Laurel and Hardy to Edinburgh in 1932. The famous pair's other contribution to Scottish culture was in *Bonnie Scotland* (1935), a Hal Roach caper in which they journey to Scotland to collect a non-existent inheritance and wind up in India and the army. The real connections with Scotland were that Stan Laurel was brought up in Glasgow where he made his first stage appearances and James Finlayson, the partnership's perennial sidekick, was born in

Falkirk (see **Falkirk**). Further Scottish 'authenticity' was added by the appearance of David Torrence (who was born in Edinburgh) and Mary Gordon (from Glasgow).

From the sixties, The Playhouse was regularly used by the Edinburgh Film Festival for screenings of major premières. *Easy Rider* (1969) had one of its first European performances in The Playhouse, an occasion made memorable by the presence not only of one of the stars, Peter Fonda, but by the attendance of large numbers of Hell's Angels who filled Leith Walk with their bikes.

In 1973 The Playhouse ceased to be a cinema and in the following years there was frequent talk of its demolition. There were several changes of ownership between public and private bodies, but by becoming a major venue for opera, ballet, stage shows and other entertainment it has survived. The Film Festival continued to use it for important screenings and *E T* (1982) provided another splendid première.

Edinburgh's most outstanding film performance for decades (certainly for the 2500 people who were lucky enough to be there) took place in the Playhouse on 23 August 1981 when *Napoleon* (1927), Abel Gance's masterpiece and arguably one of the greatest works in the medium of cinema, was screened there. The recent reconstruction by Kevin Brownlow, including the famous triptych sequence at the end, was presented with live music by the Wren Orchestra conducted by Carl Davies, who had constructed a score drawing on Beethoven, Haydn and Mozart among others. It was an epic occasion in every sense. The first of the four parts began at 10.30 am and the last, on its own the length of an average feature film, concluded at half past five. The Playhouse, itself a cinema on an epic scale, provided the ideal venue for such an historic occasion.

● *Napoleon*

France, 1927, Societé Général de Films, 313 mins. Directed by Abel Gance. With Albert Dieudonné, Antonin Artaud, Wladimir Roudenko, Gina Manès, Eugenie Buffet, Anabella, Alexandre Koubitzsky and Pierre Batcheff.

● *Bonnie Scotland*
US, 1935, MGM, 80 mins. Directed by James
Horne. With Stan Laurel, Oliver Hardy, James
Finlayson, Daphne Pollard, William Janey,
David Torrence and Mary Gordon.

Lothian Road: The Filmhouse, The Edinburgh Film Guild and The Edinburgh Film Festival

The thoroughfare running south from the west
end of Princes Street has more than its fair share
of film connections. The Caley Cinema, which
opened in 1923, for many years staged the
Sunday screenings of the Edinburgh Film Guild
and played host to major presentations during
the Edinburgh Film Festival. That function is
still performed by the MGM Cinema further up
the hill which began life as The Regal, an ABC
Cinema, in 1938. In between is The Filmhouse
which, as well as being one of the most
successful regional film theatres in the UK, is
home to the The Edinburgh Film Guild and the
Drambuie Edinburgh Film Festival (to give it its
present name).

The Filmhouse

The Filmhouse itself is in effect (despite the
difference in spelling) the third set of premises
to bear the title. The first 'Film House' was in
Hill Street (see **Edinburgh, Hill Street**) and
housed only a small preview theatre. The
second, in Randolph Crescent (see **Edinburgh,
Randolph Crescent**) began as the private
theatre for the Edinburgh Film Guild. In the
late sixties, the BFI's 'Outside London' initiative,
originally designed to bring the benefits of the
National Film Theatre to the rest of the nation,
was seized on by the Edinburgh Film Guild and
a membership film theatre established. Shortly
afterwards, the Scottish Film Council took
responsibility for Regional Film Theatres in
Scotland and was determined to create a series
of entirely public cinemas for audiences
interested in films beyond the narrow fare
offered in the commercial houses.

In 1978, Lothian Road Church was bought
with the proceeds of the sale of Film House,
Randolph Crescent. After several years in which
the new Filmhouse survived in what had been
only the back hall of the kirk (a period of
sometimes agonisingly slow fund raising and
construction), the main auditorium was
completed and formally opened by His Royal
Highness, the Duke of Edinburgh on 2 July 1985.

After that, Filmhouse quickly established
itself as one of the best film theatres in the UK.
Further development took place and under the
present director, Jim Hamilton, there are plans
for a third auditorium.

The Edinburgh Film Guild

The Edinburgh Film Guild is a remarkable
organisation; a film society with a history that
transcends all the norms for a purely voluntary
body. Even the basic facts are impressive. The
Guild was not the first film society, that honour
belongs to the original Film Society founded in
London in 1925, but it was formed as early as
1930 and has long outlasted its London
counterpart, which closed in 1939. Indeed, it
claims to be the oldest continuing film society
in the U K, and possibly in the world. Although
that assertion is hard to verify, no challenger
has emerged.

Longevity, however, is only one of the Guild's
virtues. Undoubtedly its greatest achievement
was as the agency that established the
Edinburgh Film Festival in 1947. At that time
the Guild was based in Hill Street (see
Edinburgh, Hill Street) and had a membership
of some two and a half thousand, making it
probably the largest film society in the country.
Norman Wilson and Forsyth Hardy, the two
mainstays of the Guild's development, founded
an influential international magazine of film
criticism, *Cinema Quarterly*, in the early 1930s.

More recently, the Guild was crucial to the
setting up of the Regional Film Theatre for
Edinburgh in Randolph Crescent (see **Edinburgh,
Randolph Crescent**) and played a major part in
its move to the present premises in Lothian

Road. Despite the growing competitive pressures of alternative means of access to movies, the Guild continues to flourish and retain its reputation, not least by innovation in educational and other work

The Edinburgh Film Festival

The Edinburgh Film Festival was originally a relatively modest affair. In 1947, it was formally known as the first International Festival of Documentary Film. There were just four separate programmes, organised by the Edinburgh Film Guild with the cooperation of UNESCO whose adviser on Mass Media was John Grierson. However, more than twenty feature films,

including *The Brothers* (see **Skye**), *The Silver Darlings* (see **Dunbeath**), *A Matter of Life and Death* and *Les Enfants du Paradis*, were shown in cinemas throughout Edinburgh.

The presence of film at The Edinburgh Festival represented a remarkable breakthrough. For the first time the medium was recognised as part of an international festival of the arts. Edinburgh's was the first film festival to be founded after the Second World War and, since Cannes and Venice though pre-war in origin did not resume immediately after the conflict, Edinburgh has the distinction of being the oldest continuing international film festival.

Laurel and Hardy in **Bonnie Scotland** (1935, MGM).

The history and achievements of the Film Festival are meticulously documented by Forsyth Hardy in his book *Slightly Mad and Full of Dangers* (1992). The title might seem a little wild for the chronicle of such a venerable institution, but as anyone associated with the Film Festival can testify it rather understates the position.

As it reaches its fiftieth anniversary, conveniently coincident with the centenary of cinema, the Edinburgh Film Festival is in better shape and looks more secure than it has for most of its history. With hindsight, it is extraordinary that it has survived at all.

The unique context for the Film Festival – being part of the Edinburgh Festival – has proved to be both an advantage and a burden to it. The Film Festival's contribution to the overall event has been outstanding, adding a distinctive dimension alongside the Fringe, the Tattoo and all the other manifestations of the world's largest arts celebration. The association had been beneficial in terms of international profile and in providing additional incentives for distinguished film visitors to come to Edinburgh. But not being the only festival in town, it has sometimes seemed marginalised, hence the recurring call to move it to another time of year.

There is a paradox about a country that so enthusiastically celebrates a medium in which it has done relatively little itself. Inasmuch as this book has a central thesis, it is that film culture in Scotland only becomes really worthwhile when we can be seen to be operational in all aspects of the medium. For years the Film Festival (like the regional film theatres to some extent) was primarily an excellent conduit by which world film in all its glory came to Scotland but was unable to provide a showcase for indigenous fiction film production, for the very good reason that there was virtually nothing to show.

It is hard to imagine a national film festival anywhere else in the world that would not, at least partly, exist on its ability to promote its own country's films. Yet Edinburgh survived for years virtually without that strand. The good news is that now Scottish cinema is not just a hypothetical issue but is becoming a reality as structures, stratagems and opportunities for production in Scotland increase.

Edinburgh does not have the glamour of Cannes any more than it has the weather; though there are competitions within the Edinburgh Film Festival (for British films and for animation) these are not fundamental to the event; it is by no means the largest in the world; (there are festivals such as Toronto and Montreal with ten times the audience); and there are, no doubt, other comparisons to its apparent disadvantage. Nevertheless Edinburgh's film festival has plenty of its own special virtues. It takes risks with the unfashionable and the as yet unproved. It provides a meeting-place for professionals, and the connections made can have remarkable results (the 1993 encounter between the producer Peter Broughan and the director Michael Caton-Jones led to *Rob Roy).*

Traditionally, the Edinburgh Film Festival has had a good respect for its audience rather than for convention or authority. In the past, there were regular minor confrontations with the Town Council, usually over matters of censorship. One for example, resulted in victory for the Film Festival and the tabloid headline, 'Uncensored – The Festival Nude goes on!'

The Film Festival's character, or at least its programme policy, has changed greatly over the years as the organisation has evolved from an essentially collective event run by volunteer enthusiasts to a fully professional operation dependent on grant income as much as box office revenue. Over the first two decades, the centre of gravity moved from documentary to features and from executive decision making by committees in London and Edinburgh to day-to-day control in the hands of a Festival Director (initially a part-time appointment).

The main period of transition was in the late sixties and early seventies as Murray Grigor, the part time Director at the time, brought in a new generation of young cinéastes determined to re-invent the Film Festival as a much more radical event. Cinema was examined as a social and psychological phenomenon in which the role of the audience was diminished but the excitement of debate greatly enhanced. This allowed areas of cinema, such as the work of American directors like Sam Fuller, Monte Hellman, Roger Corman, Douglas Sirk, Frank Tashlin and Raoul Walsh to be explored seriously (in some cases for the first time) and attracted new attention to the Edinburgh Film Festival as an event at the forefront of thinking about the medium.

In 1973, one of Grigor's new movers, Lynda Myles (who has since become a successful producer), was appointed as the Festival's first full-time Director. This represented a breakthrough engineered by the Scottish Film Council, which was only able to provide significant funding for the event from the late 1980s, but had been a key supporter of it throughout its history, not least by providing personnel (including two part time directors, Don Elliot and Ronnie Macluskie, on secondment). In 1981, Myles was succeeded by Jim Hickey, and Hickey was succeeded in turn, in 1992, by Penny Thomson. Thomson was Director of the Scottish Film Production Fund from 1989 to 1991 and both had been part of Grigor's original group. In 1995 a major constitutional, financial and managerial restructuring took place and, under the Chairmanship of Gus Macdonald of Scottish Television, Mark Cousins and Ginnie Atkinson were appointed as Director and Producer.

Edinburgh Film Festival and all its directors and supporters over many years have had an overriding enthusiasm for the medium of film. It has been enough to transcend all the difficulties and to earn the accolade of the great John Huston who memorably declared the event to be, 'the only Festival worth a damn'.

Manor Place: The Scottish Arts Council

Through no fault of its own, The Scottish Arts Council (SAC) has had a slightly curious role in the development of film culture, particularly film production. To begin with, as was the case with its former parent body, The Arts Council of Great Britain, its remit excluded film. That was the business of the British Film Institute (BFI) in the south and the Scottish Film Council (SFC) north of the Border.

However, the SAC needed to be concerned with film in order to promote the other arts. It was quite entitled to sponsor and encourage films about art, as opposed to film for film's sake, a distinction sometimes hard to draw if the art was drama or literature. While the Scottish Film Council had the remit, it had (to poach the expression originally applied to the Films of Scotland Committee) no remittance.

Aware of this, in 1980 the SAC set up its own Film Committee, under the able chairmanship of Rod Graham, and shortly afterwards helped fund *Another Time, Another Place* (1983) (see **The Black Isle**). By then, however, the fundamental anomaly of the situation had been recognised. In 1982 joint action by SAC and SFC with the promise of additional funds from the Scottish Office led to the creation of The Scottish Film Production Fund, based at the SFC. The first Chairman was Professor Ian Lockerbie of the University of Stirling. (For more about the Production Fund and other initiatives in support of production, see **Glasgow, Dowanhill**).

With the establishment of the Production Fund, the SAC's concern for film was ostensibly removed but it still retained an interest in moving images as a component in the visual arts. Since the making and manipulation of film and video, particularly in a progressive or experimental mode, can impact on the 'workshop', art-house or sometimes even mainstream areas of film this puts the SAC in an ambiguous position.

In 1995, the SAC found itself once more with a very central and important concern for all aspects of film and cinema when it was appointed as one of the bodies to distribute funds from the new National Lottery. The way the Government set things up funding for film production, as well as support for capital projects associated with film exhibition and other film activities, was not handled by film agencies, but embraced within the remit of the new Arts Councils for England, Wales, Scotland and Northern Ireland.

Now SAC, working closely with the film agencies, finds itself disbursing money for film on a larger scale than it could have dreamed of. The first such award, made in August 1995, was one million pounds towards the production of *Poor Things* (based on Alastair Gray's novel). By mid 1996 over twenty awards had been made to film projects of major cultural significance, including John Byrne's *Slab Boys* and a proposal by John McGrath to make a new version of Neil Gunn's *The Silver Darlings* (see **Dunbeath**).

Morningside: The Dominion

The douce southern suburb, where Finlay Currie (see **Inverary**) was an organist and choirmaster, boasts a unique treasure - the Dominion Cinema. Suburban cinemas have almost died out as a breed and the Dominion must be virtually the last of the species; a great pity since the idea of a cinema related closely to its host community has always been extremely important to the best exhibitors.

Opened in January 1938, the Dominion was one of the last pre-war cinemas. It was architecturally a perfect specimen for its time. Very much a family concern, it was built for W M Cameron. After his death in 1942 it was run successively and often in tandem by his brother, Hector, his widow Jenny, his son Derek and his grandsons Michael and Al. The grandsons are now joint managing directors with Derek as chairman. They have successfully maintained the tradition of providing cinema for the community with the best in film entertainment. In 1972 the cinema was twinned and, in 1980, stole a march on its rivals by opening a third screen using video projection, an experiment which lasted for four years before a return to 35mm.

The Dominion prides itself on its policy of films for the family, eschewing more violent films despite the temptation to do otherwise. Its restaurant is called the Spool Room.

The Mound

The artificial roadway linking the Old Town with the New appears conspicuously in many films, including *The Battle of the Sexes* (1960), *Restless Natives* (1985) and *Blue Black Permanent* (1992) The Mound also shares with Calton Hill (see **Edinburgh, Calton Hill**) a stake in the prehistory of cinema. For many years in the middle of the nineteenth century a strange wooden building housing a Panorama stood at the top of the Mound.

Napier University: a film school

One of the most obvious and necessary components for any film culture is a mechanism to ensure the best possible supply of new blood to the production sector, and indeed to other sectors. The most acute need, however, is for as many young film-makers as possible to be enabled to learn their trade in their native land, informed by the particular circumstances of its culture and history, and in close proximity to the best current practitioners.

For years, the only way of learning film production in Scotland was to find one of the few outfits engaged in the trade and be lucky enough to be taken on at the lowest possible grade and wage. How that was changed, largely by the industry itself, is discussed elsewhere in this book (see **Glasgow, Park Terrace, Scottish Broadcasting and Film Training**).

The idea of a Film School for Scotland is not new. It was first proposed in the early days of film and again, soon after the Second World War, by Joseph Macleod and the promoters of the Scottish National Film Studios. It was considered once more (and rejected) at the time of the founding of the National Film School at Beaconsfield and it has recurred regularly ever since.

Napier University has the distinction of being one of the few places to actually do anything about it. In its previous incarnation, as Napier College, it ran the Scottish Projectionists Training School, which was discontinued in the 1970s. In the late eighties, an attempt to link with Duncan of Jordanstone College of Art in Dundee to create a two-campus national film school was not very successful, but by establishing an MSC in Film

Restless Natives (1985, Oxford). On the Mound.

Photography and Television and a postgraduate MSc in Film and Television Production, Napier has provided vocational courses at a high level and has begun to produce individuals of ability who can genuinely contribute to the development of film in Scotland.

The Secretary of Napier College from 1974 was Wilf Stevenson (born 1947). In 1987 he left to become Deputy Director of the British Film Institute (see **London**) and the following year was appointed Director, maintaining the tradition of Scots in very senior positions in the media in the UK.

Nicolson Street: Empire Palace Theatre, William Kennedy Laurie Dickson and The Great Lafayette

What is now the Edinburgh Festival Theatre has been transformed and rebuilt several times since it was the Empire Palace Theatre in which film made its first Scottish appearance, challenging traditional forms of entertainment. In fact, there is some doubt about where the first moving picture show in Scotland really took place. The argument turns on definitions of what constitutes a film show and even what qualifies as film.

Film as a fairground novelty, at the level of peep-show, existed in one form or another before the end of 1895. The Scottish Film Council's 1946 booklet, written by Charles Oakley to mark *Fifty Years at the Pictures*, suggests the Carnival Ground near the Gallowgate in Glasgow as the first place in Scotland where showmen presented the new medium.

For the purposes of celebrating the Centenary of Cinema, however, some consensus has emerged that to qualify for the accolade of being 'first' a presentation had to be of projected moving pictures on film to a paying audience. By that definition, the performance at the Empire Palace Theatre on 13 April 1896, seems to have been the first film screening in Scotland. It was not a great success. The account in *The Scotsman* of 14 April is moderate in its rapture.

The great advertised attraction for this week at the Empire is an exhibition of the 'Cinematographe' – a kind of electric magic lantern by which the patancaneous [sic] photographs of Edison's wonderful Kinetoscope are thrown upon a screen in the sight of the audience. The Cinematographe has been a great success at the London Empire, and Mr. Moss is to be complimented for his enterprise in securing the first appearance of it in the provinces.

Unfortunately in Edinburgh last night the exhibition somehow missed fire. These instantaneous photographs are, it may be recalled, printed on a celluloid ribbon, which in the Kinetoscope was made to fly across the lens by means of an electric motor. Underneath was a powerful electric lamp, which rendered the celluloid quite transparent, and a sharp silvery vision was the result. In the Cinematographe views the light seemed not to be powerful enough to render celluloid sufficiently transparent, and a somewhat indistinct picture in consequence appeared upon the screen - such as might have been thrown if the instrument had not been properly focused.

Another defect was that the photographs were passed too slowly before the lens, so while the action was lifelike, it was, in the dancing and pugilistic scenes especially, of too funereal a character....

The Scotsman's critic goes on in similar vein, but concedes (ungrammatically) that 'There is, unquestionably, great possibilities in this interesting scientific toy'.

What *The Scotsman* failed to make clear, leading to confusion among film historians and others for the subsequent hundred years, was that although one of the films on show at the Empire on 13 April was from Edison all the rest were by the British pioneers Robert Paul (1869-1943) and Birt Acres (1854-1918). Moreover, the equipment used on that historic occasion was not Edison's Kinetoscope (primarily a peepshow machine) or the Lumière Cinematographe, but in all probability Acres' Kineoptikon, which was indeed prone to poor performance. The Edison film was *A Cockfight* made for the Kinetoscope but capable of being shown on Acres' machine. The Paul/Acres titles included *The Policeman and the Sailor, The Shoeblack, The Dancers* and *Boxing*.

The main rival system was that of the Lumière brothers whose demonstration of their Cinematographe in Paris in late December 1895 marked the genuine beginnings of cinema as we know it today. By the end of the 1896, most towns and several smaller places in Scotland had experienced cinema in one form or another. The first major Glasgow screening (Lumière system) was on 16 May 1896 in the Ice Skating Palace, Sauchiehall Street (see **Glasgow, Sauchiehall Street**), and Robert Paul's was probably the one first seen in Aberdeen later in the year.

There was an important Scottish connection with Edison, however. William Kennedy Laurie Dickson (1860 – 1935) was not born in Scotland, nor lived or died here, but was very proud of his ancestry – the 'Laurie' in his name indicated his descent from a great family – and it is therefore surely only a minor liberty to claim him as one of ours. In fact he was born in France and died in England.

His father died while William Dickson was still a child and he and his mother emigrated to the United States in 1879. In 1883 he joined Thomas Edison and in just two years Dickson had contributed crucial work towards the development of moving pictures as a practical proposition. In particular, he designed the Kinetoscope (patented by Edison) which not only proved successful as a peepshow but, with its 35mm film and double row of sprocket holes, was the basis for cinema of the future.

Dickson's parting from Edison led him to devise his own, more sophisticated, systems (avoiding Edison's patents) and to the foundation of the American Mutoscope and Biograph Company. In 1897, Dickson joined British Biograph and subsequently become the first cameraman to cover a war - the Boer War. His exploits in South Africa are recounted in *The Biograph in Battle*, originally published in 1901 and recently reissued in facsimile with an excellent introduction by Richard Brown.

The Empire Palace Theatre has another (and rather bizarre) connection with film thanks to The Great Lafayette, his dog and his lion. In early May, 1911, The Great Lafayette, an escapologist and illusionist in the same league as his contemporary, Houdini, was playing at the Empire Palace Theatre. Unfortunately his dog, a faithful and much loved companion, died. Lafayette in his grief wished it a proper burial in an Edinburgh cemetery but this proved awkward to arrange. However, a Glasgow taxidermist was engaged to prepare the animal for burial.

On 9 May, a fire in the Empire Palace, although confined to the stage area (thanks to quick thinking on the part of the management), led to the death of ten members of the company including Lafayette. Both the aftermath of the disaster and The Great Lafayette's funeral on May 14 were filmed. *Theatre Fire in Edinburgh* includes shots of the burned interior of the building and of the remains of Lafayette's lion, whose disappearance had provided the climax of his act. *Funeral of the Great Lafayette* shows a brief shot of the hearse entering the gates of Piershill Cemetery. With it is a brass band and a wagon bearing a floral tribute with the legend 'The Last Act'. Lafayette was buried with his dog.

Picardy Place: Sir Arthur Conan Doyle

The statue of Sherlock Holmes in Picardy Place must come as a surprise to many visitors to Edinburgh. Holmes seems so completely London metropolitan that you feel that he would be a little out of place strolling down Leith Walk, (presumably not so Dr Watson). But the Edinburgh link is even stronger than the fact that their creator, Sir Arthur Conan Doyle (1859-1930), was born at 11 Picardy Place. By Doyle's own account, it was the experience of his time as a student in the Medical Faculty of Edinburgh University, and the influence of his Professors, notably Dr. Joseph Bell, that shaped him as a man and a writer. The result could be read as one of the movies' greatest debts to Edinburgh.

The statistics to do with Sherlock Holmes and the film business are astonishing.It has been estimated that no fictional character has been portrayed more often on the screen by as many different actors. There must be at least two hundred films featuring Holmes (there were well over a hundred silents). There are over thirty with his name in the title, the first being *Sherlock Holmes Baffled*, a half minute fragment, circa 1900, which was followed by the slightly more substantial *The Adventures of Sherlock Holmes (The Sign of Four)* (1905). There are Sherlock Holmes's from Britain, the USA, France, Germany, Czechoslovakia, Italy, Australia and many more countries. There are a dozen versions of *The Hound of the Baskervilles* alone. Some of these are dreadful, but they include the John Barrymore silent version of 1922 (with David Torrence) and the classic Basil Rathbone and Nigel Bruce collaboration in 1939 with Glasgow-born Mary Gordon as Mrs Hudson.

Later derivatives have Holmes battling with Nazis and turning up in unlikely periods and places, including Washington, New York and Algeria. That all this began in Edinburgh is remarkable considering that Holmes never crossed the Border into Scotland (though see **Loch Ness**).

Holmes gave rise to an industry which spanned literature, film and television, but Doyle's other fiction also found its way onto the screen. *The Lost World* was originally made into a film in 1925, then remade in 1960 and 1993. The earliest version had the odd distinction of being the first film to be shown in an aeroplane. *The Fires of Fate* was made by Tom Terriss in 1923 and, in 1927, Donald Crisp (see **Aberfeldy**) directed *The Fighting Eagle*, based on *The Adventures of Brigadier Gerard*, Doyle's Nalopeonic epic. A 1970 version of the same story was directed by Jerzy Skolimowski and starred Eli Wallach, Claudia Cardinale and Jack Hawkins.

● *The Adventures of Sherlock Holmes*
U.S, 1905. Directed by J Stuart Blackton. Adapted from the Conan Doyle story, 'The Sign of Four'. With Maurice Costello.

Recycled Teenagers. Video in Pilton's '50 Plus Group' in France.

● *The Adventures of Sherlock Holmes*
US, 1939, Twentieth Century Fox, 81 mins. Directed by Alfred Werker. With Basil Rathbone, Nigel Bruce, Ida Lupino and Mary Gordon.

Pilton: Video in Pilton

Formed in 1981, Video in Pilton (VIP) is one of Scotland's seven main Film and Video Workshops. Incorporated as an independent Workshop supported by the Union (ACTT) in 1984, in 1988 it received Urban Aid funding to establish itself as a full-scale video resource providing equipment, training and production.

VIP's success in making the means and methods of media production accessible to its host community has been very impressive. Not only has it provided training and expertise but enthusiasm in quantity. The result is that in addition to documentaries, mainly concerned with problems of the community, it has graduated

to fiction including *Beatha Ur* (1989) and *The Priest and the Pirate* (1993), a drama set in a future Scotland on the brink of political upheaval.

One of VIP's most innovative developments has been the formation of the Pilton Over-50s Video Group whose first major documentary enjoyed the title *Recycled Teenager* (1990). *From Muirhouse to Macon* was a thirty eight minute documentary for Channel 4 which followed the making of *Recycled Teenager* and traced the journey of the group to Macon for a 'Third Age' European Festival of the Arts.

Portobello: Harry Lauder

Sir Harry Lauder was born in Portobello in 1870. He was so closely identified with the image of Scotland abroad that it is astonishing how little evidence of him there is on film, particularly since he himself was very keen on the medium (his estate contained large amounts of amateur film, much of it on the obscure and obsolete 17.5mm gauge).

Apart from various newsreel and short film appearances, such as his first pantomime appearance at the Theatre Royal, Newcastle, there seem to have been only a couple of forays into feature film. The first (certainly it was billed as such) was in *Huntingtower* (1927), directed by George Pearson, and was adapted from the novel by John Buchan. It starred Lauder as a Glasgow grocer who, aided by a bunch of lads known as the 'Gorbals Die-hards', rescues a Russian princess from the hands of the Bolsheviks. Whether or not the film (or Lauder) was any good, we will probably never know. *Huntingtower* is one of those potentially significant films which, despite popular success at the time of its release, has disappeared from view entirely. All that remains is a group of stills.

In 1929, Lauder starred in *Auld Lang Syne*, also directed by George Pearson. The talkies were in process of ousting silent films and some fairly desperate attempts were made to come to terms with the new situation. Thus *Auld Lang Syne* was made as essentially a silent film but with songs recorded on wax discs and subsequently transferred to a sound-track.

● *Huntingtower*
GB, 1927, Welsh-Pearson-Elder, 80 mins. Directed by George Pearson. From the novel by John Buchan. With Harry Lauder, Vera Voronina, Pat Aherne and Nancy Price.

● *Auld Lang Syne*
GB, 1929, Welsh-Pearson-Elder, 76 mins. Directed and written by George Pearson. With Harry Lauder, Dorothy Boyd, Pat Aherne and Dodo Watts.

Randolph Crescent: The Films of Scotland Committee

In 1958, the original Film House in Hill Street (see **Edinburgh, Hill Street**) was sold by the Edinburgh Film Guild in favour of the much larger and more convenient premises at 3 Randolph Crescent. There was room in the basement for a small cinema which was used by the Guild and by the tenants of the premises who included the Edinburgh Film Festival and the Federation of Scottish Film Societies. Ten years later, the cinema became the first regional film theatre in Scotland.

Occupying the top floor of the building were the offices of the Films of Scotland Committee whose Director, H Forsyth Hardy (1910-94), had been a major force in the creation and sustenance of all the other organisations in the building as well. Films of Scotland was, in fact, the second committee bearing that name, the first having been formed to produce films for the 1938 Empire Exhibition (see **Glasgow, Bellahouston**).

This second Films of Scotland Committee was set up in 1954. Technically, it was a sub-committee of the Scottish Council (Development and Industry) whose assessor, John Donachy, was, many years later, to become Chairman of the Scottish Film Council. The relationship between the Committee and the Scottish Council was not an easy one with Hardy constantly seeking more support from the Council than it was able to give.

Films of Scotland's Chairman was Sir Alexander B King, one of the most successful

independent exhibitors and a man of considerable influence in the trade. The Treasurer was Hugh Fraser, who made a gift of £10,000 to the new enterprise. It was the only money that the Committee ever received gratis and it was Hardy's proud boast that twenty years later, after a hundred and fifty films had been made, the original donation remained intact. There was also some help in kind from the House of Fraser, but the Committee was given the remit to 'promote, stimulate and encourage the production of Scottish films of national interest', without any other visible means of support. The in-joke was that it was 'a remit without a remittance'.

Forsyth Hardy's own writings (see **Bibliography**) have documented the rather astonishing way in which business and public agencies, large and small, were coerced, persuaded or flattered into sponsoring films on a range of topics that reflected a broad spectrum of Scottish life. Just as remarkable was the success Sir Alexander B King and his committee had in finding cinema distribution for films almost all of which had some sort of ulterior motive – the promotion of tourism, of an industry or even of a specific product.

Much of the output was related to tourism, as the titles show - *Ayr from the Auld Brig, Beyond the Grampians, Highlands, Busman's Holiday, A Pride of Islands, Travelpass, The Line to Skye,* and *The Quiet Country.* They were tailored to the commercial cinema market for supporting short films and many were released with popular major films. They were mostly well made (though some were fairly awful) and among them were some distinguished pieces of film-making.

The Heart of Scotland (1961), about Stirling and the surrounding area, was directed by Laurence Henson, filmed by Eddie McConnell to a treatment by John Grierson and had a score by Frank Spedding. Murray Grigor's *Clydescope* (1974), featured an early screen appearance by Billy Connolly in a subversive

attempt to change the style of tourist films. Grigor and Connolly subsequently worked together very succesfully (outwith Films of Scotland) on *Big Banana Feet* (1977) a film record of the comedian's Irish tour, which pulled in huge audiences. Connolly later became a significant actor in straight roles, notably in the work of John Mackenzie (see **Glasgow, City Chambers**).

About a third of Films of Scotland's films were sponsored by industry and they often deal with new industrial developments. *The Hollow Mountain* (1966) described the pump-storage hydro-electric scheme in Ben Cruachan (see **Cruachan**); *Young in Heart* (1963) marked the launch of the Hillman Imp at the newly created Linwood car plant. One of the most ambitious and certainly one of the best, *The Big Mill* (1963), directed by Laurence Henson for Templar Films, was about steel-making at Ravenscraig. There were also films on more traditional pursuits such as carpet-making (*Glasgow Green to Bendigo* (1961) (which was released with *Spartacus*)) and the woollen trade (*Weave Me a Rainbow* (1962)). There were films to promote New Towns, whisky distilleries and a range of other commercial activities.

As Films of Scotland's reputation grew, it was able to encourage more public agencies to back other kinds of film. The Scottish Arts Council provided funding for a number including *Three Scottish Painters* (1963), which dealt with John Maxwell, Joan Eardley, and Robin Philipson; *Mackintosh* (1968), Murray Grigor's first major film on architecture which he followed up with *The Hand of Adam* (1975); and a film on William Gillies, *Still Life with Honesty* (1970) by Bill Forsyth. A few films were produced using the Committee's own resources. *A Kind of Seeing* (1967) was an abstract account of the colour of Scotland by Eddie McConnell who also made *Amazing Moments of the Great Traction Engines* (1969) in which he experimented with multi-image lenses. *The Sun Pictures* (1965) told the story of the pioneer photographers, David Octavius Hill and Robert Adamson.

(left) Harry Lauder in an unidentifed film.

Films of Scotland: (top left) **Busman's Holiday** (1959), (top right) **Enchanted Isles** (1957), (bottom left) **Spirit of Scotland** (1979), (bottom right) **Seawards the Great Ships** (1960, Templar).

(top left) Billy Connolly in Murray Grigor's **Clydescope** (1974, Viz).

(top right) Filming **Clydescope.** Director Murray Grigor on right. (bottom) **The Duna Bull** (1972, IFA Scotland). A prop.

The most significant excursion into funding its own work was when Films of Scotland turned from documentary to fiction. Laurence Henson's *The Duna Bull* (1972) and Robin Crichton's *The Great Mill Race* (1975) were indicative of where Hardy wished the Committee to be heading, encouraged by the evident success of Scottish film-makers' work for the Children's Film Foundation. In a way they revealed the agenda behind the years of short film-making and invited an assessment of Films of Scotland's achievements which goes beyond the track record of the producer of a large number of successfully placed sponsored films.

In the late 1950s there were precious few film-makers in Scotland. Indeed, when Films of Scotland sought to place its first commissions it felt it had to go south to get the pictures made. At least Anglo-Scottish Pictures was run by Scots. As for native producers, Thames and Clyde Films, Templar Films (see **Glasgow, Lynedoch Street**), and Campbell Harper Films (see **Edinburgh, Hill Street**) had little experience of making cinema documentaries (though Campbell Harper had in fact achieved cinema distribution for *The Freedom of Aberfeldy* (1943)). On this rather unpromising foundation, a small documentary film industry was built. The Scottish companies recruited young film-makers, some with amateur and art college backgrounds, but all with enthusiasm. They, in due course, set up their own companies with names such as IFA, Tree, Ogam, Viz, Martyr and Pelicula. Others, such as Edinburgh Film Productions, emerged and together these constituted the workforce of independent film-making in Scotland (see **Edinburgh, Calton Studios**).

Films of Scotland was therefore directly responsible for the growth of the sector, for encouraging new talent and for establishing standards of excellence - production values that ensured its films would be acceptable to distributors and exhibitors throughout the world and would win awards at international festivals. It was an exceptional achievement deserving proper recognition. To apportion credit is perhaps invidious, but Forsyth Hardy deserves most for driving the operation with such effective ambition and determination.

The Committee had its critics, particularly among the film-makers, mainly because of the dominant position it held in Scottish film production and because it seemed less than generous in its dealings with them. The Committee almost invariably retained all the rights in a film so that whatever its success there was no related financial return to the production company. Nevertheless, in John Grierson the Committee had the greatest documentarist of all and his status was of enormous importance to the credibility of the whole operation. The knowledge that their work was to be scrutinised by Grierson had a wonderful way of concentrating the minds of young film-makers.

Misunderstanding Films of Scotland was (and still is) easy. It looked like a Government body, but wasn't. It seemed to exist to promote film-making in Scotland, but its prime function was actually to get sponsored films onto as many public screens as possible. Strictly speaking, therefore, the Committee's development of film-making was a means to further that objective. That there were larger ambitions in the background was almost incidental. If Films of Scotland did seem too dominant it was because it was virtually the only body in the land commissioning films; if it was accused (not without justification), of paying too little for its films it was because it never had a great deal of money.

Films of Scotland's success was manifested in several ways. Crucial, in terms of its economy, and therefore for film-making in Scotland, was its capacity to do distribution deals. The fact that many of the productions achieved circuit releases or at least substantial cinema bookings was extremely important; a tribute to the Committee's connections and to Hardy's negotiating skills. A different, but also important kind of success, was in the public showings of new films that Hardy organised and toured both in this country and overseas.

Halls in Canada, the United States, Australia and England were packed to capacity on a regular basis, and not only by expatriates.

Films of Scotland's most celebrated success was the Oscar-winning *Seawards the Great Ships* (1961) (see **Clydebank**). It was made at a time when cinema documentary was just about to be overtaken by television and, with the possible exception of *The Big Mill* (1963), was the last of the major industrial shorts to make it to the cinema screen. Hypothetically, the best thing that could have happened to Films of Scotland in the afterglow of Hollywood triumph would have been for it to have gone broke dramatically.

Films of Scotland was a Government-approved body set up to promote Scotland without Government funding; it was a sub-committee of The Scottish Council, Development and Industry; its Director was appointed from the Civil Service (there was an understanding that, should the enterprise fail, he might be retrieved by St. Andrews House); a senior Scottish Office official, Willie Ballantine, sat on the Committee. Yet with all these connections, and the obvious success of the enterprise, it still could not attract government funding, the breakthrough that could have changed the history of film in Scotland. Perhaps only the loss of Films of Scotland at its moment of greatest success, and therefore greatest potential political embarrassment, could have created a situation in which the Government might have felt obliged to intervene with cash. Institutional change of that sort, and significant public money for film-making, did not come about for another thirty years.

Three cameramen (c1980). Michael Coulter, Oscar Marzaroli and David Peat.

Towards the end of his life, Forsyth Hardy suggested in his book, *Scotland in Film*, that maybe setting up Films of Scotland had been a mistake. 'If the Scottish Office wanted films made in the national interest it ought to have found money to pay for them. The longer I succeeded in making them the less was the likelihood of this happening'.

It is a sad, and incorrect, analysis. The fact is that in 1954 when the Committee was set up there was no possibility of Government funding for film, promotional or any other sort. The established position on film, that its only use to the Government was for propaganda purposes or revenue, was then no different than it had always been. It was therefore necessary to demonstrate that there was in Scotland the professional capability to make films to the highest technical and aesthetic standards. That was achieved; the Oscar for *Seawards the Great Ships* proved it in the most public way possible. The tragedy is that at that moment the political will and imagination required to capitalise on the achievement and all the energy and talent that it represented, was totally absent.

As it was, the Committee continued to operate successfully for many years. In 1974, Forsyth Hardy retired and was succeeded by Lawrence Knight. In 1976, Neil Paterson (see **Crieff**) became Director, followed in 1978, by Jim Wilson. By the early 1980s, however, cinema documentary was long gone and the television market was proving a much less willing recipient of the Committee's work. Films of Scotland formally ceased trading in 1982.

Regent Road: The Scottish Office.

St Andrew's House is the seat of Government in Scotland. Film legislation, on the other hand, is a matter for the UK as a whole. Whenever there has been any distinction in policy interpretation between north and south of the border it has been in the context of film as culture rather than as commerce. Only in recent years has film's economic role in Scotland become an issue of interest to politicians. In fact, historically, British

political action on film has been more about safety and censorship than encouragement and development. For most of the last hundred years, film in the UK has had an extraordinarily poor deal from Governments of every shade, certainly in comparison to the treatment afforded the film industries of other developed countries.

The temptation is to ascribe the reason for this to some form of prejudice agin the medium because of its humble origins in fairgrounds and peepshows. But that history applies equally in other countries. It didn't stop the Americans enacting laws to encourage the development of the film industry, particularly in relation to its export. America recognised that film's mass appeal provided a tremendous opportunity to spread their culture and with it their commerce; we didn't.

John Grierson found the most vivid way of expressing the problem. He had been a main instigator in the National Film Board of Canada and knew all about politics. In a letter to *The Saltire Review* in June 1960 he said that there would be no progress towards a film industry in Scotland (he could have meant Britain) until the public authorities are 'persuaded'. He went on to say how unlikely that was because 'the will is not there'. He even speculated that something in the Presbyterian soul is inimical to such an enterprise.

It was not an encouraging analysis. Studios, Grierson argued, were not a necessary component for film in Scotland when London was just an hour away by air. Being a Scot was no impediment to success in the movies so long as you had talent and were prepared to move to where the action was. In any case there were some activities that could be successfully pursued at the highest level without leaving Scotland at all. Neil Paterson had won an Oscar for the screenplay of *Room at the Top* (1958) without abandoning Crieff.

In the most important matter Grierson was absolutely correct. Small countries wanting to make films about themselves can only do so with Government will translated into financial backing. Economics dictate that a population as small as Scotland's cannot generate sufficient domestic box-office revenue to pay for the making of even a fairly modest feature film. Therefore, it would follow that the motive for backing film-making must be 'other', if not quite ulterior. In many small countries, a film industry is partly a defence against the erosion of national culture, particularly language. Norway provides a good example. Not only does the state system encourage film-making with a very high (by our standards) proportion of subsidy but there is further money available to the film-maker who chooses to make films in New Norwegian, roughly the equivalent of Lallans. Beyond the domestic need, there is the possibility that a few films, maybe only a very few, will have export potential, with the chance of financial returns and improved international status for the country and its films.

Arguing for film other than for its own sake has its problems. Too great an emphasis on the economic benefits of promoting the arts carries the danger that the arts will seek money before excellence. Nevertheless there is no doubt that public authorities are most susceptible to persuasion when the arguments combine the cultural, the economic and the political. In contrast to the situation in Grierson's day such arguments have begun to gain ground in Scotland.

The Scottish Office has always had an interest in film for education and publicity. It sponsored many remarkable documentaries in the thirties and forties including the outstanding *Children of the City* (1944) (see **Dundee**), about juvenile delinquency, and several concerned with health and education such as *Highland Doctor* (1943). The 'old' Scottish Film Council (see **Glasgow, Dowanhill**) existed on Scottish Office support (through the Education Department) for film as an audiovisual teaching aid. However, The Scottish Office did not sponsor either the pre-war Films of Scotland Committee or its more famous successor (see **Edinburgh, Randolph Crescent**). St. Andrew's House approved of the latter, gave it a remit and even seconded Forsyth Hardy to run it, but put up no money.

It would be hard to identify exactly why and when, but during the 1980s Scottish Office attitudes to film became more supportive. The persuasion of the public authorities began to show in the setting up of the Scottish Film Production Fund and, in 1990, in the constitutional change to the Scottish Film Council making it an independent body able to facilitate the creation of other important agencies and projects, notably Scottish Screen Locations and Scottish Broadcast and Film Training. The period also saw a significant growth in government funding for the SFC. Other public authorities also showed interest in film for virtually the first time; the success of Scottish Screen Locations, for example, is due almost entirely to local authority support (see **Glasgow, Dowanhill**).

What precisely persuades Governments to support the film business will probably remain a mystery, but there is no doubt that the huge success of a film of Scottish origins such as *Rob Roy*, or at least with Scottish connections, such as *Braveheart*, will help. Grierson also remarked that film was the only business in which one swallow *could* make a summer. On the other hand, it is an old British Government ploy to argue that if a film can win an Oscar without Government support then clearly Government support for the entire industry is quite unnecessary. The trouble about the one-offs, especially in Scotland, is that they do not create the critical mass necessary to sustain even a small 'industry' and keep the talent at home. The real test of a Government policy for film in Scotland will be whether or not it can do just that.

By the end of 1995, Scottish Office interest in film had reached unprecedented levels. The regular quinquennial Review of the Scottish Film Council (a process to be undergone by all semi-autonomous agencies) became linked with a major reappraisal of the whole scene in a report costing many tens of thousands of pounds. It was commisioned from Hydra Associates by Scottish Enterprise and Highlands and Islands Enterprise at the request of the Secretary of

State for Scotland, Michael Forsyth, who in the late eighties had been the key figure in granting autonomy to the Scottish Film Council. Forsyth had made a point of involving himself in film matters, most publicly in associating himself with Mel Gibson and *Braveheart* (see **Glen Nevis**). His Minister with responsibility for the arts, Lord James Lindsay, undertook investigative visits to Canada and Los Angeles and for the first time a senior civil servant was given exclusive responsibility for film matters.

On 18 April 1996, in New York, where he was attending a preview of *Loch Ness* (see **Loch Ness**) for American tourism executives, the Secretary of State announced a radical reorganisation of the agencies dealing with film in Scotland. The functions of the existing four bodies - The Scottish Film Council, The Scottish Film Production Fund, Scottish Screen Locations and Scottish Broadcast and Film Training - would be taken over by The Scottish Screen Agency, providing a single focus for all public financial support for film. Funding was increased for various aspects of film production and promotion and for the Drambuie Edinburgh Film Festival; it was suggested that Scottish Screen Locations appoint a 'scout' based in Hollywood to alert them to films which could shoot in Scotland; and a thorough investigation of the potential for a new studio complex was promised. Concerns were expressed that the package lacked the promise of a new tax regime for film production, a cornerstone in the strategy of almost every country eager to promote its film industry and particularly successful in the Republic of Ireland but the contrast between this dynamic form of intervention and the previous lack of Government interest could scarcely be more marked, or more welcome.

Amid the euphoria, though, a deep worry lingers about the amount of emphasis placed on a commercial rather than a cultural approach to film in Scotland. It would be ironic if the effort to persuade the authorities that film in Scotland was a serious business in which they had a stake was too successful, tipping the balance between art and money, so crucial to a healthy cinema culture, too far in the economic direction. The danger that only commercial, 'theme park', movies could be made in Scotland is already real enough. Scottish film must be enabled to reflect all aspects of our culture. Nothing less will do.

Rose Street: Margaret Tait and women in Scottish film

Many years ago, before Rose Street was pedestrianised and trendy, it was more like a village community than a busy thoroughfare less than a hundred yards from one of the world's most famous streets. Margaret Tait, film-maker and writer lived there.

Tait was born in 1919 in Orkney (see **Orkney**) and studied at the Centro Sperimentale di Cinematographia in Rome. Most of her films – syntheses of poetry and visual images – were made in Orkney but she filmed in Rose Street too, very much as an insider, observing minor domestic comings and goings in a gentle way.

Tait's training as a film-maker was only given full rein when she was over seventy years of age. With the encouragement of Barbara Grigor as producer, she made her first feature film, *Blue Black Permanent* in 1992. Set in Edinburgh and Orkney at three distinct periods, the thirties, the fifties and the nineties, *Blue Black Permanent* tells the story of a woman seeking her mother's past and her own identity. Its first screening at the 1992 Edinburgh International Film Festival was received with tremendous enthusiasm.

In the history of film in Scotland there have been disappointingly few women film-makers but those who have worked here or have their origins in Scotland have produced distinctive, but sadly often undervalued, work. In Margaret Tait's generation there were several significant characters such as Jenny Gilbertson (1903-90) (see **Shetland**), the Grierson sisters, Ruby (1904-40) and Marion (born 1907) (see **Cambusbarron**) and Brigid ('Budge') Cooper (1912-83), who were very much part of the documentary movement. Helen Biggar's (1909-53) name is closely associated with that of Norman McLaren (see **Glasgow, School of Art**) and a specially radical approach to the medium with films like *Hell Unlimited* (1936) and *Challenge to Fascism* (1938). Another Glasgow film maker, with a primarily arts and education interest, Louise Annand (born 1915) made one of the first films to examine the work of Charles Rennie Mackintosh.

Recently, following a period of years when there were very few women in senior positions in film in Scotland, there has been a welcome growth in their numbers, particularly in the disciplines associated with production. Among those in a position to influence the course of Scottish film have been Lynda Myles (see **Filmhouse, Lothian Road**), Paddy Higson, the late Barbara Grigor (see **Inverkeithing**), Christeen Winford, Andrea Calderwood, Penny Thomson, Kate Swan and the animator, now CD-Rom producer, Lesley Keen (*Taking a Line For a Walk* (1983), *Orpheus and Euridice* (1984) and *Ra: The Sun-God* (1990)).

● *Blue Black Permanent*
GB, 1992, Viz Productions for Grampian Television, Channel Four et al. 84 mins. Written and Directed by Margaret Tait. Produced by Barbara Grigor. Cinematography by Alex Scott. Music by John Gray. With Jack Shepherd, Celia Imrie, Gerda Stevenson, James Fleet and Sean Scanlon.

South Bridge: Edinburgh University

In May 1958, at the height of the degree examinations, there was a major distraction for students who should have been working their hardest. The University's Old Quad became the set for the opening and closing scenes of the Jules Verne epic, *Journey to the Centre of the Earth* (1959). What damage it did to that year's academic results is not known, but some Edinburgh graduates remember being an extra in the movie among the highlights of their time at university.

Gerda Stevenson in **Blue Black Permanent** (1992, Viz).

Journey to the Centre of the Earth (1959, Twentieth
Century Fox). Studio reconstruction of the Old Quad,
Edinburgh University.

● *Journey to the Centre of the Earth*
US, 1959, Twentieth Century Fox, 129 mins.
Directed by Henry Levin. With James Mason,
Arlene Dahl and Pat Boone.

Waverley Steps

Waverley Steps (1947) has a decent claim to be
the best film ever made about Edinburgh. It was
unique for a number of reasons. The last film
made for the Government to boost civilian
morale, it was in a way a leftover from the war.
In that respect it fell into the same category as
the sometimes excellent series on urban and rural
Britain which included such films as *Children
of the City* (1944) (see **Dundee**) and *Highland
Doctor* (1943). Like them, it was overseen at
the Scottish Office by Forsyth Hardy.

On a visit to Stockholm, Hardy had seen Arne
Sucksdorff's *Rhythm of a City* which, if not a
model for the Edinburgh film, strongly influenced

it (Robert Siodmak's *Menschen an Sonntag*
(1929) was the famous Berlin equivalent). The
idea was developed for a film about Edinburgh
which would eschew the conventional tourist
approach and look more to Continental
Europe for its style than to the traditions of
British documentary. *Waverley Steps* was
directed by John Eldridge of Greenpark
Productions, who subsequently went on to
direct features including *Laxdale Hall* (1952)
(see **Applecross**), and combined elements of
documentary and feature film-making. Without
commentary, the film observes an ordinary day
in Edinburgh. A number of individuals are
followed to their work and their recreation and
the pattern of life in the city is traced from
dawn to dusk. Social contrasts are pointed up -
the driver of the overnight express from
London returns to his wife in the morning,
tenement dwellers wait as an elderly neighbour
dies in bed, a banker lunches at The New Club,
students in the Medical Faculty attend their
lectures. An outsider, a Danish seaman,
wanders the Capital. He visits the usual sights,
the Castle and the High Street; glimpses the

interior of St. Giles Cathedral (where a young Herrick Bunney is playing the Widor *Toccata* on the organ), and ends up in a friendly pub.

In order to provide the film with identifiable characters, the makers turned to the redoubtable Sadie Aitken of the Gateway Theatre who supplied amateurs, of variable talent, to fill the various roles. Despite the odd lapse, *Waverley Steps* is a remarkably fine film, as successful an evocation of a city as you are likely to come across anywhere.

Behind appearances there lurks another story to which Forsyth Hardy would sometimes admit, though never in print. Apparently, the production was troubled by a continuing tension between the film-makers and the Edinburgh establishment. For example, the original treatment proposed that the first citizen the Danish seaman should meet on leaving his vessel in Leith was a 'lady of the night'. Understandably, the Town Council were not too happy about that. Relations were also a little difficult with the New Club who insisted that no actual members be shown. The cut from the actor playing the banker at lunch to a horse with its nose in a trough was a little

Waverley Steps (1947).

unkind, but the clearest rude gesture was reserved for Princes Street. As the camera tracks along the posh shops and elegant shoppers a small boy very visibly relieves himself in the gutter.

Wester Hailes: *Restless Natives*

In the wake of Bill Forsyth's early success, particularly with *Gregory's Girl* (1980), a small group of films appeared trying to capitalise on the new-found audience for gentle whimsy with a Scottish accent. (In this, incidentally, they suffered a misapprehension that all there was to Forsyth was charm and no substance). Most of these films had a decidedly West of Scotland flavour, but *Restless Natives* (1985), directed by Michael Hoffman was an exception. The plot concerned two youthful and well-meaning motorcycle bandits, played by Joe Mullaney and Vincent Friel, who, from a base in a peripheral housing scheme in Edinburgh, make sorties to the Highlands, where they relieve tourists, mainly American, of their money. They become such celebrities on account of their daring and effortless success in baffling the Constabulary that the tourists become ever more willing victims.

The script, by Ninian Dunnett, provided moments of genuine comedy and won the Lloyd's Bank National Screenwriting Competition. It was perhaps better than the resulting film which, looking back, seems very much a product of its time. Incidentally, it was not as pure Edinburgh as it appeared; much of the urban material was shot in Glasgow; an Edinburgh Corporation bus was even removed from its natural habitat to be filmed in the other city's streets.

Among the film's virtues were a sound-track by Big Country and the fact that it provided invaluable experience for its young cast and crew.

● *Restless Natives*
GB, 1985, Oxford Film Company/Thorn EMI, 89 mins. Directed by Michael Hoffman. Produced by Rick Stevenson. Associate Producer, Paddy Higson. Written by Ninian Dunnett. Music by Big Country. With Vincent Friel, Joe Mullaney, Teri Lally, Ned Beatty, Robert Urquhart and Mel Smith.

Edinburgh Zoo

One of Edinburgh's most famous attractions has been the subject of several promotional films such as *Zoo Year* by Campbell Harper Films for Films of Scotland in 1965. It was also central, by inference, to Brian Crumlish's *Tickets for the Zoo* (1991) (see **Edinburgh**).

EILEAN DONAN CASTLE

The restored castle by Dornie where Loch Duich meets Loch Alsh has been so heavily filmed and photographed it is surprising that it has not worn away. Sitting on its own islet with a magnificent mountain backdrop it dares the onlooker not to expose their film and professional film-makers and amateur photographers have been equally susceptible to its charm.

Nevertheless, it tends to appear in supporting rather than starring roles – sometimes just single shots. And substantial feature footage of Eilean Donan is not easy to find. In addition to television - *The Avengers* and *Oliver's Travels*, for example - the castle appeared in the Errol Flynn *Master of Ballantrae* (1953), Peter Yates' *Year of the Comet* (1992) and *Loch Ness* (1996) starring Ted Danson, in which it doubled for the less substantial Castle Urquhart.

Eilean Donan's biggest role was in the first of the *Highlander* films (1986), starring Christopher Lambert and Sean Connery. The mixture of science fiction and more traditional fantasies, with a dash of tartan kitsch, made for a successful movie which generated two sequels (see **Glencoe**).

ERISKAY: Dr Kissling

The island on which the S S Politician foundered in the early hours of 5 February 1941, providing Compton Mackenzie with the basis for *Whisky Galore!* (see **Barra**), has another unlikely film connection.

In the summer of 1934, a German aristocrat, Dr Werner Frederick Theodore Kissling, sailed to Eriskay in a hired yacht and became so attached to the place and its people that they were to dominate his life for years afterwards. Kissling was a film-maker and photographer with a strong interest in anthropology. On Eriskay he found a population with a style of life utterly different from anything he had seen before, one that was slowly adapting to the modern world, leaving behind traditions of behaviour that had remained unchanged for centuries.

The title of his film *Eriskay – a Poem of Remote Lives* (1935) does rather indicate his attitude to the local population, but the intensity of his interest and the detail with which he recorded every aspect of the community made his account invaluable. The film was premiered in London, in the presence of Ramsay MacDonald and the Queen Mother, at the annual Hebridean Concert of the London Gaelic Choir who had contributed to the soundtrack. Kissling then used the film to raise money for the island.

Kissling continued his anthropological pursuits in New Zealand but returned to London only to be interned in the Tower (he was, after all, an aristocrat) on the outbreak of war. He was soon released. Some idea of his political orientation may be judged from the fact that his brother was part of the plot to assassinate Hitler in 1944 and, on its failure, committed suicide.

After the war, Kissling visited the Uists and Eriskay on a regular basis. In the 1950s, he bought a hotel in Melrose which was not a success. He died in poverty in Dumfries in 1988. In 1996, Michael Russell, the former director of Cinema Sgire (see **Benbecula**), produced a television documentary on Kissling, telling the full story for the first time.

ETTRICK: *Confessions of a Justified Sinner*

Despite plans, treatments and scripts by several film-makers, some of them eminent (the late Lindsay Anderson and Bill Douglas, for example), James Hogg's *The Private Memoirs and Confessions of a Justified Sinner*, written in 1824, remains one of Scotland's unmade feature films. Hogg, 'The Ettrick Shepherd' (1770-1835), may have predated the cinema by some time but his masterwork has many characteristics which make it a natural candidate for cinema realisation.

Certainly no Scottish film has yet probed the native Presbyterian soul as Hogg's book did. Although we have had glimpses of what we might do with certain kinds of horror (*The Wicker Man, Shallow Grave*) we have yet to approach the gates of Hell, as we would have to for this extraordinary tale. All we can hope is that someone out there is working on it.

EYEMOUTH: *Depth Charge*

Eyemouth on the Berwickshire coast was the location base for *Depth Charge* (1960) a short semi-factual feature about a fishing boat which trawls up the unexploded depth charge of the title. The *Good Hope's* skipper was played by Alex McCrindle (1911-90) whose career off-screen, as a campaigner for freedom of the press and the arts (he was allegedly removed from the BBC on government pressure), was as eventful as some of his screen roles. In 1953 he was appointed the first Organiser in Scotland for Equity, the Actors Union. In film he appeared in (among others) *The House in the Square* (1951) (as James Boswell), *Trouble in the Glen* (1954), Bill Douglas' *Comrades* (1986) (see **Newcraighall**), *The Private Life of Sherlock Holmes* (1970) and as General Dodonna in *Star Wars* (1977). An older generation will remember him as Jock Anderson in the great radio serial *Dick Barton-Special Agent* which had three inferior film spin-offs without the radio cast.

● *Depth Charge*
GB, 1960, President, 55 mins. Directed by Jeremy Summers. Screenplay by Jeremy Summers and Kenneth Talbot. Music, Muir Mathieson. With Alex McCrindle, David Orr, Elliot Playfair, Alex Allan and John Young.

Eriskay – a Poem of Remote Lives (1935).

Ff

FALKIRK: Finlayson and Campbell

James (Jimmy) Finlayson was born in Falkirk on 27 August 1887. Instead of going to university in Edinburgh and joining the family firm as his relations intended he took to the stage and, in 1916, ended up in Los Angeles where he became a regular with Mack Sennett and, later, with Hal Roach.

In 1920 he appeared in *Married Life* and, thereafter, in a string of comedies with titles such as *Home Talent* (1921) and *Do Detectives Think?* (1927). He is best known for his association with Laurel and Hardy, appearing in many of their most famous films including *Bonnie Scotland* (1935) and *Way Out West* (1937). His appearance – bald head, moustache and a bit of a squint – made him an admirable foil for whatever comedy was going on.

At the end of a very long career in movies, he appeared as a London cab driver in the Stanley Donen romance *Wedding Bells* (1950). He died in 1953.

Falkirk also gave birth to another early Hollywood pioneer. Colin Campbell (1883-1966) is not to be confused with the director Colin T Campbell from Edinburgh. The Falkirk Campbell's career stretched from *Tillie's Tomato Surprise* (1915) to *My Fair Lady* (1964) in which he appeared in the Ascot scene. He played numerous character parts, mostly in fairly minor movies.

FASLANE

The vast British nuclear submarine base at Faslane, a few miles west of Helensburgh on the Gareloch, looks as though it could be a movie set. It is full of sinister looking machinery, not least the huge black vessels with their Polaris and Trident Missiles which can be seen regularly slipping out into the Clyde. A sequence in *The Spy Who Loved Me* (1977), the James Bond movie starring Roger Moore, was shot in the dry dock at Faslane.

Nuclear catastrophe films are good box-office. The cinema would be decimated by a ban on end-of-the-world scenario movies, but in the Scottish context there has been little of that sort of film-making beyond the occasional use of a remote Scottish location for a chase.

Until 1996 one of the ancillaries of Faslane was the Peace Camp at the South Gate. Scottish film-makers have tended to address the serious questions raised by Faslane's existence rather than looking at it as the setting for a thrilling adventure (see **Dunoon**).

One of the most comprehensive accounts of Scotland's role in the defence of the realm was the documentary *Northern Front* produced by Edinburgh Film Workshop Trust in 1986 (see **Edinburgh, Albany Street**).

FLOORS CASTLE: Tarzan

The great Border mansion near Kelso provided the setting for the Scottish episode in *Greystoke: The Legend of Tarzan Lord of the Apes* (1984) in which the child brought up by apes in the African jungle is brought face to face with his aristocratic birthright. The original Greystoke Castle is actually south of the Border but was deemed insufficiently grand for movie purposes. The Director Hugh Hudson is better known in a Scottish context for *Chariots of Fire* (1981) (see **St Andrews**).

● *Greystoke: The Legend of Tarzan Lord of the Apes* GB, 1984, WEA Records/Warner Brothers Pictures, 130 mins. Directed and Produced by Hugh Hudson. From the novel by Edgar Rice

Burroughs. With Ralph Richardson, Ian Holm, James Fox, Christopher Lambert, Andie MacDowell and Ian Charleson.

THE FORTH RAILWAY BRIDGE:
The Thirty-Nine Steps

Apart from all the tourist films The Bridge has one outstanding feature appearance to its name. *The Thirty-Nine Steps* (1935) brought together a collection of superlatives: the greatest adventure writer of his age, John Buchan; his most ripping yarn, full of spies, mysteries and terrific action; the most accomplished screen hero of his day, Robert Donat; the greatest-ever director of suspense, Alfred Hitchcock with his best British production; and one of the most famous landmarks in the world.

The Thirty-Nine Steps (1935). In the studio.

The ever-resourceful Richard Hannay (Donat), wrongly suspected of murder, seems trapped by his pursuers on a train crossing the bridge but manages to escape by forcing his attentions on Madeleine Caroll, causing chaos in the dining car, and finally pulling the communication cord before leaping out to dice with death among the high girders.

There were two remakes of *The Thirty-Nine Steps*, in 1959 (with Kenneth More) and in 1978 (with Robert Powell) but, enjoyable as they were in their own right, the comparison with Hitchcock's work was never going to be to their advantage.

● *The Thirty-Nine Steps*
GB, 1935, British Picture Corporation, 87 mins. Directed by Alfred Hitchcock. From the novel by John Buchan. With Robert Donat, Madeleine Carroll, Godfrey Tearle, Lucy Mannheim, Peggy Ashcroft and John Laurie.

● *The Thirty-Nine Steps*
GB, 1959, Rank, 93 mins. Directed by Ralph
Thomas. From the novel by John Buchan. With
Kenneth More, Taina Elg and Brenda de Banzie.

FOULA: *The Edge of the World*

Michael Powell's *The Edge of the World*, about
the last days of an island community separated
from the mainland by miles of Atlantic Ocean,
was different from any other film of its time,
and arguably from any other film ever made in
Scotland. Although born and brought up in
Kent, Powell was fascinated by Scotland long
before he first came north of the Border. In
June 1930 he saw an item in *The Observer*
about the evacuation of St Kilda (see **St Kilda**)
and became determined to make a film on the
subject.

At the time, Powell was only just setting out on
his directing career and it was several years before
the opportunity arose to fulfil his ambition. That
he did so, in 1936, was due to more than the
usual quantities of luck, ingenuity and persistence
needed for any production. Powell documented
the entire process in one of the most entertaining
and enlightening film books, originally published
in 1938 as *200,000 Feet on Foula* and reissued in
1990 as *The Edge of the World*.

Among the many obstacles that had to be
overcome was the small matter of being refused
permission to film on St Kilda which, since the
story was specific to the island's recent history,
had entirely determined the script, down to the
last detail. The owner of St Kilda was the Earl
of Dumfries who had purchased it to be a bird
sanctuary. The last thing he wanted was an
invasion of film-makers. Within a period of
twenty four hours, Powell was formally refused
access to St Kilda and given clearance to make
the film on another island (which he had never
heard of).

The substitute was Foula, which exhibited
many of the same physical characteristics as St

The Thirty-Nine Steps (1959, Rank).
Kenneth More on the Forth Bridge.

Kilda – size, remoteness, height of cliffs – but
in human terms could scarcely have been more
different. Powell had to amend his conception
of the story to take account of a Norse rather
than a Gaelic culture. The name of the island
remained 'Hirta' as in the main island of the St
Kilda group (in any case a Norse word), but
where the script had called for MacDonalds
and Fergusons there now had to be Grays and
Mansons and all thought of Gaelic had to be
abandoned.

On the benefit side, whereas on St Kilda
there was nothing left but the Earl of Dumfries'
birds, on Foula Powell was at least able to
count on local inhabitants to assist in the film
making. The changes were so substantial that
the finished production (down from the
200,000 feet exposed to 7,300) was more of a
Foula than a St Kilda film.

The logistics of filming on a Shetland island
twenty miles from its nearest neighbour would
be formidable today. In 1936 the difficulties
included not only the frequently hostile weather
but transporting and accommodating an entire
cast and crew with their gear (including sound).
In the event they had to be sustained on
location for no less than five months. Filming
on remote islands was not unknown (Powell
had been close to Flaherty at Gaumont-British
when the great documentary film-maker was
laboriously editing *Man of Aran*), but it was
usually for documentary rather than fiction.

The Edge of the World had a relatively
simple narrative structure. The story is
prefaced by a scene in which a yachtsman
(played by Powell himself) lands on the
deserted island of Hirta with two companions,
one his wife (Frankie Powell) and the other a
seaman who had lived there and who
proceeds to tell the tale of its abandonment.
We learn of families and generations divided
on whether or not to leave the island and of
an intense love story all but thwarted by
human intransigence and fate. The story and
the drama of the place – the storms, the
deaths on the cliffs, the sense of isolation -
still has impact sixty years later.

The Edge of the World (1937). Finlay Currie and John Laurie.

For *The Edge of the World* Powell assembled a cast as committed to the adventure as he was. As the family heads, Manson and Gray, he had the excellent John Laurie and Finlay Currie, both convincing as Shetlanders. Their sons were played by Eric Berry and Niall MacGinnis, and Manson's daughter, Ruth, by Belle Chrystall, the least believable import. Many of the other players were not professional actors and most of the island's population played a part either in front of or behind the camera.

The uniqueness of *The Edge of the World* stems from the passionate compulsion of one individual to tell the dramatic, even shocking, story of the death of a community. Powell was in no doubt that the experience of making the film changed his life. His attachment to Scotland

and its islands was reinforced by it and he returned north to make *The Spy in Black* (1939) in Orkney (see **Orkney**) and *I Know Where I'm Going* (1945) on Mull (see **Mull**), both in partnership with Emeric Pressburger.

A more literal account of the evacuation of St Kilda, Bill Bryden's *Ill Fares the Land* (1983), had also to be filmed elsewhere (see **Applecross**).

● *The Edge of the World*
GB, 1937, Joe Rock Productions, 80 mins. Written and directed by Michael Powell. Produced by Joe Rock. Cinematography, Skeets Kelly, Ernest Palmer and Monty Berman. With John Laurie, Finlay Currie, Eric Berry, Niall MacGinnis, Belle Chrystall, Kitty Kirwan, Grant Sutherland, Campbell Robson and George Summers.

Gg

THE GAIDHEALTACHD

Strictly speaking, the Highlands are the Gaidhealtachd, but the term tends to be associated with those parts of Scotland where Gaelic culture has been at its strongest. If in global terms Scottish cinema has to be thought of as a marginal phenomenon, Gaelic language cinema, in the sense of films in that tongue made specifically for the big screen, is practically non-existent.

Hero (1982), by Barney Platts-Mills was a full length feature film about love and adventure set in an indeterminate Gaelic Scotland. A mediaeval myth with modern references, it was a very bold attempt to develop a particular style. The use of Gaelic was a striking, almost defiant, gesture. In fact, the film-maker assembled a cast of non-Gaelic speakers who had to be taught the language.

There were no such problems for *Hallaig: the Poetry and Landscape of Sorley MacLean* (1984), the memorable documentary by Tim Neat (see **Skye**). Edinburgh Workshop Trust was responsible for *Uamh an Oir* [Cave of Gold] (1995), a 'visual pastiche of Gaelic legend and contemporary life'. A crucial contributor to that project and to two other feature films substantially in Gaelic – *As an Eilean* (1993) (see **Aultbea**) and *Mairi Mhor* (1994) (see **Skye**) – and central to the remarkable growth of television in Gaelic, was Comataidh Telebhisein Gaidhlig (CTG) (see **Stornoway**).

A recent initiative by the Scottish Film Production fund and the CTG will result in new short Gaelic-language films being produced at the rate of at least two per year. Short fiction films in Gaelic are not entirely new. In 1993, Douglas Mackinnon, (who also made *Home*, the memorable television documentary series on Skye) wrote and directed a fifteen minute fable, *Sealladh* [*The Vision*] with Domhnail Ruadh, Dolina MacLennan and Peter Mullen.

● *Hero*
GB, 1982, Maya Films for Channel Four, 92 mins. Written and directed by Barney Platts-Mills. Original Story by J F Campbell. With Derek McGuire, Caroline Kenneil, Alastair Kenneil, Stewart Grant, Harpo Hamilton and Danny Melrose.

● *Uamh an Oir*
GB, 1995, Edinburgh Film Workshop Trust for Channel Four and CTG, 55 mins. Directed and produced by David Halliday. Script by David Halliday and Domhnail Ruadh. Cinematography by Sam Maynard and Maxim Ford. Edited by Cassandra McGrogan.

GLASGOW

Glasgow's contribution to the history of cinema includes the origins of many people who made their way in the movies. Stan Laurel (1890-1965) was brought up in the city and Mary Gordon (née Gilmour) (1882-1963), a perennial Hollywood character actor who often played Scots and Irish supporting roles, was born there. Mary Gordon was an ideal Mrs Hudson to Basil Rathbone's Sherlock Holmes and she appeared with Laurel and Hardy in *Bonnie Scotland* (1935). She also connected with another Glasgow native when she appeared in *Rulers of the Sea* (1939) (see **Greenock**) directed by Frank Lloyd (1888?-1960). To this day, the tradition of emigration continues. George T Miller, one of Australia's best known contemporary directors (*The Man From Snowy River* (1982)), left Glasgow as a child in the 1940s. Other Glasgow-born actors include Gordon Jackson (1923-90) and David McCallum (born 1933).

At the end of cinema's first hundred years Scotland's largest city hosts the greatest amount of film activity in the country. Edinburgh film and television makers become understandably annoyed when it seems that their contributions to the scene are overlooked or their interests subordinated to those of the battalions in the West, but in any mapping exercise or historical perspective on Scottish film culture, Glasgow inevitably bulks larger than the capital.

The main national film media institutions, the new Scottish Screen Agency (incorporating the Scottish Film Council, Scottish Film Archive, Scottish Film Production Fund, Scottish Screen Locations and Scottish Broadcast and Film Training), BAFTA Scotland, PACT, many independent producers and the headquarters of both the major broadcasters, BBC Scotland and Scottish Television, are all located in Glasgow. Before the Second World War, Glasgow was the home of one or two small studio operations

That Sinking Feeling (1979).

and from the mid fifties onwards, most of the Films of Scotland films were made by Glasgow-based companies such as Templar and IFA.

This accident of history, has the effect that much of Scottish feature film-making takes place in Glasgow, a fact reflected in the number of indigenous movies made in and around the city in the last twenty years. With the notable exception of Tavernier's *Deathwatch* (1979) (see **Glasgow, Finnieston**) and the occasional use of Glasgow buildings as surrogates for famous edifices elsewhere (see **Glasgow, City Chambers**), a high proportion of Glasgow film-making has been native endeavour. Tavernier himself remarked that Edinburgh may be beautiful but that Glasgow was 'dramatic'. It is as a 'dramatically' modern city that Glasgow has tended to be represented.

However, it was not at the heavy end of the scale that Glasgow emerged in the 1980s as a film-making city. Almost the reverse. Bill Forsyth's debut feature, *That Sinking Feeling* (1980), is a gentle comedy about a group of unemployed

The Girl in the Picture (1985, Antonine).

youths whose raid on a kitchen and bathroom fittings warehouse leaves them with the problem of how to dispose of the loot. It came as a revelation. For some time previously the only Scottish feature-length fiction film-making was under the auspices either of the Children's Film Foundation (*Flash the Sheepdog, Mauro the Gypsy, Nosey Dobson* etc) or Films of Scotland (*The Duna Bull* and *The Great Mill Race*). Here was an independently made fiction film that drew on local talent for all aspects of its production. Moreover, it had great style in the writing, the direction, the performances and the entirely authentic use of contemporary Glasgow locations and humour. What others had said was possible only if the right public funding could be achieved, Forsyth had gone out and done. He did it so well that *That Sinking Feeling* set him and Scottish film-making on a new road.

Forsyth's next film, *Gregory's Girl* (1981) (see **Cumbernauld**) caused even more of a stir. In its wake came a minor spate of light comedies, not all of them Scottish, doing their best to

capitalise on a public appetite for amusing, non-violent films concerned with enjoying the daftness of the human condition. One such was *The Girl in the Picture* (1985), whose links with Forsyth's early work included casting John Gordon Sinclair in the lead part of a young photographer with problems of the heart as well as the darkroom. If the American Cary Parker, who wrote and directed the film, evoked an extremely pleasant sense of life in Glasgow's West End, a lot was due to an excellent cast of the famous and soon to be famous. *The Girl in the Picture* was also notable as the first feature produced by Paddy Higson of Antonine Films (see **Glasgow, Springfield Road**), a Glasgow company that was to be central to the development of the city's film scene.

A more substantial version of Glasgow was portrayed in two films by Forsyth's former colleague, Charlie Gormley. *Living Apart Together* (1983), about a rock singer (played

Living Apart Together (1983, Legion/Film on Four).
B A Robertson.

by B A Robertson) who returns to Glasgow
with the hope of sorting out his marital
problems, was much more Glasgow-by-night
with the sense of a real city and real and
difficult personal problems. Three years later,
Heavenly Pursuits (1986) for all its jokes about
miracles and the absurdities of institutionalised
education and religion, retained an atmosphere
that was recognisably, and not superficially,
Glasgow (see **Glasgow, City Chambers**).

Bill Forsyth's own return to the city of *That
Sinking Feeling* took the form of a Christmas
story. *Comfort and Joy* (1984) was, to some
extent, the victim of one of those accidents of
history where life and art imitate each other to
nobody's benefit. Alan 'Dickie' Bird (Bill Paterson),
a disc jockey seeking meaning in his life after
the abrupt departure of his girl friend with
virtually all the contents of their flat, becomes
involved in a dispute between rival gangs over
which areas their ice-cream vans can cover.

Although it was not widely known outside the
West of Scotland, around the time of the film's
release a real, violent and distinctly unfunny,
ice cream war was in progress in Glasgow.

Some critics saw it as remarkable that the
setting was both specific (the locations were
clearly Glasgow) and universal (Glasgow was
standing in for any large town that had high-
rise office blocks, peripheral housing estates
and leafy suburbs). What made the film
extremely watchable was the central performance
by Bill Paterson as a man whose job it was to
wake the city every morning with great good
cheer, particularly at Christmas time, whatever
misery he himself might be suffering.

Like so much else about Glasgow its movie
image has been transformed over the last
twenty years. The city has been thoroughly
documented by factual film-makers. Its social
and educational progress, its football matches,
its transport and even just the look of the place
(see **Glasgow, Great Western Road**). But its
representation as essentially a hard place for
hard men is difficult to shake off. Film has

sometimes contributed to that perception in, for example, *The Big Man* (1990), and *Silent Scream* (1990) (see **Barlinnie**). But there are now alternative accounts of the culture, and the more Glasgow films there are the greater the odds that balance will prevail.

The most immediate proof that this could be the case came with the release, in March 1996, of *Small Faces*, Gillies MacKinnon's striking evocation of Glasgow in 1968. *Small Faces* is the story of a teenager growing up in a city where gang culture permeates all aspects of life, so that career ambitions or personal relations were equally affected by the environment of threatened violence. There was no distance between the world of the Art School and the tenement close. *Small Faces* was a new kind of film for Glasgow. Its antecedents (insofar as there were any) were to be found in the work of Terence Davies and Bill Douglas as much as in Bill Forsyth or the 'hard school' films, and was as remote from the old tartanry images as is most ordinary Scottish life.

Perhaps the most atmospheric Glasgow film was also one of the smallest. *Dear Green Place* (1960) was produced and directed by Oscar Marzaroli and Michael Pavett. Lasting just fifteen minutes, it consisted of black and white stills set to the songs of Ewan McColl.

Marzaroli was one of the great characters of film-making in Scotland from the sixties until his death in 1988. A brilliant photographer who captured his adopted city and its people – street children from Gorbals to Castlemilk, artists, football crowds and, it seemed, virtually everyone who made up the place – Marzaroli worked with most of the film-makers of the time. While at Templar Films he worked on *Seawards the Great Ships* (see **Clydebank**), appearing for once in front of the camera, albeit very briefly, as a burly figure high on a crane. Later he and Martin Singleton set up Ogam Films and produced

Comfort and Joy (1984, Lake).
Bill Paterson receiving a request.

films for the new Highlands and Islands Development Board including *A Pride of Islands*, a spectacular aerial vision of the Hebrides. However, it is for his large personality and his photographs, as published in his books *Shades of Grey* (1987) and *Shades of Scotland* (1989), that he will probably be best remembered.

Glasgow was the ultimate destination for the leading character, played by Peter Capaldi, in *Soft Top, Hard Shoulder* (1992). This story of a young Glasgow Italian who is obliged to return home from London to attend his father's birthday celebrations rang only partly true but Capaldi's next personal move was to become the director of *Franz Kafka's It's a Wonderful Life*(1995), one of the most successful short films ever made in Scotland (see **Glasgow, Queen Margaret Drive**).

● *That Sinking Feeling*
GB, 1979, Sinking Feeling Films, 93 mins. Written and directed by Bill Forsyth. With Tom Mannion, Eddie Burt, Alex Mackenzie, Margaret Adams, Kim Masterton and Richard Demarco.

● *Living Apart Together*
GB, 1983, Legion Productions/Film on Four, 105 mins. Written and directed by Charles Gormley. Edited by Patrick Higson. With B A Robertson, Barbara Kellerman, Judi Trott, David Anderson, Jimmy Logan, James Cosmo and Peter Capaldi.

● *Comfort and Joy*
GB, 1984, Lake/Thorn EMI and Scottish Television, 106 mins. Written and directed by Bill Forsyth. With Bill Paterson, Eleanor David, C P Grogan, Alex Norton and Patrick Malahide.

● *The Girl in the Picture*
GB, 1985, Antonine /NFFC. 91 mins. Produced by Paddy Higson. Written and Directed by Carey Parker. With John Gordon Sinclair, Irina Brook, David Mackay, Gregor Fisher, Paul Young and Rikki Fulton.

Anniesland: Edinburgh translated

One of Edinburgh's most archetypal institutions – the New Town flat – was built in an industrial unit in Glasgow's Anniesland for the filming of *Shallow Grave* (1994). The lack of proper studio facilities (or the Edinburgh ambience) seemed to have no detrimental effect on the film, which was a great success.

Figment Films next venture, *Trainspotting* (1996) (see **Leith**), was an even greater triumph. Its interiors, too, were shot in Glasgow, in the old Wills factory in Alexandra Parade.

Barlinnie: hard men

One of the penalties of a low volume of film production is that two or three films with roughly the same theme are liable to be identified as a significant trend which can easily become a new stereotype. With the diversity of subject matter that greater numbers of films offers, the opportunity for such fixations diminishes. Moreover, the over-heated expectations, praise or opprobrium heaped on a particular Scottish film, if it is the only one around at the time, may be replaced by more mature and balanced consideration when it is one of a number on offer.

In the 1980s, there was a period when it looked as though our screen media had become hooked on West of Scotland violence. The 'Hard Man' image of Scotland was taking over from the innocence of the beginning of the decade when it seemed that Bill Forsyth and his followers were the only depictors of how we were.

As they do, the academics sought a label for the 'hard' version of Scotland. 'Clydesidism' was about working class violent crime with overtones of poverty, sectarianism and stubborn refusal to be beaten by the system. Barlinnie and the story of the Special Unit, Jimmy Boyle, Larry Winters and their contemporaries, were central to this thesis. The two key films were *A Sense of Freedom* (1981), made for television, and *Silent Scream* (1989).

Silent Scream (1989, Antonine). The dream sequence.

The actor and director, David Hayman, a passionate advocate of a viable Scottish film industry with control of its own resources was a key figure in this area. Hayman played Jimmy Boyle in *A Sense of Freedom* and directed *Silent Scream* which was voted Best British Film at the 1990 Edinburgh International Festival and won Iain Glen the *Evening Standard* Best Actor award and the Silver Bear at the 1991 Berlin Film Festival for his performance as Larry Winters. In 1995 Hayman directed the highly atmospheric *The Near Room*, about a journalist's search for his daughter in a Glasgow underworld of drugs and criminality.

But there were other films and television dramas with violence at their core. Based on the William MacIlvanney novel, *The Big Man* (1990), the story of a former miner turned bareknuckle prize fighter was not short on violence but its harsh reflection of the reality of at least one aspect of West of Scotland life made it well worth watching. *The Big Man* cast and crew list is interesting. The lead was the Irishman,

Liam Neeson, who would return spectacularly to another Scottish part in *Rob Roy* (1995). Billy Connolly appeared in one of his most effective straight roles. The music was by Ennio Morricone, more usually associated with the wide open spaces and guns of the spaghetti western than the tight clandestine world of bareknuckle fighting in North Lanarkshire.

The Big Man was not particularly well received by the critics but regarded as a mini-genre, the 'hard man' film has had a fair degree of success.

● *A Sense of Freedom*
GB, 1981, Scottish Television, 105 mins. Produced by Jeremy Isaacs. Directed by John Mackenzie. Script by Peter McDougall from the autobiography of Jimmy Boyle. With David Hayman, Jake d'Arcy, Sean Scanlon, John Murtagh, Roy Hanlon, Fulton Mackay and Alex Norton.

● *Silent Scream*
GB, 1989, Antonine Productions for BFI and
Channel Four, 85 mins. Directed by David
Hayman. With Iain Glen, Paul Samson,
Andrew Barr, Bobby Carlyle and Tom Watson.

● *The Big Man*
 GB, 1990, Palace/BSB/Scottish Television, 116
mins. Directed by David Leland. Written by
Don MacPherson, from the novel by William
McIlvanney. Music by Ennio Morricone. With
Liam Neeson, Joanne Whalley-Kilmer, Billy
Connolly, Ian Bannen, Maurice Roeves, Kenny
Ireland, John Beattie and Amanda Walker.

● *The Near Room*
GB, 1995, Inverclyde Productions, 90 mins.
Directed by David Hayman. Produced by
Leonard Crooks. Screenplay by Robert
Murphy. With Adrian Dunbar, David O'Hara,
David Hayman, Julia Graham, Tom Watson,
James Ellis, Robert Pugh and Peter McDougall.

A Sense of Freedom 1981, Scottish Television).

Bellahouston: The Empire Exhibition

The 1938 Empire Exhibition remains firmly in
the memory of Glaswegians, and many others,
as one of the greatest events ever staged in
Scotland. It is still a point of reference for
large-scale enterprises and the nostalgia it
evokes is wonderfully potent, even among
those who could not possibly have experienced
it first hand.

The Empire Exhibition provided a rare
opportunity to promote Scotland and Scottish
endeavours to a wide audience. At the time, the
documentary movement led by John Grierson
was at the height of its development. Grierson
proposed that a series of films be made to be
shown in the specially constructed, six hundred
seat, Empire Cinema in Bellahouston Park. As
a result of his persuasion, the Scottish Office
set up the first Films of Scotland Committee
which, like its successor in 1954, included Sir
Alexander B King among its members, thus
ensuring the likelihood of cinema distribution
for whatever it produced.

The Committee produced seven films intended for the Exhibition and one other, about Dundee. The most important were: *Wealth of a Nation*, directed by Donald Alexander, a survey of industrial Scotland with an eye to its future; *They Made the Land*, directed by Mary Field, depicting new methods supplanting old in the struggle to produce a modern agriculture in often intractable terrain; *The Children's Story*, outlining the history and contemporary strength of education in Scotland; and *The Face of Scotland*, directed by Basil Wright.

The last of these, a perhaps slightly pretentious attempt to define what makes a Scot, still stands up remarkably well. The film contains more than enough historical rhetoric but there is also an attempt to let the camera find out who we are and many of the images are superb. The final sequence, of a sea of mens' faces (exclusively mens') at a major football match, is one of the most telling passages in Scottish cinema history. *The Face of Scotland* may not quite live up to its lofty intentions but considered without prejudice as a documentary of its times, it is really remarkable.

The Face of Scotland was to be shown at the World Fair in New York the year after the Empire Exhibition, but the British Council's Film Committee in London decreed that this powerful and serious film full of working class faces was not appropriate to represent Britain (England?). Something of a tourist nature with Beefeaters would be screened instead. However, Forsyth Hardy records that Grierson had the last laugh. The Bellahouston films were shown in New York after all, not in the British Pavilion but, through his influence, in the pavilion devoted to American Science and Education.

It has to be recorded that the Empire Exhibition film series also contains one of the most inadvertently funny films ever made. *Scotland for Fitness* begins with a small, rather unhealthy-looking member of the aristocracy sitting behind a large desk and telling us in a very drawly upper-class accent how important fitness is for all of us. The sudden appearance of a man in a kilt, apparently using the baronet's study as a short-cut on his hill walk,

fails to surprise him and the two proceed to study a map... .

● *Wealth of a Nation*
GB, 1938, Strand Productions, 18 mins. Directed by Donald Alexander. Produced by Stuart Legg (Film Centre). Commentary spoken by Harry Watt.

● *They Made the Land*
GB, Gaumont British Instructional, 1938. Directed by Mary Field.

● *The Children's Story*
GB, Strand Productions, 1938. Produced by Stuart Legg. Directed by Alexander Shaw.

● *The Face of Scotland*
GB, Realist Film Unit, 1938, 20 mins. Directed by Basil Wright. Produced by John Grierson.

Blythswood Square: *Madeleine*

An innocent-looking house on the corner of Blythswood Square holds a terrible secret. It is alleged that through the bars of the basement window young Madeleine Smith handed a poisoned chocolate drink to the Frenchman, Emile L'Angelier, her inconvenient and unfortunate lover.

Madeleine (1949) was David Lean's version of the 1857 trial of the presumed murderess (played by his then wife, Ann Todd). Critics of the time were not entirely happy with it, or her, complaining that she was too old for the part and that the ending was unsatisfactory. With a verdict of 'unproven' it was hardly likely to be otherwise.

Next door is the building which now houses the Scottish offices of the Independent Television Commission.

● *Madeleine*
GB, 1949, Cineguild, 114 mins. Directed by David Lean. With Ann Todd, Ivan Desny, Norman Wooland, Leslie Banks, Elizabeth Sellars, Jean Cadell, André Morell and John Laurie.

Madelaine (1949, Cineguild). Ann Todd.

Broomielaw: setting sail

The enduring film image of the Broomielaw is of smoky steamers full to the gunwales with passengers setting off 'doon the watter' to resorts on the Clyde estuary. Archive footage from the early years of the century, such as in *Glasgow and the Clyde Coast* (1910) and *St Kilda, Britain's Loneliest Isle* (1923), carries a heavy charge of nostalgia. More recently, the Broomielaw provided the point of departure for the lowly puffers including *The Maggie* (1954) (see **Islay**).

Fitba' Daft (1921), one of the more significant missing-presumed-lost Scottish films, contained a sequence in which a young woman jumped into the Clyde at the Broomielaw (see **Ibrox**).

Celtic Park: at the Odeon

One Sunday in 1967 probably set the record for attendances in one day at a Glasgow cinema. The cinema was the Odeon before it was tripled and its capacity reduced. The movie, shown three times to a total audience of nine thousand, doesn't appear in the film encyclopedias. It was *The Celtic Story* (made by IFA (Scotland) on 16mm) which told the history of the club, climaxing in its triumph in the European Cup that year.

City Chambers, George Square: *Heavenly Pursuits*

Glasgow's magnificent seat of civic power has the curious distinction that it's marble pillars and echoing corridors have masqueraded as both the Vatican and the Kremlin.

Heavenly Pursuits (1986) was Glasgow film-maker Charlie Gormley's second feature film based in the city. The story concerns a teacher in a Roman Catholic school who finds himself the innocent agent of miraculous happenings. As the school and the church are looking for evidence of divine intervention to upgrade their Blessed Edith Semple to Sainthood (hence the need to visit the Vatican), the timing could not be better.

Though billed as a comedy and containing some very funny moments, *Heavenly Pursuits* was not merely a spin-off from the early films of Gormley's former partner Bill Forsyth. It had a serious streak to it (how could a Glasgow film about religion and education be otherwise?). Moreover, in Tom Conti and Helen Mirren it had two excellent leads.

An Englishman Abroad (1983) concerned an episode in the life of Guy Burgess in Moscow. The interior of the Kremlin was provided by the City Chambers. The pedestrian suspension bridge over the River Clyde also featured and some of the other exteriors were filmed in Dundee.

There was a glimpse of the City Chambers in John Mackenzie's *The Long Good Friday* (1979). Mackenzie (born in Edinburgh in 1932) is a director usually associated with action and crime thrillers. Over many years he has built a reputation for movies such as *The Honorary Consul* (1983), *The Fourth Protocol* (1987), *Ruby* (1992) and television films such as *The Cheviot, the Stag and the Black, Black Oil* (1974), *Just Another Saturday* (1975) and *A Sense of Freedom* (1981), often in collaboration with Peter McDougall (see **Greenock**).

● *Heavenly Pursuits*
GB, 1986, Produced by Michael Relph and Island Films for Film Four International, 91 mins. Written and Directed by Charles Gormley. With Tom Conti, Helen Mirren, Brian Pettifer, David Hayman, Dave Anderson and Jennifer Black.

Heavenly Pursuits (1986, Island).
Tom Conti and Helen Mirren.

● *An Englishman Abroad*
GB, 1983, Directed by John Schlessinger. With Alan Bates and Coral Browne.

Cowcaddens: Scottish Television

Scottish Television Plc is the largest of the three ITV Companies covering Scotland. The others are Grampian, based in Aberdeen, and Border, based in Carlisle. Scottish, by virtue of covering central Scotland where the bulk of the population lives, has the biggest share of the market. It began transmission in August 1957.

Historically, the relationship between cinema and commercial television in Scotland has probably not been very different from elsewhere. Television was the major contributor to the decline of cinema from the fifties onwards, though there were other factors; it has been suggested that the decline in cinema attendances is more closely paralleled by the spread of domestic central heating than by the rise in the sale of television sets and cinema owners contributed to their own downfall by failing to invest in audience comfort when they had the chance.

Scottish Television (it used to be commonly known as STV) began with an oblique connection to the cinema. Its owner, Roy Thomson (later Lord Thomson of Fleet), engaged John Grierson to present a series, *This Wonderful World*, in the station's early years. Grierson's material, appropriately for the 'Father of the Documentary', was largely factual. For STV, the making of fiction films was another matter.

Television has an enormous appetite for feature film. Movies are a crucial part of any station's schedule and regularly reach bigger audiences than other programmes. Only a few major sporting or other sensational events surpass viewer ratings for movies. Television therefore needs feature films just as much as feature films require television as a market beyond the cinemas and as a means of promotion.

John Grierson (right) with Laurence Henson at STV.

Most movies on television, as in the commercial cinema, are American. In the 1995 Christmas period, some eight hundred films were on offer to viewers in Scotland who had access to all the terrestrial and satellite channels. Yet, as a leading nationalist politician pointed out (no doubt seeking the appropriate effect), within that list only three – *Highlander, Whisky Galore!* and *The Maggie* were remotely on Scottish subjects, and none of these were truly indigenous productions. If television has any pretensions to reflect its host culture, this survey indicates that it is failing miserably.

Logic suggests that if television wants audiences to identify with a station it should provide them with locally-made feature films on a regular basis, even if that means making them itself. In theory at least, if they made a lot of feature films, some would succeed at the box office and some would certainly fail, but they would all be available for television screening, with a fair chance of economic equilibrium and cultural gain. Unfortunately the real world gets in the way of such a vision. The comparative costs of making films or producing drama 'in house', as opposed to buying in even a major movie, make such a strategy appear unviable to most broadcasters. The fundamental problem is the size of the country and the broadcasting economy. As Gus Macdonald, Chairman of Scottish Television, keeps pointing out, unless Scottish broadcasters and independents produce films that sell outside Scotland such film-making has no future. Productions aimed purely at the Scottish market have to be made at a cost consistent with the size of a Scottish audience, which means very cheaply. On the other hand, good quality television drama can sell abroad, (*Taggart* proved it). The difficulty in penetrating the market is such that even achieving a minimum exposure on the ITV Network, let alone selling abroad, requires immense effort and, in the commercial television sector, the market, not the culture, dictates. Fiction film made in Scotland must therefore have clear potential elsewhere if it is to have any chance of getting its money back, and that applies whether the target is the large or the small screen.

The independent film companies, most of them very small, view the position differently from the broadcasters. They see a political as much as an economic problem in which television has the power and the resources to transform fiction film-making in Scotland into a full scale industry should the television companies wish it. They note the commitment to feature film of broadcasting systems in other countries. They also worry about the amount of money available for 'domestic' production, which many of them rely on to keep going.

The situation is complicated by the activities of the other ITV player, Channel Four, which transformed feature film-making in Britain when it arrived on the scene in 1982. Channel Four has its own approach as a 'publisher' of television programmes, not as a producer. It is too easy to talk, as some did, of it being 'the saviour' of the British film industry, but it has been a most important stimulus to low and medium budget film-making. Inevitably, Channel Four was, and continues to be, accused of 'London bias'. Equally inevitably its performance in commissioning Scottish work is compared favourably with the record of the local broadcasters.

Channel Four has played a very significant role in feature film development in Scotland. Not only is it involved closely with the Scottish Film Production Fund, but it has its own special development fund for Scotland. As a result, a very large proportion of Scottish films acknowledge Channel Four's backing in their credits. The list is an honourable one including, for example, *Another Time Another Place, As an Eilean, Blue Black Permanent, Conquest of the South Pole, Heavenly Pursuits, Ill Fares the Land, Shallow Grave, Silent Scream, Venus Peter* and *Trainspotting*.

Production aside, Scottish Television has done much to its credit in supporting Scottish film culture. In common with the other broadcasters, Scottish has participated increasingly in efforts to develop the infrastructure, for example in new training arrangements (see **Glasgow, Park Gardens**). Scottish itself played a key role in the reorganisation of the Edinburgh International Film Festival – now the 'Drambuie' Edinburgh Film Festival – with Gus Macdonald, then Managing Director of Scottish Television, taking over the Chairmanship from Murray Grigor in 1994. The company has also been a strong supporter of the development of the Scottish Film Archive and has collaborated with the Scottish Film Council and the Scottish Film Production Fund on various projects, notably the schemes 'First Reels' (which gives a platform to film makers at the very beginning of their careers) and 'Prime Cuts' (for more advanced practitioners).

Scottish *has* participated in the funding of feature films, though most have been 'TV movies', that hybrid form of production which only occasionally gets onto cinema screens, and there is no doubt that the decision to back *Gregory's Girl* (1981), *A Sense of Freedom* (1981), *Ill Fares the Land* (1982), *Comfort and Joy* (1984), and *The Big Man* (1990) benefited Scottish film- making as well as the company. The one instance of Scottish Television producing a feature film on its own (through Scottish Television Enterprises) ended unhappily. *Killing Dad* (1989) was just not good enough to make it to commercial cinema screens. Had it been a resounding success, the story of Scottish Television's involvement in movies might have been very different. As it is, the number of significant feature films produced in Scotland (even including the contribution of Grampian Television (see **Aberdeen**)), either directly by, or funded by, the indigenous independent broadcasters over the last thirty years has not been impressive.

There is another dimension to television's significance to film production. Television companies provide employment and training, and help to sustain a pool of actors and technicians with the skills to make cinema films in Scotland. Unfortunately, cutbacks in all broadcasting organisations are currently undermining even that function.

The issues outlined here generate tensions within the film and television industry. Although this is most obvious in relations between the independent film/programme makers and the broadcasters there is also rivalry between the television organisations themselves which becomes public from time to time. To the detached observer, this must seem obscure and internecine, but television is so vital to Scottish film culture that it is never good news when relationships on our small patch are fraught. The hope must be that all concerned will come together in taking the long-term view that a 'slate' of indigenous feature film productions, not just the occasional one-off, is the way forward, allowing the inevitable peaks and troughs in the business to balance out. The announcement, in July 1996, of a scheme whereby six ITV companies, including Scottish, would pool their resources to fund a series of films for cinema was an encouraging sign that this might happen.

There are other positive signs too. Scottish Television has pursued enlightened policies and been innovative in many areas of broadcasting and has employed independents to undertake some highly original documentary work, particularly in the arts, where, for example, it has provided an outlet for the work of Viz Films (see **Inverkeithing**). Its support of Gaelic culture is well recognised and its coverage of cinema events such as the Drambuie Edinburgh Film Festival is often very good. A similar commitment to the making of feature films in Scotland could transform the scene.

Dowanhill: the film organisations

The tree-lined streets to the west of Byres Road house a large part of Glasgow's academic community in a mixture of elegant terraced villas and student bed-sits. It is good territory for film-making and hardly a week goes past without some film crew or other's pantechnicons blocking the streets. Usually the activity is for the benefit of television (BBC Scotland is only a few hundred yards away and Scottish Television favours Dowanhill for *Taggart*, for example) but several movie sequences have been filmed in the area including parts of *Deathwatch* (1979) and *Heavenly Pursuits* (1986).

Towards the top of Dowanhill, the former Notre Dame teacher training college houses the Scottish Council for Educational Technology (SCET), whose tenants, in 1996, included most of the key Scottish film organisations – The Scottish Film Council (including the Scottish Film Archive), The Scottish Film Production Fund, Glasgow Film Fund, Scottish Screen Locations, Producers Alliance for Cinema and Television (PACT) and BAFTA Scotland as well as a number of independent producers (see also **Glasgow, Park Terrace, Scottish Broadcast and Film Training**).

The Scottish Film Council (SFC)

At this point, it is only fair to offer the reader a word of caution. I was first employed by the Scottish Film Council in 1969, brought in by the Director, R B Macluskie, to develop the Council's cultural work. SFC became SCET, of which I was Depute Director, and was subsequently re-established as the new SFC, of which I was Director from 1986 to 1994. What follows is therefore an inside view.

A full account of the complex history of the Scottish Film Council would require a volume on its own and is beyond the scope of this overview of film culture in Scotland. It began in the 1930s and, although there have been times when its main achievement was survival rather than progress, continues, increasingly optimistically, through the 1990s. The optimism which started the SFC was generated by a group of individuals enthused at the prospect of what film could do for society as entertainment and, even more so, as a means of communication. This was, after all, the era of the documentary when film was beginning to show its strength as a social force. Even at the outset, therefore, the emphasis was on film as a tool rather than as an end in itself. Thus for many years the first stated aim of SFC was 'to encourage the use of film as an educational and cultural medium'. This teleological approach

determined the Council's relatively narrow role for much of its existence and ensured its survival. It also distinguished it from the British Film Institute, whose remit was more clearly in favour of 'the art of the film'.

The formation of the SFC was very much bound up with the origins of the BFI. In November 1929, a Commission on Educational and Cultural Films was established at a UK conference by some one hundred educational and scientific bodies. Two and a half years later the Commission produced a report, 'The Film in National Life'. Public meetings were held, including one in Glasgow chaired by the Principal of the University, Sir Robert Rait. The upshot was the formation of the British Film Institute, which was formally incorporated on 30 September 1933. The BFI's first chairman was the Duke of Sutherland.

There was no question of Government finance for the new body which had to be funded from a levy on Sunday cinema shows. Since there were no such performances in Scotland, there was at once an issue for minor cross-border tension. However, the BFI immediately set about creating 'Councils' throughout the UK to further its work and, not surprisingly given that many of the most enthusiastic supporters of its creation were Scots, one of these was in Scotland. 'The Scottish Film Council of the British Film Institute' held its first meeting in September 1934 in Glasgow. The first Chairman was John Buchan M P. Buchan's novel *The Thirty-Nine Steps*, was being filmed at that time by Alfred Hitchcock, but his association with SFC lasted only a year before, as Lord Tweedsmuir, he departed to be Governor General of Canada.

According to Charles Oakley(who chaired the SFC from 1939 to 1975) in *21 Years of the Scottish Film Council 1934-1955*, the BFI 'did not envisage the Scottish Film Council developing into anything more than its link with Scottish interests'. In fact, with the enthusiastic participation of the film society movement, led by Forsyth Hardy and Norman Wilson of the Edinburgh Film Guild, and Charles Oakley and

John Buchan and Alfred Hitchcock (c1935).

Tom Hutchison of the Glasgow Film Society as well as educational and cinema trade bodies, it quickly established its own agenda.

The SFC set up four 'Panels' (a good Scottish word for a committee) the names of three of which signify clearly where the priorities lay. These were the Education Panel, whose remit was, among other things, 'to influence public opinion to appreciate the value of films in education'; the Social Service Panel, mainly concerned with ensuring that young people saw 'suitable' entertainment films; and the Amateur Cinematography Panel to foster just that.

The fourth panel was the only one which seemed to connect with film as art and even then in a slightly strange way. It was called the Entertainment Panel and was chaired by Forsyth Hardy. Its job was 'to secure the views of the public as to the type of film required; to encourage the repertory cinema movement in Scotland; and to obtain public support for films of unusual merit which did not obtain appreciation from the ordinary cinema-going public'. Over thirty years later, following the BFI's 'Outside London' initiative, SFC decided to devote all its energy to setting up film theatres throughout Scotland, probably its most important policy decision up to that point and certainly one of its most successful, as Glasgow Film Theatre, Filmhouse in Edinburgh and the other Regional Film Theatres demonstrate.

In 1937, Russell Borland, a former schoolteacher, was appointed as the SFC's first employee and within two years, thanks to a grant from the Carnegie Trust, the Scottish Central Film Library was founded. The pattern was therefore established which would last for the best part of forty years, strengthened in the 1940s by Borland's successor, D M Elliot. The SFC was primarily concerned with film in support of education (and as such was funded by local and central Government) as well as having wider interests including film in industrial training, health, and community issues. It retained an interest in film culture but at a much lower level than the other considerations.

It is important to note two things: firstly, that, as an agency concerned with film in the service of the community, the SFC was immensely successful. The Scottish Central Film Library supplied every school, and practically every other sort of organisation, in the land. It grew to be possibly the largest 16mm educational film library in Europe (see **Glasgow, Woodside Terrace**). The SFC and its associated bodies such as the Scottish Educational Film Association were world leaders in the innovative promotion and application of visual aids in education and at one point in the 1980s the Director, Ronnie B Macluskie, held the presidency of the International Council for Educational Media. The second significant fact is that, within the limits of SFC's funding (given that virtually none of its resources were specifically for the promotion of film culture), it succeeded in sustaining a connection with film as art. Its principal cultural interests were in supporting the Edinburgh Film Festival; running a repertory season of foreign-language films (e.g. the films of Luis Bunuel, in 1969); and supporting and organising the Scottish International Amateur Film Festival, an event of world standing which provided an invaluable showcase for aspiring Scottish film makers by not only giving them a public platform but, under the festival's unique judging system of engaging a celebrity adjudicator, letting their work be seen and commented on by some of the most distinguished film-makers of the day. Thus it was that Norman McLaren was 'spotted' by John Grierson in 1936, when his *Colour Cocktail* was among the prize winners. Other adjudicators included Victor Saville, Anthony Asquith, Alfred Hitchcock, Michael Powell, Alberto Cavalcanti and Alexander Mackendrick.

Strong support for the film society movement, through the Scottish Group of the British Federation of Film Societies, and growing interest in media education were other manifestations of the SFC's connection with mainstream film. More direct involvement came through 'Educational Films of Scotland', the Council's programme for making classroom films (which employed many independent film-makers (on miniscule budgets), including Mike Alexander, Bill Forsyth, Charlie Gormley, Robert Riddell Black and Douglas Gray) and occasional projects such as the joint short film competition with BBC Scotland's 'Scope' programme in 1972 and 1974 which had a jury, chaired on one occasion by Joseph Losey.

The central paradox remained that the body which looked equivalent to the BFI and whose title suggested it should be there to promote film in all its aspects was simply not set up to do that job. The reason, the same one that had prevented the Films of Scotland Committee from realising its potential, was that the Government, however willing it was to put money into film for education and training, would not fund film culture in Scotland. The excuse was that the BFI should take care of it (which it patently didn't). This explanation was often difficult to get across to unhappy film-makers and others, and the situation was to become even more opaque before the problem was finally resolved.

In the late sixties and early seventies, the technology of education began to change dramatically. 'Educational Technology' embracing 'audio visual aids' was the expression to cover all forms of mechanical and electronic devices applied in the classroom. But educational technology, we were told, was not machines, it was a systematic approach to learning, a state of mind integral to the development of open learning, distance learning, learning by computer and so on. A Council for Educational Technology was set up for Britain but, given Scotland's independent status in educational matters, a body was needed north of the border. Given that the SFC was an acknowledged leader in the field, it was the natural candidate.

So, in 1976, the SFC became The Scottish Council for Educational Technology (SCET). The benefits to the organisation were very considerable, not least in the increase of staff and the move from Woodside Terrace to Dowanhill. From a film culture perspective, the change, with its apparent loss of status for film interests was not as bad at it looked. As part of the deal, SCET had to sustain a statutory committee known as the Scottish Film Council, chaired by Professor Ian Lockerbie. Its sole remit was to foster film culture and it had a budget with which to pursue its programme. The SFC was now part of a much larger economy.

There were, of course, huge difficulties of perception and practice. Even before SCET was formed, one angry and frustrated film-maker demanded to know how it was that with 'all those hundreds of people up there' the SFC was doing nothing for film-makers. In fact in 1975, the 'hundreds of people' were the forty working in the Scottish Central Film Library. Film as film was the full-time responsibility of just one member of staff, John Brown, an assistant director who also had other responsibilities, with one assistant, Ken Ingles (later Director of GFT), and some input from senior colleagues including the present author, Tom Clarke (now an MP) and Dick Tucker, an educational technologist who came from film teaching and had a book on Japanese cinema to his credit.

On the other side, there were educationalists who thought that the staff of SFC and SCET were really only interested in film, and there were endless debates about the educational benefit of the SFC's activities. This matter was of more than academic interest since all the Government money they received came from the Scottish Education Department, a problem partly solved when, in 1986, SFC was given a separate earmarked grant for its activities. This was a significant move achieved by R B Macluskie (Director of SFC/SCET from 1968 to 1986) on his retirement and it laid the foundation for formal independence in due course. Macluskie, an accountant by training was an enthusiast for all aspects of film culture. The survival of a national film culture agency in Scotland was largely due to his calm persistence.

Despite all the problems, there were many significant advances. The decision to prioritise public access to film in the 1970s had led to the setting up of a network of highly successful regional film theatres. The politically grey area

of media education – was it education, was it film? (it was both) – had progressed as effectively in Scotland as anywhere in the world. Production support was beginning to become rational with the creation of the Scottish Film Production Fund. The future of Scotland's moving image heritage was becoming more secure with the establishment of the Scottish Film Archive in 1977. Thanks to Macluskie's enthusiasm for film heritage, and his reluctance to throw anything away, there was also the core of a Scottish Film Museum in formation (see **Coatbridge**).

A series of short-term projects and appointments also helped advance the cause. The Scottish Film Archive (see below) was the outcome of one such initiative and from the late seventies a number of enterprising individuals, including Peter Broughan, Lesley Keen, Martyn Auty, John Adams and Sheena McDonald (who went on to careers in the industry), found themselves on the staff of SFC for various periods of time. Lynda Myles, Director of the Edinburgh Film Festival was also made a full-time member of staff. Of the long-term members, John Brown, who had joined the Council in 1970, played a crucial role in determining cultural policy throughout the seventies and eighties. He left in 1989 to become a successful television screenplay writer.

Nevertheless, the cohabitation of educational technology and film culture was unsatisfactory to both sides. The clear need for a separate national agency to promote film as art and industry pointed categorically towards some new arrangement. After a Scottish Office review, it was agreed that SFC would become fully autonomous and, in 1990, that was finally achieved. The first Chairman of the new board, whose membership was composed largely of established film and television professionals, was John Donachy, a volunteer stalwart of Scottish film culture for many years who, as Chairman of SFC under the previous arrangement, had successfully argued the case for SFC's independence. In 1992 he was succeeded by Allan Shiach, Chairman of the MacAllan-Glenlivet Whisky and a Hollywood screenwriter (see **Hollywood**) under the *nom d'écran* Allan Scott. It was a new deal, a new beginning, and was marked as such by the Scottish Office with a programme of increased funding over the next four years.

Fom the late eighties onwards the prospects for SFC and its role in promoting film culture, including the economic aspects, were greatly improved. Specifically, SFC's enhanced status allowed it to work with other bodies such as Scottish Enterprise in promoting and setting up new and desperately needed professional agencies to deal with training (see **Glasgow, Park Terrace, Scottish Broadcast and Film Training**) and screen locations (see below **Scottish Screen Locations**). It also enabled it to strengthen its existing work in exhibition, media education and archiving, and increase its involvement in production-related activities such as the collaboration with Scottish Television on 'First Reels', a low budget film competition for entrants to the business devised by Erika King, SFC's new Deputy Director.

Independence clarified SFC's position as a national cultural body for Scotland. Its relationship with its progenitor, the British Film Institute, though for the most part excellent at officer level, was sometimes troubled by the issue of the 'Britishness' of the BFI (see **London**). The creation, on the demise of the Arts Council of Great Britain, of an autonomous Scottish Arts Council funded, like SFC, by the Scottish Office, and the formation of Film Councils in Wales and Northern Ireland has opened up and diversified British cultural funding in an entirely healthy way. In 1994 SFC acquired a new Director, Maxine Baker, who had a background in both film and television.

As to the future, although the situation for film in Scotland is much improved, not least institutionally, with the promise of a new Scottish Screen Agency (see **Edinburgh, Regent Road**), there is still an enormous amount to be done before the nirvana of a complete Scottish film culture is achieved. SFC, and its heirs and allies, will continue to bear the obligation to provide the engine to drive things forward.

The Scottish Film Archive (SFA)

The Scottish Film Archive was set up in 1976. Together with the creation of the regional film theatres it was the most important film cultural achievement of the nineteen seventies. In a classic SFC bricks-without-straw manoeuvre it was started as a temporary job creation scheme under the Government's new initiative of that year. Three young unemployed people were recruited, two of whom, the curator Janet McBain and her assistant Anne Johnson, are still in post twenty years later. By the time the job creation money had run out, the need for the archive had been so comprehensively demonstrated that the Scottish Office agreed to increase SFC's grant to keep it going as a permanent part of the Council.

Although there was more than a hint of opportunism in the archive's birth, the case for such a facility had been well established in the previous year by an SFC working party chaired by the late Professor Denis Roberts, Librarian of the National Library of Scotland. They found that Scotland's moving-image heritage was being lost at an alarming rate, particularly through the decomposition of inflammable nitrate stock. A visit to the National Film Archive in London (who were extremely supportive of the idea of a Scottish Archive) convinced the working party that something drastic had to be done.

The National Film Archive had a responsibility to preserve films from Scotland, but given its other huge concerns it could not reasonably be expected to devote time and resources seeking out materials on the ground, which was what was urgently required. Moreover, they could not be expected to have the local knowledge to determine, for example, which of two films on ploughing from Aberdeenshire and the Borders was the more worthy of preservation to represent Scottish ploughing in the UK national collection. A Scottish Film Archive should be able to tell the difference and would want to preserve both.

To begin with, the bulk of the Archive's holdings was redundant material from the

Scottish Central Film Library which R B Macluskie had refused to discard. Although much of this was educational, indeed classroom, film, there were also four hundred reels of 35mm nitrate film, some of it there by chance rather than by design. Interestingly, there had been a genuine concern for old film on the part of some of the SFC's founders in the 1930s, particularly the late Charles Oakley and, although a great deal of original footage had been lost, some important compilations had survived such as *Glasgow's Yesterdays, Glasgow and the Clyde Coast,* and *Aberdeen 1906.*

A public appeal for old film was so successful that the rate of acquisition was well beyond the staff's capacity for accession.This continues to be the case and subsequent bulk deposits and individual donations have increased the Archive to well over 20,000 reels of which 15,000 have not yet been fully catalogued. Within the holdings are several particularly important collections such as the complete Films of Scotland output and major deposits from all the Scottish broadcasting organisations and many the independent producers.

The Archive is, in effect, the audio visual record of Scotland in the twentieth century. (Actually the oldest film – Dr McIntyre's experimental X-ray footage – dates from March 1896, a month before any film was publicly shown in Scotland). It is almost entirely a documentary archive and holds very little fiction or feature film.

Like most film archives, SFA's activities are conditioned by the need to balance the imperative of preservation at all costs with the need to provide access to what is preserved; a dilemma made acute by the need to generate income, mainly by making materials available for television. The immediate physical problems of having to store priceless footage in the basement of a Victorian terrace, despite the best mechanical techniques for sustaining low temperatures and humidity, are obvious. The point at which unfortunate circumstances and inconvenience tip over into national disgrace may not be far off, but it has to be hoped that the heightened attention paid to archive film brought about by the Centenary of Cinema may provide the trigger for a major improvement in the Archive's situation.

The Scottish Film Production Fund (SFPF)

The birth of the Scottish Film Production Fund was only marginally less accidental than that of the Scottish Film Archive, despite the fact that it, too, had long been desperately needed. It came about partly due to the curious and debilitating anomaly that the Scottish Film Council, charged with the job of promoting Scottish film culture (which obviously had to include film production), had no money to do so, while the Scottish Arts Council (see **Edinburgh, Manor Place**), whose remit excluded the art of film, could support film production so long as it was promoting another art form, was keen to back high quality film projects and did have money.

This impossible situation was resolved in the early 1980s. Joint action by the SAC and the SFC resulted in SFC taking responsibility for a new production fund to be financed partly by the SAC from the money it had already allocated to film production and partly by new money from the Scottish Education Department which funded SFC. SFPF held its first meeting in 1982. The Chairman was Professor Ian Lockerbie (the former chairman of SFC) and the Fund Secretary was John Brown, SFC's Assistant Director. In 1989, Sir Denis Forman became Chairman. Sir Denis (born in Dumfriesshire in 1917) had been Director of the BFI (1948-55), its Chairman (1971-74) and Chairman of Granada Television (1974-87). Just as important, he has been a life-long supporter of Scottish film. In 1992 he was succeeded by Allan Shiach (see **Hollywood**).

In 1989, the Fund appointed Penny Thomson as its first full time Director, (see **Edinburgh, Lothian Road**), followed in 1991 by another independent producer, Kate Swan, and in 1994 by Eddie Dick, previously Media Education Officer at SFC. The effect of the new kind of executive arrangement was beneficial in various ways, not least in allowing the fund to gain a higher profile and become a more influential force in Scottish, and indeed British, film-making. The membership of the board also changed. To reflect the composition of the film scene in Scotland there were more broadcasters, writers and independent film makers as well as representatives of key London bodies on it.

Until the fund was set up, the only likely source of public funds for Scottish fiction film-makers had been the BFI Production Board, but the success rate of Scottish applicants had been very low to the point that very few applied to it. The SFPF's initial grant from the public purse was a modest £80,000. It only exceeded £100,000 six years later, though by that time other money, particularly from television, increased the total. By 1990, the figure was £216,500. Under Eddie Dick, the rise became more dramatic. In January 1994 the total was £340,000; exactly two years later SFPF had £735,000 at its disposal, albeit that £378,000 of that was tied to specific deals (for instance with BBC Scotland for the 'Tartan Shorts' scheme).

The Tartan Shorts scheme brought about SFPF and BBC Scotland's most spectacular success. One of the first three films it backed, Peter Capaldi's *Franz Kafka's It's a Wonderful Life*, won an Academy Award in 1995, proving what can be done with enough talent and the right package.

In its early days SFPF's shortage of cash ('penury' was the Chairman's word) prevented it from making a serious impact on film production. Circumstances dictated that this was to be a development fund which would intervene in production when it could. The most notable example, in the early years, of its doing so was in Ian Sellar and Christopher Young's *Venus Peter* (1989) where the SFPF contribution was crucial in unlocking other money from BFI, British Screen, Channel Four and the local authority (see **Orkney**).

The danger of this strategy was illustrated the following year when SFPF allocated almost half its annual budget to the same team to go towards the production of *Prague*. The perceived difficulty was that the film's Scottish connections were not strong - the production team and the principal actor, Alan Cumming, were Scots but not much else was. The co-stars were Sandrine Bonnaire and Bruno Ganz, the setting and crew were Czech, so why was such a large proportion of the small amount of Scottish public money for film being spent on such a project? Despite being a legitimate example of how any ambitious film had to be made in 1990s Europe and the fact that it was a rather good film, *Prague* became a stick to beat the SFPF with. It should, it was argued, confine itself to script development and purely indigenous movies.

Within the limitations of its resources, however, SFPF has been remarkably successful. Its remit, 'to foster and promote film and video production as a central element in the development of Scottish culture, by the provision of financial assistance to such individuals, production companies, production groups or cultural bodies as are deemed appropriate', may sound worthy, but SFPF's Committee has not only been conscientious but genuinely excited by the opportunity to back native talent. Much of the reason for this was that the Committee included in its membership a majority of individuals who were practising film-makers or closely associated with film-making, such as Charlie Gormley, Iain Smith, Paddy Higson, Liz Lochhead, Bernard MacLaverty, Clare Mulholland, Colin Young, Mike Alexander, Bill Forsyth, Lynda Myles and Christeen Winford. This was also manifest in SFPF's support for new entrants to the business, with grants being awarded to National Film and Television School students from Scotland to complete their graduation films. In that category were Michael Caton-Jones for *The Riveter*, Gillies Mackinnon for *Passing Glory* and Ian Wyse for *Fall from Grace*.

The proof of the Fund's success lies not just in its ability to spot winners, though it has had its share. In a dozen years, SFPF's energy and money has been applied to a whole range of projects, mostly in the form of development funding. Its name now appears regularly in films with Scottish origins or connections and it has been in at the beginning of many of the significant films of recent years including *Venus Peter, Silent Scream, Rob Roy* and *Shallow Grave*.

Film production being a very expensive business compared to most art forms (grand opera is the only rival), the amount of money required to make a decisive impact on Scottish feature film production was almost always going to be beyond the resources of SFPF. Other public authorities would have to be persuaded to put significant sums of money into film-making. *Venus Peter* demonstrated in Orkney that feature film-making, whether native or imported, could have a major economic impact on a place and the success of Scottish Screen Locations (see below) in attracting lucrative foreign film production to Scotland went a long way to bring the powers that be round to putting their hands in their pockets to support the movie business.

The Glasgow Film Fund (GFF)

The Glasgow Film Fund, founded in 1990, was the first regional film fund in Scotland to make a major impact on indigenous film-making. Run by SFPF but with its own rules which confine it to providing funds for film shot in Strathclyde or made by Strathclyde based film-makers, it provided an excellent complement to the older fund's activities. Financed by the Glasgow Development Agency, Glasgow City Council, Strathclyde Regional Council and the European Regional Development Fund, it could devote its entire annual budget, initially of £150,000, to one film. The first project GFF chose to back it was a winner; *Shallow Grave* (1994) returned GFF's investment within two years.

In GFF Glasgow and Strathclyde provided a model for local authority involvement in film production. The next stage was to encourage others to do likewise with the ultimate objective the creation of a pan-Scottish fund with sufficient resources to be a major player in feature film finance. By 1995, progress towards that goal had been made, but the suspicion remains in many quarters that only further government intervention, perhaps in the context of a Scottish Parliament, would finally achieve it.

Scottish Screen Locations (SSL)

Scottish Screen Locations (SSL) is the body charged with the task of attracting 'foreign' (that is anyone from furth of Scotland) film-makers to shoot in Scotland. It was set up in 1990 with funding from virtually all the local authorities in Scotland and the support of other public agencies including the Scottish Film Council. The formal launch took place at the European Film Awards in Glasgow. SSL maintains a comprehnsive database of possible film locations and acts as the first stop for film-makers considering Scotland as a place to shoot their movies.

The arguments which persuaded the public authorities to finance and support SSL were simple and based on demonstrable precedent. The case for a 'film commission' for Scotland had been articulated for several years. It had been made in a report prepared by Robin Crichton of Edinburgh Film Productions, who had witnessed how such a system operated very successfully in various parts of Australia. Further evidence and encouragement came from North America and from the Association of Film Commissions International.

The heart of the matter was that if a major film production is based in a community, even for just a couple of weeks, there can be substantial short-term benefit to the people and place concerned. Should the resulting film be an international success, the tourist-related earnings can be very large indeed. An example of the first part of the proposition could be found in Orkney where the local authority contributed £60,000 to the production of *Venus Peter* (1989) which was based in Stromness. Five or six times that amount was spent by the film-makers on local services, labour, accomodation, food and so on. Two years later, Zeffirelli's *Hamlet* (1991) had an even larger impact on Stonehaven.

Longer-term benefits are harder to demonstrate in statistical terms but there is plenty of

The Launch of Scottish Screen Locations in 1990. The Scottish Office Minister for the Arts, Lord James Douglas-Hamilton, with Lee Leckie and Lord Richard Attenborough.

anecdotal evidence concerning such places as Pennan, whose village telephone-box played a central role in *Local Hero* (1983). There is no doubt that Glencoe and Glen Nevis, indeed the whole of Scotland, have benefitted enormously from internationally successful films such as *Rob Roy, Braveheart* and *Highlander.*

There are those who worry that Scottish Screen Locations, ably run in its early years by Lee Leckie and now by Celia Stevenson, is wholly devoted to the commerce of film and television. Some say that it does little for culture and may even contribute to the promotion of a stereotype of Scotland. The answer to such criticism is that, while attracting ten times the previous best estimate of film-making spending in Scotland SSL also encouraged the import of work and valuable experience for indiginous film-makers.

Scottish Screen Locations is, therefore, one more vital piece in the jigsaw of our film culture. Its greatest contribution may be that in making local councillors and officials consider film as an economic possibility it is promoting the medium as less of a foreign intrusion and more as something that truly belongs to us.

The Producers Alliance for Cinema and Television (PACT) Scotland

The Producers Alliance for Cinema and Television, have their Scottish office within the warren that is the Dowanhill complex. The role of the independent producers in advancing the cause of film in Scotland is an honourable one and is discussed elsewhere (see **Edinburgh, Calton Studios**). PACT (Scotland) was also founded in 1990 to promote the producers' commercial interests to broadcasters, Government and others.

The British Academy of Film and Television Arts (BAFTA) Scotland

BAFTA Scotland is the Scottish presence of The British Academy of Film and Television Arts which combines a reputation for staging glamorous events with the serious business of promoting the film and television industries. BAFTA Scotland has proved to be very useful indeed in creating opportunities for film and television professionals from all over the country to meet regularly on neutral ground.

Set up in 1986 with the present author as its acting Chairman, it was seen to fill a gap in the Scottish media scene. The splendid London headquarters of BAFTA in Piccadilly was too remote from most Scottish film and television professionals with the result that Scotland was severely under-represented in BAFTA activities, not least in connection with the prestigious annual awards. However, it was also the lack of BAFTA's social dimension in Scotland that prompted calls for a branch to be created north of the border.

Under the direction of the energetic Linda Pearson, BAFTA Scotland's main function is to bring the tribe together, usually for previews and premieres but also for events such as the annual Edinburgh Film Festival Lecture whose list of past speakers includes David Puttnam, Lindsay Anderson, Michael Winner, Michael Caton-Jones and John McGrath.

To the general public, BAFTA is synonymous with colourful and sometimes lachrymose award ceremonies, but it was with serious intent that BAFTA Scotland established the bi-annual Scottish Awards, first held in 1991. The idea that Scotland required or even had the talent and self-confidence to mount a regular showcase was greeted with scepticism in some quarters but the outcome has vindicated the organisers and provided proof of Scotland's growing strength in media production.

Finnieston: *Deathwatch*

Finnieston, famous for its crane which hoisted mighty locomotives built in Springburn on to the decks of ships bound for the farthest reaches of Empire, was one of the locations for a movie which affected the course of Scottish film, and the perception of Glasgow, in several ways.

Bertrand Tavernier's search for a setting for *Deathwatch*, his film version of David Compton's novel, *The Continuous Katherine Mortenhoe*, led him to Glasgow. Originally he had intended to shoot in Berlin but, invited by Professor Ian Lockerbie to visit Scotland for screenings of his work at the Glasgow and Stirling film theatres, he was excited to 'discover' Glasgow, which, he said, was better than Berlin because his audience would not recognise it! In Forsyth Hardy's book *Scotland in Film*, Tavernier is quoted as saying that Glasgow 'impressed me so forcefully: a rich nineteenth-century town, now strangely depopulated'. The powerful contrast between Glasgow's combination of astonishing Victorian architecture with gap-site waste-land and the Mull of Kintyre, was crucial to the film's ending.

Deathwatch (1980) was set in a future where medicine had made death from disease so rare that it was the subject of popular fascination and media technology was so advanced that the last three weeks of a woman's life could be monitored for a TV programme by a man with a camera implanted in his brain. Although the woman originally agrees to being filmed, she changes her mind and decides to flee the city.

In addition to being being a rare example, at that time, of a major European production choosing Scotland for its locations, *Deathwatch* provided extremely valuable, if sometimes painful, experience for local film-makers. In particular, it marked the beginning of the career in feature films of Iain Smith who was born and brought up in Glasgow and whose job in *Deathwatch* was to manage the local arrangements. The demands of an international film company provided Smith with the steepest of learning curves. The benefit to him and several others associated with the production was reaped later. Smith got the job of location manager on *Chariots of Fire* (1981) (see **St Andrews**) and subsequently established himself as a line producer of major international projects on *Local Hero* (1983), *The Killing Fields* (1984) and *The Mission* (1986).

In more general terms, the presence in Glasgow of a significant project like *Deathwatch* had the effect of bringing closer to home the idea that film-making at this level was a legitimate part of the Scottish cultural experience and did no harm to Glasgow's reputation as a European city.

● *Deathwatch (La Mort en Direct)*
France/Germany, 1980, Selta Films, 128 mins.
Written and directed by Bertrand Tavernier.
From the novel *The Continuous Katherine
Mortenhoe* by David Compton. With Romy
Schneider, Harvey Keitel, Harry Dean Stanton
and Max von Sydow.

Gibson Street: the Kelvin bridge

A chilling little cameo marked Michael Caton-
Jones (see **Broxburn**) as a director to watch.
At the beginning of the television drama serial
Brond (1987) a young boy is tipped casually
over the parapet of the bridge by a smiling
villain (Stratford Johns). It is a scene once seen,
never forgotten. As is the way in movies, the
apparently simple is often only achieved with
great effort. It took three successive Sunday
shoots to get this one right.

Glasgow School of Art: talent

The creative energy that flows from Garnethill
seems to be greater than from most art
colleges. Not content with supplying the
country with painters, sculptors and architects,
Glasgow School of Art (GSA) has made a
major contribution to film in Scotland.
Although film-making does not appear on the
curriculum many talented people have found
the Art College a good environment to develop
their skills.

That great talent hunter, John Grierson,
raided the GSA more than once. The first time
was in 1936 when he was the adjudicator at the
third Scottish Amateur Film Festival, an event
that had a quite disproportionate effect on film-
making in this country. Two years earlier, a

Norman McLaren.

The Gorbals Story (1949). Isabel Campbell, Eveline Garrat, Jack Stewart and Russell Hunter.

group of students and staff at the GSA had formed an amateur film-making unit. The group included Norman McLaren, Stewart McAllister, Helen Biggar, William J Maclean and Violet Anderson. Grierson's enthusiastic response to the work they submitted to the Festival led to offers to McLaren and McAllister of professional training and apprenticeships at the GPO Film Unit.

McLaren, who later joined Grierson at the National Film Board of Canada, became one of the world's leading animators. McAllister moved on to become boss of British Transport Films. Many years later, Grierson helped launch the film-making career of another GSA student. Eddie McConnell and his non-GSA partner, Laurence Henson, showed Grierson their short film, *Broken Images*, an impressionistic account of a drunk coming to in George Square, Glasgow to be confronted with the images of nobility in the square's statues. The film had already won

an award as one of the UK 'Ten Best' amateur films of the year. With Grierson's encouragement Henson and McConnell became key contributors to the development of Scottish film during the Films of Scotland period and beyond.

Arguably Scotland's greatest director (despite being born in America and making only a couple of films in Scotland), Alexander Mackendrick was a student at GSA from 1926 to 1929. He left (without qualifications) to join the J Walter Thompson advertising agency in London.

More recently the GSA has produced another highly successful animator, Lesley Keen. Keen's *Ra The Sun God* (1990) was the biggest single animation project ever commissioned by Channel Four.

Peter Capaldi, director of the Oscar-winning short, *Franz Kafka's It's a Wonderful Life* (1994), is another GSA alumnus, as is Sandy Johnson, director of the BBC Television series *Roughnecks* and many other programmes. GSA has also produced many distinguished screen actors and writers including Capaldi, Robbie Coltrane and

John Byrne. Alasdair Gray, one of GSA's most distinquished alumni is likely to make an impact on screen; a film version of his novel *Poor Things* was in development in 1996 and received a major grant from the National Lottery.

The GSA's extraordinary Mackintosh building has often appeared on film and television as setting or background, for example in *Small Faces* (1996) and has a starring role in *Mackintosh* (1968), Murray Grigor's first major architectural film.

Gorbals: *The Gorbals Story*

Described and dismissed as 'a curiosity' by some who should have known better, *The Gorbals Story* (1949) may not be a great movie but is significant for its connection with a fascinating episode in Scottish theatre history.

Glasgow Unity Theatre's roots were firmly in working-class Glasgow, a long way from the romantic view of Scotland characterised by the 'Kailyard' writers. *The Gorbals Story*, a play by Robert McLeish based on an artist's reminiscences of his upbringing in a Glasgow slum (a distant precursor of *Small Faces* (1996), see **Glasgow**), was first produced by the Unity Theatre in September 1946. *The Gorbals Story* was more performed and more toured than any other play they did and a run at the Garrick Theatre in London's West End led to the making of the film version. The film was much watered down from the play and, despite some encouragement in the trade journals, did not impress the critics or the public. The film soon disappeared into obscurity and Glasgow Unity Theatre did not last much longer.

Except for some establishing shots of Glasgow *The Gorbals Story* was filmed at Merton Park Studios in London. It was very much a studio-bound affair with all the inhibiting characteristics of a filmed play. Perhaps its most interesting feature is the cast list, which included several actors later to emerge as important figures on stage and screen.

Huntingtower (1927). The Gorbals Diehards.

Another film reference to Gorbals presents a somewhat more romantic version of Scotland than *The Gorbals Story*. In *Huntingtower* (1927), the adventure film (now lost) starring Harry Lauder, the tribe of stout-hearted, kilted, urchins who defy the Bolsheviks are known as the 'Gorbals Die-hards'.

● *The Gorbals Story*
GB, 1949, New World Pictures, 75 mins. Directed by David MacKane. From the play by Robert McLeish. With Russell Hunter, Roddy McMillan, Betty Henderson, Isabel Campbell, Archie Duncan and Andrew Keir.

Great Western Road: a Sunday in 1914

Great Western Road earns its place in the history of film in Scotland for a remarkable sequence shot one Sunday in 1914 just after the kirks had released their congregations into the sunlight. It was made by James Hart, the manager of the Grosvenor cinema nearby in Byres Road, and consists of no more than a tracking shot taken from the back of an open car. It shows the bourgeoisie of Glasgow's West End dressed in their Sunday best walking along Great Western Road between the junction with Kirklee Road and Kelvinbridge.

It is a piece of minimal film-making in which the camera is an innocent observer of a slice of very ordinary pavement life, no creative documentary here. The sense of immediacy, of almost direct contact with a large number of people of all ages who are surprised and curious at being filmed takes the viewer back to the very beginnings of cinema.

In 1922, Hart returned to Great Western Road to re-shoot almost exactly the same sequence, this time from a tram. But the First World War had changed everything. The crowds are smaller, the outfits much less flamboyant. And, poignantly, there seem to be very few young men.

● *Great Western Road 1914*
Filmed by James Hart. Silent.

Hillhead: The Salon

The Salon Cinema, prized as one of the oldest purpose-built cinemas in the country, first opened in October 1913. Described by one authority as 'a small posh cinema', its architects were Brand and Lithgow who specified concrete as the main building material when it was still relatively unusual. With some modification, its capacity by 1938 was 544. It closed on 13 October

Great Western Road (1914).

1992. Despite resolute attempts by the local

1992. Despite resolute attempts by the local community to save it, which included public appeals, recruiting sympathetic celebrities, the involvement of the District Council, and various radical plans to modify its use while retaining its original function, in 1996 it remained empty.

Ibrox: *Fitba' Daft*

Ibrox Stadium, synonymous with Rangers Football Club, was the setting for part of the now lost *Fitba' Daft* (1921), a very successful film in its time, running for six weeks at the Regent Cinema in Renfield Street. The Ibrox episode featured the famous Alan Morton demonstrating his 'Morton Lob', a technique designed to fool advancing goalkeepers.

The German documentary film-maker Joachim Kreck expressed his devotion to football in a series of films on the game. One of these was an attempt to understand the history and psychology of the two great Glasgow clubs, Rangers and Celtic. *The Big Clubs* (1974) not only showed the passion of an 'old firm' game from other than the standard perspectives but allowed managers and others, including Willie Waddell, Jock Stein, Desmond White, Jimmy Reid and Cliff Hanley, to expound on the centrality of football culture in all its virtues and vices to Glasgow and to disuss issues such as sectarianism in the game.

● *The Big Clubs*
Germany, 1974, Joachim Kreck in association with IFA (Scotland), 39 mins. Directed and Produced by Joachim Kreck. Photography, Eddie McConnell and Rudiger Laske. Sound Cyril McConnell.

India Street: Scottish Film Productions

Of the pre-war film companies in Scotland, possibly the most successful was Scottish Film Productions (1928) Ltd which had a studio in India Street. The company was the brainchild of Malcolm Irvine, a campaigner for film in Scotland, who was later joined by Stanley

Russell, originally an amateur like many in the film business at the time. Scottish Film Productions not only did their own processing but they developed their own sound system, the 'Albion Truphonic', with which they produced short films starring well known Scottish music hall entertainers and actors such as Dave Willis and Alec Finlay.

Although these particular films do not seem to have been very successful, Scottish Film Productions (like Campbell Harper in Edinburgh) did well in the field of sponsored and documentary productions with films for Glasgow Corporation and companies such as Beardmore, Templeton and Colville's. In 1936, they produced the first edition of *Things That Happen*, a monthly cine-magazine, to be shown in the Glasgow cinemas. The first edition began with sensational footage of the Loch Ness monster, the supposed authenticity of which has only recently been undermined by the admission of the cameraman, Graham Thompson, that the blurred pictures of something strange on the surface of the water were actually filmed on Loch Lomond.

At some point before the Second World War, Malcolm Irvine left Scottish Film Productions and Stanley Russell set up Russell Productions, which in turn became Thames and Clyde. In 1961 Thames and Clyde made *Ayr from the Auld Brig* and *Playing Away* for Films of Scotland. Somewhat later, Russell advertised for a trainee; the young man who got the job was Bill Forsyth.

Lynedoch Street: Templar Films

Templar Film Studios was set up in 1949 by Robert Riddell Black. As a maker of good quality sponsored films for local authorities, businesses and other agencies Templar would have an honourable place in Scottish film history, but one film took their reputation much further. *Seawards the Great Ships* (1961) (see **Clydebank**) was one of sixteen films Templar made for the Films of Scotland Committee. A number of these were fairly routine, but *Seawards* was not Templar's only major industrial documentary to win awards.

The Big Mill (1963).

The Big Mill (1963), directed by Laurence Henson, with Eddie McConnell as cameraman, looked at steelmaking at the new Ravenscraig and Gartcosh facilities in Lanarkshire. Hindsight tells us that both *The Big Mill* and *Seawards the Great Ships* were about industries shortly to face decline, and were made at a time when cinema documentary itself was on the very edge of extinction, but they represent the best industrial documentary film-making that Scotland produced.

Of the other Templar productions for Films of Scotland at least three are worth special mention. *The Heart of Scotland* had an outline treatment by John Grierson (see **Cambusbarron**); *Weave Me a Rainbow* was an evocative promotional piece for the wool industry; and *Three Scottish Painters* broke new ground in art documentary in Scotland.

Like Campbell Harper Films in Edinburgh's (see **Edinburgh, Hill Street**) Templar played a very important role in developing new talent.

Many of the significant Scottish film-makers from the mid-sixties and thereafter began either at Templar or in one of the small companies set up by its former employees. So, for example, Henson and McConnell's IFA (Scotland), formed in 1963 - the name was suggested by Grierson from his own 'International Film Associates' in America - later included Bill Forsyth, Charlie Gormley, Oscar Marzaroli, Gordon Coull, Jon Schorstein (who subsequently formed another company with Iain Smith) and Michael Coulter.

For several years, Templar Film Studios made a regular vital contribution to Scottish cultural life. Their cameramen and 16mm processing plant (in the basement at Lynedoch Street) provided BBC Scotland viewers with their essential football coverage on television.

The Necropolis

There must be thousands of films and television plays which begin in a graveyard. Glasgow has several peculiarly photogenic cemeteries and the Necropolis – the one by the Cathedral – is a favourite haunt of television and film crews. One of the most interesting to have chosen this particular setting was Bertrand Tavernier whose *Deathwatch* (1979) cast Glasgow in an entirely new light (see **Glasgow, Finnieston**).

Perhaps the most unusual use of the Necropolis, however, was in *Ring of Truth* (1996). When Bill Douglas (see **Newcraighall**) died in 1991 he left a small number of unrealised scripts, including one he had completed for his students while he was Carnegie Visiting Fellow in the Department of English Studies at Strathclyde University in 1990. Five years later, the film – a comic tale of life, death and cinema – was made by Richard Downes with a cast including Jimmy Logan and his sister Annie Ross – the first time they had appeared in a film together. The project was also the first film to be completed with funding from the National Lottery (see **Edinburgh, Manor Place**).

This grand city of the dead did miss out on one film credit. The distinction of being the setting for the opening scene of *Tutti Frutti*, the best Scottish television drama of the eighties, went to the Eastern Necropolis in Parkhead.

● *Ring of Truth*
GB, 1996, Lomond/BBC Scotland/Strathclyde University/BFI, 30 mins. Directed by Richard Downes. Written by Bill Douglas. Produced by Alastair Scott. With Jimmy Logan, Annie Ross, Libby McArthur and Craig Hemmings.

Park Gardens: the training story.

Until relatively recently, determination, luck and who you were or knew, were almost more important qualifications than talent for a start in the film business. Determination remains vital, but the rest has changed. Opportunities for aspiring film-makers in Scotland are better and more varied than ever, largely due to the establishment of proper training facilities. The opening, in May 1993, of Scottish Broadcast and Film Training (SBFT) at 4 Park Gardens was a tribute to the determination of Scotland's film and television professionals and meant that Scotland had, at last, a full-time agency devoted to ensuring film practitioners received the best possible training to pursue their careers and advance standards of film and television programme making.

Thirty years ago, formal training for a career in film-making was not available outside the confines of the BBC and STV and even these organisations expected some evidence of previous ability for most disciplines. So it was customary for film-makers to learn their trade by persuading their way into a company such as Templar Films (see **Glasgow, Lynedoch Street**) or Campbell Harper (see **Edinburgh, Hill Street**) whose experienced people could pass on their skills, however informally. The alternative for a few was to make a film as an amateur that was so noticeable it led to being hired by a broadcaster or an independent film company. Others sought experience or training ouside Scotland: Iain Smith, now a successful international producer, gained a place at the London International Film School, a unique institution at the time, essentially

aimed at overseas students; Lesley Keen, following in the footsteps of Norman McLaren, largely taught herself animation while a student at Glasgow School of Art, before going to Prague to study at Jiri Trnka's Brothers-in-Tricks Studio, one of Europe's most distinguished animation centres; many went to foreign film schools from Poland to the west coast of America.

Progress towards something less random first occurred in 1965 with the setting up of the Lloyd Committee, a Government initiative to look into the possibility of creating high-level training for the British film industry. There were two Scots on the Committee: George Singleton, the owner of the Cosmo cinema in Glasgow, who was prominent in the Cinematograph Exhibitors Association (CEA) and a member of the Films of Scotland Committee, and George Reith, former Director of Education in Edinburgh and a member of the Scottish Film Council with a specific interest in the production of educational films. The Lloyd Committee concluded that the needs of the film industry would be best met by establishing a single National Film School. They were not persuaded that there was a case for a separate institution for Scotland which, given the low volume of Scottish film-making at the time, may have been reasonable, if regrettable. In 1971, therefore, the National Film School was established in former studios at Beaconsfield in Buckinghamshire. In 1983 it became known as the National Film and Television School (NFTS).

Scottish concerns about being left out of this extremely important development were considerably assuaged when the first Head turned out to be a Scot. Colin Young had been a student at the University of California at Los Angeles in the early fifties and later joined its staff, becoming head of its Film School in 1964 and Chairman of the Department of Theater Arts the following year. One of those keenest to persuade Young to take the job in Beaconsfield was the Oscar-winning screenwriter Neil Paterson (see **Crieff**) who had met him in California. Young duly made the move and held the post with great distinction for over twenty years until his retirement in 1992. His determination that the School should always draw on the best talent from throughout the United Kingdom and his tireless ability to maintain contact with all aspects of film in Scotland, including taking on the Chairmanship of the Edinburgh International Film Festival, ensured that Scots were unlikely to regard the NFTS as unsympathetic to them or their culture.

The National Film and Television School was very successful in training those destined to be the elite of British film-making, the directors and producers who would provide the energy and ideas to move the British industry forward. Early students (though that term may be inappropriate for an institution that was more studio than school) included Bill Forsyth, Michael Caton-Jones and Michael Radford. Forsyth, in fact, already had some film-making experience and was only at the School for a year.

What NFTS could not provide was training on their home ground for 'technicians' (as those involved in the 'craft' disciplines were known), though it later became very successful in organising 'short courses' for them. In Scotland, action on that front came about through a remarkable enterprise in self-help by the workforce of the fledgling Scottish film industry. With the closure of Templar and Campbell Harper there was no longer any natural point of entry for beginners and, as the industry was starting to expand, there was a pressing need for people at the lowest grades in the business. The Technician Training Scheme, launched in 1978 by the film-makers trade union (ACTT) and the Scottish Film Council, was an ingenious plan under which two trainees were 'adopted' by virtually every participant in the industry, including the Producers' Association and the Union. Those chosen were paid a basic allowance and put at the disposal of whoever might need them as supernumeraries. In the event of their being employed in a role that entitled them to payment, their earnings were ploughed back into the Scheme. Remarkably, it worked very well and a high proportion of those who entered the business by this

unconventional route have progressed with distinction. They include Andrea Calderwood (now head of drama at BBC Scotland), Christopher Young (producer of *Venus Peter* and *Prague*), Des Bradley (a director of Skyline Television), Grant Cameron (a leading cameraman), Sheena McDonald and Cy Jack (who runs an independent sound recording studio).

The Technician Training Scheme operated on a relatively informal basis, managed by officers of SFC, but there was a clear need for a more permanent structure which, as well as overseeing the Scheme, could engage with wider training issues. Other training initiatives, including the beginnings of practical courses (of variable quality) within further education, were being taken but a national strategy was still a distant prospect. So the formation, in 1982, of the Scottish Film Training Trust (SFTT) chaired by Iain Smith and later by Paddy Higson, was an important step on the road to a rational arrangement covering all aspects of training. The Scottish Film Council, the Scottish Arts Council, Goldcrest and, later, Thorn EMI Elstree Studios gave financial support to SFTT which funded the Technician Training Scheme and undertook to help finance Scottish students at the National Film School.

Increasing willingness on the part of the television organisations to become involved in discussion and practical arrangements about training was encouraging and, in 1985, SFC and SFTT convened a conference at the Glasgow Film Theatre which commissioned a study group, chaired by Dr John Izod of Stirling University, to consider the possibility of establishing some form of film school for Scotland. The result was the Meech Report which later became the basis for arguments in favour of a joint initiative between Duncan of Jordanstone College of Art in Dundee and Napier College (now University) in Edinburgh. The plan was for a Scottish Film School operating on two campuses with, roughly speaking, Duncan of Jordanstone dealing with electronic media, in which it had already established a very fine reputation, and Napier focusing on traditional film-making, some aspects of which were already being taught there. The Scottish Office Education Department provided capital for the project and the Scottish National Film School was formally launched in the 1990-91 academic year.

It is fair to say that there were difficulties at several levels in this exercise, including funding. Not everyone was happy that the scheme should promote itself as a Scottish National Film School, at least not until it had earned that status. By 1994, however, with restructuring (Napier and Duncan of Jordanstone were now operating independently of one another) the problems diminished. In the meantime, other training initiatives had begun to appear. These were mostly within the colleges, but an increasing amount was being done by the Workshop movement, particularly by Glasgow Film Workshop, Video in Pilton and Edinburgh Video Access, whose Director, John McVay, later become the Director of SBFT.

In 1990 the Government announced the allocation of £9.5 million to the new Gaelic Television Committee (CTG). Here were new training needs to be addressed. Once again SFC brought the parties involved together, this time in Stornoway. By now, such gatherings had become much larger and their concerns more diverse. A follow-up meeting in Glasgow revealed how dramatically the perceptions of academics and practitioners differed on training matters, but at least they were talking to each other. A need had arisen to make a clear distinction between courses in media studies - an academic discipline which had grown very large in the previous decade and courses designed to be vocational. There was genuine concern that young people might believe non-vocational courses could get them into the business when in fact they provided no real practical experience.

Two developments of major importance grew out of these encounters. One was the creation of a Scottish Screen Training Forum which would continue to bring the parties together on neutral ground and keep them in touch with developments. The other was the commissioning, in 1991, of the Scottish Development Agency 'Frontline' consultancy, based on a brief devised by Andrea Calderwood for the Scottish Film Training Trust. The SDA's report recommended the setting up of Scottish Broadcast and Film Training.

Queen Margaret Drive: BBC Scotland

Since the arrival of television in the early fifties the BBC has been central to the film scene. Although BBC Scotland's business is broadcasting, not cinema, it cannot avoid being a key player in the Scottish film business. Because Scotland is so small the BBC's influence as the public sector broadcaster is disproportionately great, affecting all aspects of our cultural life. Its policies and practices substantially affect the health of the other audio-visual media since it provides a large proportion of the available opportunities for employment and expression. Without it even a minimal Scottish film industry might be impossible.

– Richard E. Grant in **Franz Kafka's It's a Wonderful Life** (1994, Conundrum). (photo – Oliver Upton).

To begin with, the small independent film sector proved a vital recruiting ground for the BBC with its constant need for 'stringers' (freelance people on the spot) to cover, for example, news items and football matches. This meant that almost everyone in the film community worked for the BBC at some point in their career. Those that didn't, worked for Scottish Television.

In pre-tape days BBC Scotland's interest in film was primarily as a recording medium. Film was only the medium of choice when the circumstances were appropriate, for example for drama. Neverthless there was excellent film-making within the BBC and its long gone film unit produced first class results.

The distinction between film and television production could sometimes be fairly academic where drama was concerned. When Bill Forsyth made the George Mackay Brown story *Andrina* for BBC Scotland he was working as a film-maker; it was just that the means of delivery to the public was the small rather than the big screen. On the other hand James McTaggart and other major television drama producers shot much of their work on film and they deserve to be recognised as legitimate contributors to Scottish film culture. Indeed, while Hollywood and London made intermittent forays into the field, there were long periods when the only Scottish screen fiction was produced by the BBC.

In recent years BBC Scotland has increased its role in the institutions and agencies which form the infrastructure of the Scottish film business and is represented, as are the commercial broadcasters, on bodies such as Scottish Broadcast and Film Training (see **Glasgow, Park Gardens**). Collaborations of this sort help to define BBC Scotland's distinct cultural identity in the face of London's centripetal influence.

BBC Scotland has also become increasingly directly involved in productions with the potential for cinema release. Although Queen Margaret Drive has a track record of making single 'TV film' dramas, such as those of John Mackenzie, the BBC was also successfully involved in 'real' movie-making with the Oscar-winning *Franz Kafka's It's a Wonderful Life* (1995), directed by Peter Capaldi. The film was one of the first 'Tartan Shorts', a joint BBC Scotland/Scottish Film Production Fund scheme to promote short film production and the talent associated with it. Although not the first short film competition it had been involved in (there was one with the Scottish Film Council as early as 1970 under the auspices of the late W Gordon Smith's arts programme, *Scope*), there could not have been a more spectacular proof that BBC Scotland had a stake in the Scottish film business.

Franz Kafka's It's a Wonderful Life defied all the conventions and looked like a winner from first viewing. In a splendidly surreal way it drew on Kafka's *Metamorphosis* for its central idea of a writer struggling desperately to complete the first line of a story. He knows that he wants his hero to awake in bed one morning transformed into something extraordinary but only reaches the conclusion that it must be as an enormous insect after some agonising encounters with the other inhabitants of his dark tenement. A curiously sinister Scottish tone (Glasgow accents predominate) and an absurdly happy Capra-esque finale, set it apart. Its 'Best Short' award at BAFTA 1994 and its Oscar in 1995 were thoroughly deserved and a great boost for Capaldi and the Scottish film-making community.

1995 saw the first instance of BBC Scotland commissioning a feature film for cinema. *Small Faces* (1996) (see **Glasgow**), directed by Gillies MacKinnon, was a great success and must have encouraged the Corporation to commission more films. The involvement of a Scottish-based producer, Steve Clarke-Hall (a great contributor in many ways to the native film scene) was important. However, at much the same time BBC Scotland was shedding operational facilities, a move which could only have a negative effect on the general situation. If Scotland is to achieve critical mass in film culture it needs to retain all the personnel and talent it can.

Small Faces (1996, BBC Scotland).

Television in the 1990s is proliferating in every aspect, from production to the coming plethora of channels, but in one crucial regard the BBC remains unique. As the public service broadcaster it is, at least in theory, advised and governed by boards drawn from the community, including a Broadcasting Council for Scotland, which can ensure that it does not lose sight of its obligations to its Scottish audience and to Scottish interests. Unhappily, advising is one thing and exercising real power another. If at times, the Broadcasting Council for Scotland has seemed impotent in the face of metropolitan pressures to cut and conform (for example in the run up to the Charter renewal), the blame does not necessarily fall on the members of such boards, but with the system. The remedy must be to encourage the Secretary of State for Scotland to take the sort of direct action on broadcasting in Scotland that is now envisaged for film in Scotland. The health and strength of BBC Scotland is incontrovertibly vital to all aspects of our audio visual culture, and to much else besides.

● *Franz Kafka's It's a Wonderful Life!*
GB, 1994, Conundrum Films, 24 mins. Written and directed by Peter Capaldi. Produced by Ruth Kenley-Letts. With Richard E Grant, Elaine Collins, Ken Stott, Phyllis Logan and Crispin Letts.

● *Small Faces*
GB, 1996, BBC Scotland/Glasgow Film Fund, 108 mins. Directed by Gillies MacKinnon. Produced by Billy Mackinnon and Steve Clark-Hall. Written by Billy and Gillies Mackinnon. Music by John Keane. With Ian Robertson, Joseph McFadden, J S Duffy, Laura Fraser, Garry Sweeney, Clare Higgins, Kevin McKidd and Mark McConnochie.

Renfield Street: Green's Playhouse

This monumental 4,200 seat cinema in Renfield Street, opened in 1927, was the most spectacular achievement of one of the great Scottish cinema

Charlie Chaplin and Fred Green.

families. George Green came from Lancashire. Before the turn of the century his fairground Cinematograph provided a superior version of the bioscopes which were popular throughout the country and he soon graduated from travelling showman to cinema owner.

Green's first permanent cinema venture opened in 1902 in the Whitevale Theatre in the east end of Glasgow. The business expanded not only in exhibition and renting but into services to the trade and even film production. *Scottish Moving Picture News* a regular newsreel which later became *British Moving Picture News* began around 1918 and continued into the 1920s. By that time the business was being run by George Green's sons, Bert and Fred, with sundry other family members involved as managers, 'ticket wifes' and sweet sellers.

A fine sense of style was evident in all the Greens did. Their motto 'If it's Good, it's Green's', was woven into the carpets in their cinemas and printed on the dishes in their restaurants. Their empire extended beyond Glasgow and their second biggest hall was a super-cinema in Dundee. Their interests even extended as far as Hollywood. A famous photograph shows Fred Green with Charlie Chaplin and it is generally believed that the Greens invested in United Artists Corporation, founded in 1919 by Chaplin, Fairbanks, Pickford and Griffith.

The Playhouse Cinema closed in 1973 to reopen shortly afterwards as The Apollo which became a celebrated rock venue. The Apollo was finally demolished in the 1980s.

Riddrie: The Vogue

The Riddrie, one of Glasgow's best known cinemas, has been described as architect James McKissack's masterpiece, though he designed many other splendid ones, including The Cosmo in Rose Street. The Riddrie opened on 1 March 1938 with an early John Wayne film, *I Cover the War*. In 1950, it was bought by George Singleton (who owned The Cosmo) and was renamed The Vogue, very appropriate for such a sylish art deco building.

The Vogue, Riddrie during the filming of **Silent Scream** (1989).

The Vogue suffered as much as any suburban cinema from the decline in audience numbers brought about by television and other social factors and its eventual conversion to bingo was almost inevitable. Bingo at least ensured the survival of the building and it was only in 1994 that George Singleton's son, Ronald, sold it on. It is still a bingo hall.

The Vogue itself featured in a movie. In *Silent Scream* (1989) (see **Barlinnie**) it appeared in a sequence purporting to be set in London, an illusion reinforced by the presence of an imported London bus.

Rose Street: Mr Cosmo and the GFT

On 18 May 1939, a rather special new cinema opened in Glasgow. The 800 seat Cosmo in Rose Street, just off Sauchiehall Street, was unique in Scotland and rare even in United Kingdom terms. The architect was James McKissack (1875-1940), who was responsible for a number of fine Scottish cinema designs, but The Cosmo concept was the brainchild of George Singleton (1900-1995), a pioneer exhibitor with an eye for commerce wedded to a love of the arts. An admirer of the Curzon Cinema in London, Singleton felt that there was a gap in the market in Glasgow for films of 'quality' beyond what was on offer in the main commercial cinemas, several of which he himself owned. The Cosmo was the most important cinema built by the Singleton firm and arguably the most important cinema for the development of film in Scotland.

'Cosmo' was short for 'cosmopolitan' and the films on offer at the new cinema were what was usually referred to as 'continental', that is mainly foreign language, with a preponderance of French and Italian titles. The first film screened was *Un Carnet de Bal* (1937). George Singleton's own favourite was Tati's *Jour de Fête* (1948).

The Cosmo, Rose Street, Glasgow (c1959).

George Singleton was one of the great characters of the cinema business. Born in Main Street, Bridgeton, in Glasgow, on the morning of 1 January 1900 he lived to over ninety-five. He became involved in the cinema trade when his father, who as a hobby played the piano for silent films, gave up his printing business in favour of the new entertainment. The young Singleton learned the business of operating a cinema so thoroughly that he could do every job in the place, including covering for absent pianists (with a repertoire of three tunes).

His first venture on his own was in a converted United Free Church in the Gorbals. By 1924, he had, in his own words, 'two Empires – Napoleon had nothing on me!'; his Empires were cinemas of that name in Coatbridge and Dundee. They were to form the basis of a group of fourteen halls throughout Scotland. In 1937, Oscar Deutsch (of Odeon fame) acquired the Singleton circuit, whereupon Singleton started again by building in Govan the huge and stylish 2500 seat Vogue cinema, famous for its neon lighting.

Despite his other activities Singleton's name will always be remembered in association with The Cosmo in Rose Street. The Cosmo's strength lay in the fact that although its speciality was foreign language films it was never regarded as snobbish. The atmosphere was always entirely friendly and never exclusive. It was even referred to as 'the working man's education'.

The Cosmo's greatest days were after the Second World War but it flourished for three decades until economic circumstances dictated that it could no longer survive in its original form. Thanks to its sale to the Scottish Film Council in 1972 – a move that pleased Singleton greatly as it ensured that the audience he had developed and cherished would continue to see films outside the commercial mainstream – the building still operates as a cinema, the Glasgow Film Theatre, one of the most successful regional film theatres in the UK.

The late Charles Oakley (another Glasgow nonagenarian with a passion for the cinema) drew a cartoon figure to be the cinema's symbol. The dapper, bowler-hatted little figure was based on George Singleton; both came to be known as 'Mr Cosmo'.

Although cinema was his business, and his passion, George Singleton had a wide interest in the arts. He was a member of the Lloyd Committee (1965-67) which led to the setting up of the National Film School, and was prominent on the Scottish Film Council, the Films of Scotland Committee, and the Cinematograph Exhibitors Association (of which he was UK President in 1957-8). He was a member of the board of the Scottish National Orchestra and one of the founders of the Citizens Theatre.

During the early 1970s, the Scottish Film Council was establishing regional film theatres throughout the country. Recognition of their work should not be diminished by noting that this was a time of unprecedented building for the arts, making it possible to create film theatres in Stirling, Inverness, Kirkcaldy, Dundee and Irvine on the back of other new arts developments. Edinburgh already had a facility in the small basement theatre at Film House, Randolph Crescent, but finding suitable premises in Glasgow was very difficult. One scheme, quite advanced before it was abandoned, was to create a cinema in the garden space of two former houses in Woodside Terrace, a few doors along from the SFC offices. When George Singleton offered the Cosmo in 1972, however, there was no doubt it was the best available option. Not only was the building in a good location but it came with an audience, albeit a diminishing one, with a taste for foreign-language and other so-called 'minority-interest' films. A regional film theatre could hardly look for a better basis.

Charles Oakley with 'Mr Cosmo' on the cinema's last night – 21 April 1973.

That audience was not necessarily pleased by everything the Glasgow Film Theatre did. The programming was rather more radical than some of Mr Cosmo's regulars liked and for a time there was tension between SFC and *The Glasgow Herald's* film critic, Molly Plowright, who felt that as a publicly-funded cinema, GFT was insufficiently responsive to what she perceived as the Glasgow public's wishes. Then there was a radical reconstruction of the cinema's interior, reducing the number of seats to 404 to create space for a Scottish Centre for Educational Technology which was part of the funding deal with the Scottish Office (see **Glasgow, Dowanhill**).

Originally run as an integral part of SFC, after the model of the National Film Theatre in London (a division of the British Film Institute), GFT was made independent of SFC in 1986, becoming a client organisation on the same basis as the other Scottish film theatres. In this condition, under an independent board and the enterprising directorship of Ken Ingles, GFT has established itself as one of the most innovative and successful regional film theatres in Britain. In addition to its regular diet of new foreign language and independent movies, GFT offers numerous special events, previews and occasional 'festivals' of French and other films.

In 1991, the former stalls area, vacated long before by the educational technologists, was converted into a second auditorium and the Centenary of Cinema sees further capital work to restore the exterior of the building to its former glory.

Rouken Glen: *Rob Roy* (1911)

In the earlier part of Scotland's film history, 'studios' were relatively common. Glasgow hosted several at various times, some of them rather temporary, it should be said, including at Thornliebank (see **Glasgow, Thornliebank**) and in India Street (see **Glasgow, India Street**).

Rouken Glen was where the first known *Rob Roy* (1911)(see **Aberfoyle**) was made. The building had been a tram depot and remained

linked to the tramway's electrical system. The result was periodic fluctuation in the electricity supply with what must have been peculiar consequences on the set.

St Andrews Halls

Glasgwegians remember the St Andrews Halls with great affection as a venue with superb accoustics for great musical, civic and sporting events. When it burnt down in September 1962, it left a gap, in more than one sense, which remained unfilled until the opening of the Glasgow Royal Concert Hall in 1990.

Not only the hall, but also a potentially interesting film connected with it, have been lost. Produced by Elder Films (originally Elder-Dalrymple Films, set up in the 1930s to make educational pictures), *The Little Singer* (1956) was about the ambitions of a young girl, from a poor family, to sing in St Andrews Halls. The film did well locally, but failed to achieve wider release, possibly because it was perceived as too specific to Glasgow.

● *The Little Singer*

GB, 1956, Elder Films, 60 mins. Produced by Jack Elder. Directed by Clarence Elder. Adapted from the book by Isabel Cameron. With Louise Boyd, Campbell Hastie, Evelyn Lockhart, Archie Neal and the Kirkintilloch Junior Choir.

St Vincent Street: Scottish National Film Studios

121 St Vincent Street was the address in 1946 of Scottish National Film Studios. The idea was that this was only a temporary arrangement until the Studios found a permanent home in the Highlands. As it turned out, the project was as temporary as the address. In little more than a year the most ambitious plan thus far to create a 'Scottish Film Industry' had completely failed.

This particular attempt had its origins in the pre-war ambitions of a Mr T G Wolk, referred to in the *Scots Independent* as a Russian expert. Mr Wolk modestly described his plan as, 'this

The Little Singer (1956).

important undertaking for civilisation'. On 3 November 1945, a committee was formed to pursue the idea. The Chairman was Sir Hugh Roberton, of Orpheus Choir fame, and other members included the actor Moutrie Kelsall and the writers William McLellan and William Montgomerie. It seems that nobody from the small group of established Scottish film-makers or, significantly, from any arm of Government, was involved.

The key figure in the new enterprise was Joseph Macleod. Macleod had been extremely successful as one of the 'named' war-time newsreaders on the BBC where his polite accent was just sufficiently Scottish for listeners north of the Border to dentify with him but not so strong as to put off the southern majority. Macleod had recently parted from the BBC under rather tense circumstances. He had been invited to write a report on how the BBC might be improved and had unwisely told them they were out of touch with the population.

His appointment as Managing Director of Scottish National Film Studios suited his nationalism well, but he had no experience of film and little of management. Nonetheless, he could not be faulted on his dedication to the cause and was not to blame for the debacle which led to his sadly boarding the train south in March 1947 saying, "I find my native race as touchy as ever". The plan had been hopelessly ambitious. It was not just a case of intending to make feature films in Scotland; the organisers wanted studios, a film school, a national film archive, reference library, a Chair of Cinematography at a Scottish university, distribution to the far corners of the earth and the whole-hearted financial support of the Scottish people and their institutions. Any proper contact with the Scottish Office would have revealed at once how unrealistic a proposition most of it was.

The scheme was based not on common sense but on romantic patriotism of the most insidious kind. The motivation was a sensible enough desire to correct the portrayal of Scotland on the cinema screen. However, the prospectus outlined the company's belief that the undertaking would benefit from the 'loyal and maintained interest in Scotland shown by people of Scottish parentage or connection in the Dominions or in the United States of America'. Unfortunately the idea that the Scots and people of Scottish extraction throughout the World were just waiting for a Scottish Film Industry was badly misguided. The target for initial money raising was £100,000 of which about a tenth was collected or promised. A

rescue package was attempted but without success. 'Films', said Sir Hugh Roberton, 'are chancy anyway'.

Scottish National Film Studios made one film. It was not so much a feature as a dramatised documentary to promote road safety. Apart from a few production stills, all trace of it has been lost. *Someone Wasn't Thinking* (1946) featured Gordon Jackson (on loan from Ealing Studios) and Mary Walton of the Unity Players and was about the disasters that can befall the unwary on the roads. It ended with the heroine severely injured just before her marriage and her fiancé devastated.

● *Someone Wasn't Thinking*
GB, 1946, Scottish National Film Studios, 30 mins. Directed by Bladon Peak. Written by Joseph Macleod. Music by Ian Whyte, played by the BBC Scottish Orchestra. With Gordon Jackson and Mary Walton.

Someone Wasn't Thinking (1946).
Covert filming in Sauchiehall Street.

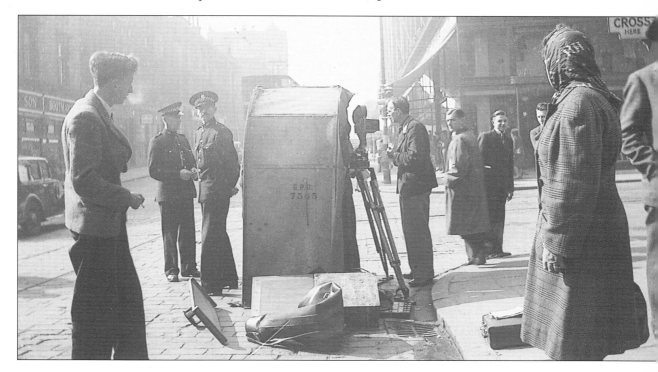

Sauchiehall Street: Glasgow's first screen

Glasgow's best known thoroughfare has appeared on celluloid plenty of times. The trams in *Glasgow and the Clyde Coast* (1910) may have been among the earliest objects of film attention but the street has a greater claim in the history of cinema. Towards the top of the street, in what is now the MGM Cinema, the first film show in Glasgow, and only the second in Scotland, took place on 25 May 1896.

The hall has had many names, uses and owners since it opened in 1888 as the Bannockburn Panorama. The one common denominator throughout its existence has been its reputation as a place of high-class entertainment bringing the Glasgow public the best and latest diversions, whether panoramas, circuses, variety acts or moving pictures.

In the spring of 1896, the building was operating as a skating palace ('the most Superb Ice Surface in Europe') with a 'Splendid Orchestra' and 'Incidental Entertainments on the Stage, Twice Daily'. On 25 May that year, the incidentals included George Meagher, 'Champion Skater of the World' and 'Direct from London, the Century's Sensation – The Cinematograph!'

The projection system employed on that occasion was Lumière's, not the Birt Acres one which had been used with less than stunning results at the Empire in Edinburgh on 13 April (see **Edinburgh, Nicolson Street**). Although Edison's Kinetoscope had been seen in Glasgow as a machine for individual viewing, the Lumière show in May was the first projected film show in the West of Scotland. It was, it could be argued, the first fully successful showing of motion pictures in Scotland. It certainly was the beginning of Glasgow's famous passion for the movies.

Sauchiehall Street figures in two of Scotland's lost movies, *Huntingtower* (1927), the John Buchan story with Harry Lauder in his first screen acting role, and *Someone Wasn't Thinking* (1946), the only production achieved by the ill-fated Scottish National Film Studios (see **Glasgow, St Vincent Street**).

Springburn: John Maxwell, Robert Clark and Alexander King

The Prince's Cinema in Springburn was not the most famous picture house in Glasgow but it is associated with the beginnings of one of the great film exhibition, production and distribution empires. John Maxwell (1877-1940) was a Glasgow solicitor whose firm, Maxwell, Hodgson & Co, handled the legal side of a number of cinema deals in the early years of the century. Maxwell recognised the commercial possibilities of the new business and, by 1912, had acquired a stake in several picture houses, beginning with The Prince's.

By 1920 Maxwell's Scottish Cinema and Variety Theatres had twenty cinemas and two years later he moved into production by setting up Waverley Films. The next major step was, like so many later film Scots, to decamp to London. There he set up Savoy Cinemas, joined the board of British National, who owned Elstree Studios, and created British International Pictures - the company that made the first British talking picture *Blackmail* (1929), directed by the young Alfred Hitchcock.

In 1928, Maxwell set up Associated British Cinemas which would build or take over hundreds of cinemas throughout the UK and his progress continued in similar spectacular fashion with the creation of the Associated British Picture Corporation (ABPC) in 1937. By the time of his death in 1940, Maxwell (invariably described as 'canny') had become one of the most powerful figures in the film industry and was generally credited with having made the cinema sufficiently financially respectable for the City to regard it as a legitimate area for investment.

Maxwell was not the only Scot to become a major player in exhibition and distribution. Robert Clark (1904-84) joined Maxwell's law firm in 1921 and entered the film business as his assistant at British Independent Pictures in 1929. By the 1940s Clark was on the board (he was later Deputy Chairman) of ABPC and in charge of production at Elstree Studios (he was executive producer of *The Dam Busters* (1954). In the Scottish context his name is best known in connection with Caledonian Associated Cinemas (CAC) (see **Inverness**). Along with Alexander B King and Robert Wotherspoon, Clark founded CAC in 1935 and was Chairman from 1949 until his death in 1984 when his son Robin took over.

Alexander King, who was Film Officer for the Ministry of Information during the Second World War, was knighted in 1944 for his extensive film and other public work. His first managerial job in cinema had been at the Grand, Cowcaddens, in 1908. Although he personally never owned cinemas, he was a director of several. His role as a booker with dozens of halls at his disposal put him in a uniquely powerful and respected position within the UK trade. He was therefore in an ideal situation to function very effectively as Chairman of the Films of Scotland Committee (see **Edinburgh, Randolph Crescent**).

Springfield Road: The Black Cat

In the east end of Glasgow, near Bridgeton Cross, the Black Cat Cinema opened in 1921. It was owned by A E Pickard, a renowned eccentric whose cinemas were often as peculiar as he was, and had plywood-backed seats which were too high for short people to see over. This odd disadvantage doesn't seem to have been too great a commercial handicap. The cinema, if not the seats, was still there in 1955, when the premises were bought by the BBC.

The BBC was not making a radical move into film exhibition but needed to find a studio for television production. Among the Black Cat's other peculiarities, it had an entirely flat floor, perfect for *The White Heather Club* which was regularly broadcast from there in the 1960s. However, there was a distinct disadvantage in the distance between Springfield Road and the BBC headquarters at Queen Margaret Drive. It was not unknown for confusion to arise about the two locations. On one occasion the producer of a live magazine programme had to go before the cameras in Queen Margaret

The Prince's, Springburn.

Drive to explain the absence of a celebrity guest who had been ferried to Springfield Road in error. By 1967 that problem had been solved by the creation of new studios at Queen Margaret Drive and, for the rest of the BBC's tenure, the Springfield Road premises were used mainly as a store.

With the final departure of the BBC, the Black Cat became a warehouse. Then, in 1984, it re-entered the film business as Black Cat Studios home of Antonine Productions. Antonine was the invention of the husband and wife team Patrick and Paddy Higson. Patrick had been an editor with the BBC, cutting most of the major drama productions, and subsequently, as a freelance, worked closely with Murray Grigor and other independents. Although his name appears on the credits of many short films his only feature film work was on *Living Apart Together* (1983)(see **Glasgow**). Sadly, he died just as Antonine was formed and Black Cat Studios came into being.

Black Cat Studios provided the interior sequences for a number of films and television productions including *Brond* (1987) and *The Girl in the Picture* (1985). As a practical, economic proposition, however, the studio had its limitations and, despite Paddy Higson's heroic efforts to keep it going, it closed in 1991.

The continuing problem of studio provision in Scotland has so far seemed incapable of satisfactory resolution. 'Studios' have been part of Scottish film for decades, though the term has been applied to a variety of operations ranging from a film company's offices (to make them sound grand) to modest versions of the real thing. In the early days of film, studios were not that uncommon (see **Glasgow, India Street, Rouken Glen** and **Thornliebank**) but in recent times the lack of modern premises with sound stage and post-production facilities has been a major drawback to Scottish film. Some film-makers sought their own solutions. Robin Crichton of Edinburgh Film and Video Productions near Penicuik (see **Penicuick**) built his own small studios in 1969 and has used them regularly ever since. But strong pressure to create large studios has arisen from the success of Scottish Screen Locations (see **Glasgow, Dowanhill**) whose overseas clients would welcome studio facilities within reach of their location work. The rival Irish set-up includes full-scale studios at Ardmore which surpasses by a long way anything on offer in Scotland.

On the other hand, with the move away from studio-based productions in the last twenty years the case for building a large complex is weakened and there are plenty examples of film-makers in Scotland adapting premises for interiors when the need arises. A Fort William warehouse was used to shoot the Houston office sequence, in *Local Hero* (1983), and the elegant Edinburgh New Town flat in *Shallow Grave* (1994) was built in an industrial unit at Anniesland in Glasgow (see **Glasgow, Anniesland**).

The fact that the television organisations have studios for their own use, and questions about how they might participate in joint action in this matter, adds to the interest. A potentially important development was the setting up, in 1995, of Sound Stage in Glasgow's Maryhill. Created by two ex-BBC employees, Alex Gourlay and Billy Mitchell, the facility's eight thousand square feet of drive-in studio space with production offices and dressing rooms, has already been well used for television production and has potential for future expansion.

The debate about the need for a full-scale studio tailored specifically to cinema film production, even a simple 'four-wall dry venue', has a chicken-and-egg feel to it. If film-makers were to be offered such a facility in Scotland would they come in greater numbers? Would indigenous companies arise on its back? Would it be a viable economic proposition? At least as the Centenary comes and goes these questions are at last being addressed seriously. In his announcement, in April 1996, of the reorganisation of the Scottish film agencies, the Secretary of State for Scotland made specific reference to an enquiry into this matter to be undertaken by Scottish Enterprise.

Thornliebank: *The Harp King*

Thornliebank was the site of one of several studios which flourished briefly in Glasgow in the silent era. It was opened in October 1919 by the Ace Film Producing Company. The first and possibly last production was *The Harp King* (1919), a romantic story of love, deception, inheritances, and harp playing.

Ace films did not lack self belief. Shortly before they went bankrupt they set up a 'college' to train actors for the screen.

● *The Harp King*
GB, 1919, Ace Film Producing Co, 56 mins. Directed and photographed by Max Leder. Written and edited by J C Baker. With Nan Wilkie, David Watt and W R Bell.

University of Glasgow

The 'University of Skerryvore', the setting of James Bridie's comedy play *What Say They?*, was a thinly disguised University of Glasgow. Some of the scenes from the film version, *You're Only Young Twice* (1952), produced by John Grierson's Group 3, were shot on location at Gilmorehill. The story was about that most

(top) **The Harp King** (1919).
(bottom) Ace Film Producing Company's studio, (c1919).

peculiar of Scottish University institutions, the Rectorship. Rectorial elections tend to generate first-class disorder, so there was immense scope for fun and games.

Unfortunately, the critics were not very keen on the result and the film became one of a number to make a loss for Group 3. However, it did provide exposure for arguably the best Scottish actor of the time, Duncan Macrae, and parts for Robert Urquhart, Eric Woodburn and Molly Urquhart. It also saw the debut of Ronnie Corbett.

For some years, Glasgow University has had a very important role in the development of film culture in Scotland. Along with the University of Stirling (see **Stirling**) and in partnership with the

University of Strathclyde Glasgow University has ensured that the study of the media has been maintained at the highest level. In 1981, an honours course in Film and Television Studies was initiated as a joint venture between the Department of Theatre, Film and Television Studies at Glasgow University and the Department of English at Strathclyde University.

In 1982, Colin McCabe was appointed to the Chair of English at Strathclyde and with John Caughie at Glasgow, proposed that a research centre be established jointly. This became the John Logie Baird Centre, under whose auspices open seminars and other events involving some of the most important figures in broadcasting and film have been held regularly. The Baird Centre is also the home of the quarterly journal *Screen*, one of the leading international publications dealing with the academic study of film.

You're Only Young Twice (1953). Duncan Macrae in the flesh and in effigy.

From 1988, a Masters course in Media and Culture was introduced and a Scottish Doctoral Programme in Media Studies was established in 1993. Thanks to these initiatives, a steady stream of graduates and postgraduates has emerged from Glasgow with an advanced understanding of the role of the media, particularly film and television, in society. Many of these young people have subsequently found their way into broadcasting and film.

A distinction has to be made between primarily academic courses run by the universities and the vocational training supplied (or often not supplied adequately) elsewhere. (For a fuller consideration of the issues, see **Glasgow, Park Terrace**).

● *You're Only Young Twice*
GB, 1952, Group 3, 81 mins. Produced by John Grierson. Directed by Terry Bishop. From the play by James Bridie. With Duncan Macrae, Joseph Tomelty, Patrick Barr, Diane Hart, Charles Hawtrey, Robert Urquhart, Eric Woodburn and Molly Urquhart.

Woodside Terrace: 'The Scottish Film Office'

From 1949 to 1979 the premises at 16/17 Woodside Terrace had a sign reading 'The Scottish Film Office', above the door. The Scottish Film Council, previously in Newton Terrace, had bought the building for £9000 from Kenneth Ireland who had made it into the little Park Theatre, giving it an auditorium very suitable as a small cinema. Ireland and his company moved on to create the Pitlochry Festival Theatre.

SFC's Director from shortly after the War until he retired in 1969 was Donald M Elliot, a former Edinburgh journalist. His assistant, Ronnie B Macluskie, succeeded him and presided over the change to the Scottish Council for Educational Technology in 1976 and the next move – to Dowanhill (see **Glasgow, Dowanhill**) in 1979.

The Scottish Film Office was closely linked with the related agency, The Scottish Central Film Library. SCFL was the province of the redoubtable Mattie B Smith, the daughter of a cinema manager, who had kept the film library going virtually single handed throughout the War.

GLEN AFFRIC: *The Kidnappers*

Scotland doubling for Canada, rather than the other way round, had Glen Affric and Glen Moriston substituting for Nova Scotia in the 1953 production *The Kidnappers*. The film had a strong indigenous input, not least in the screenplay by Neil Paterson (see **Crieff**), based on his own short story 'Scotch Settlement'.

The tale concerns two orphan boys sent to Nova Scotia and into the care of their stern grandfather. They long for a pet dog and when, in the woods, they discover not a dog but a baby, they decide that this must be their pet.

Such was the impact of the playing by the boys, Jon Whiteley and Vincent Winter, that they each received a miniature Oscar in the Academy Awards of 1954 'for outstanding juvenile performance'. They were in good company for special awards that year; the two other people who received special recognition were Danny Kaye and Greta Garbo.

The cast of *The Kidnappers* included several distinguished Scots performers led by Duncan Macrae as the grandfather, Jim MacKenzie. Macrae was widely regarded as one of the outstanding actors of his generation and although primarily a man of the theatre, where he exhibited range and power few could equal, he did appear in some fifteen films. Many of these, such as *The Brothers, Whisky Galore!, Geordie, Tunes of Glory* and *Greyfriars Bobby*, were set in Scotland, but Macrae also appeared in, for example, *Our Man in Havana* and *Casino Royale*. With the possible exception of his part in *The Brothers* (1947) (see **Skye**), none of these roles did Macrae full justice, but at least they record for posterity something of his considerable talent.

In the United States *The Kidnappers* was known as *The Little Kidnappers*. Under that title it was remade in 1990 with a curiously accented cast and Charlton Heston in the Duncan Macrae part.

The Kidnappers (1953). (left) Duncan Macrae as the grandfather, Jim MacKenzie. (top) Vincent Winter and Jon Whiteley in Glen Affric.

● *The Kidnappers*

GB, 1953, Nolbadov-Parkyn Productions, 93 mins. Directed by Philip Leacock. Screenplay by Neil Paterson. With Duncan Macrae, Jean Anderson, Jon Whiteley, Vincent Winter, Adrienne Corri, Jameson Clark and Eric Woodburn.

GLENALMOND: *The Dollar Bottom*

The famous school, which he himself attended, was the setting for James Kennaway's short story about an insurance scheme devised by a pupil as protection against corporal punishment. Translated to the screen, *Dollar Bottom* (1980) went on to win the Hollywood Oscar for best Dramatic Live Action Short Film of 1980, a tremendous achievement for director Roger Christian and his team.

In fact the film was not shot in Glenalmond (allegedly because the school's governors did not approve). Various Edinburgh schools and their pupils shared the honour, including Fettes and Stewarts-Melville, with support from the Scottish Youth Theatre.

● *The Dollar Bottom*

GB, 1980, Rocking Horse Films/Paramount, 33 mins. Directed by Roger Christian. With Rikki Fulton, Robert Urquhart, Jonathan McNeil and James Gibb.

GLENCOE

Glencoe rates among the most spectacular of Scottish locations and film-makers have frequently used it to good effect as a background to dramatic action. Hitchcock made the most of it, in 1935, as Richard Hannay, John Buchan's hero, fled from the authorities in *The Thirty-Nine Steps* (see **Forth Bridge**). More recent appearances have been in the first of the *Highlander* films (1986) (see **Eilean Donan**) and, more importantly, *Rob Roy* (1995) (see **Kinlochleven**).

The Thirty-Nine Steps (1935).
Robert Donat on the run in Glencoe.

Highlander was a curious blend of ancient and modern, high swashbuckle and computer game, whose immortal hero tracked through the wastes of the centuries, and Glencoe. If it didn't relate to Scottish culture in any recognisable form it clearly appealed to its audience, and spawned two sequels, *Highlander 2: The Quickening* (1991), shot mainly in Argentina, and *Highlander 3: The Sorcerer*, which to some extent returned to what might be called its roots. Scottish interest was mainly confined to the scenery and the reliability of Sean Connery.

The historical reality of Glencoe was as dramatic as the place itself. The infamous massacre of 1692 reached the screen in a low budget feature in the 1970s with a cast that

included James Robertson Justice and a long list of Scottish actors. Although the film failed to make a major impact in the cinema it continues to be available on video.

● *The Massacre of Glencoe*
GB, 1971, Austin Campbell Films, 58 mins. Written, directed and produced by Austin Campbell. With James Robertson Justice, Andrew Crawford, William Dysart, Sandy Neilson, Gerald Slevin, John Young, Paul Young, Michael Elder, Paul Kermack and Alex McCrindle.

● *Highlander*
GB/US, 1986, EMI, 111 mins. Directed by Russell Mulcahy. With Christopher Lambert, Roxanne Hurt, Clancy Brown and Sean Connery.

GLEN NEVIS: *Braveheart*

Fort William and its hinterland did rather well out of the film business in 1994. *Rob Roy* was shooting (see **Kinlochleven**) and in Glen Nevis a strange form of medieval encampment was built for Mel Gibson's *Braveheart*. Both films were released the following year. Despite the fact that William Wallace's is the better historically documented of the two stories, *Braveheart* was clearly the more mythical (and less satisfactory). As is often the case with movies which cost three or four times as much as their immediate competitors, it was also a bigger box office success.

The historical and cultural distortions of the $70m epic *Braveheart* and simulated Scottish accents of a rare kind did not damage its reputation with the public. Its style, its star's energy and its Anglophobia were what mattered. Audiences and politicians loved it. It went on to attract ten nominations at the American Academy Awards in 1996 and converted five of them, including Best Picture and Best Director, into Oscars. *Rob Roy* achieved one nomination, which in itself was a splendid endorsement.

Braveheart turned out to be a most important film for the progress of feature film-making in Scotland. The reason was, paradoxically, that so

little of it was filmed in Scotland and so much in Ireland. It demonstrated to the satisfaction of the Secretary of State for Scotland, Michael Forsyth, that there were great economic and other benefits (particularly through tourism) to be gained from increased film-making activity, both imported and indigenous. *Braveheart* had to move to Ireland because that country was much better able to meet the needs of the incoming film-maker. It has appropriate facilities at Ardmore Studios near Dublin and could provide armies of extras and suitable battlefields for Mel Gibson with relative ease. Ireland could also provide tax incentives although, curiously, Mr Forsyth reported Mel Gibson as saying that was not a factor in his decision to cross the Irish Sea.

Whatever the realities and unrealities of the film and its making, and whatever the discomfort it caused with its violence and chauvinism, *Braveheart* was great entertainment and certainly one of the catalysts to the creation in 1996 of the new Scottish Screen Agency (see **Edinburgh, Waterloo Place** and **The Scottish Office**) and with it the prospect of better things for film in Scotland.

● *Braveheart*
US, 1995, Twentieth Century Fox, 177 mins. Directed by Mel Gibson. Produced by Mel Gibson, Alan Ladd Jnr and Bruce Davey. Screenplay by Randall Wallace. With Mel Gibson, Sophie Marceau, Patrick McGoohan, Catherine McCormack, Brendan Gleeson, James Cosmo, David O'Hara, Alun Armstrong, Angus Macfadyen, Ian Bannen, Peter Hanly and Sean Lawlor.

GREENOCK: screenwriters and a great director

Screenwriters are Greenock's major contribution to the movies. Three of the Scotland's most successful screenwriters were born or brought up there.

Alan Sharp made his name in Hollywood but now lives in New Zealand. His many credits include *Ulzana's Raid* (1972), directed by

Frank Lloyd (with two Oscars).

Robert Aldrich, and *Night Moves* (1975), directed by Arthur Penn. For the Western *Billy Two Hats* (1973) he wrote a script featuring a Scottish outlaw. More than twenty years later his subject was another, better known, outlaw. *Rob Roy* (1995) (see **Aberfoyle**), directed by Michael Caton-Jones, gave Sharp the opportunity to write on a subject nearer home. So near home, in fact, that there is even a joke about Greenock in the film – a strangely situated milestone in the middle of Perthshire points the way to the town.

Peter McDougall's work focuses on the harder aspects of life in contemporary Scotland. *Just a Boy's Game* (1979) was set in his native town and centred on gang rivalry and violence in the semi-derelict docks. Four years earlier, MacDougall and his director, John Mackenzie, had chosen a Glasgow Orange Walk as the focus for *Just Another Saturday* (1975), but perhaps McDougall's greatest popular success (also with Mackenzie) was *A Sense of Freedom*

Rulers of the Sea (1939, Paramount).
Douglas Fairbanks Jnr and Margaret Lockwood.

(1981), the story of Jimmy Boyle. A great deal of McDougall's work, such as *Down Among the Big Boys* (1993) directed by Charlie Gormley and starring Billy Connolly, falls into the 'TV Movie' category, but much of it is close to the values of cinema and deserves mention in that context.

The Oscar winning screenwriter, Neil Paterson (see **Crieff**) came from Greenock as does Bill Bryden, who has one Hollywood screenplay – the Walter Hill western, *The Long Riders* (1980), to his credit – but is better known as a stage and screen director (see **Applecross**). However, Greenock produces more than just screenwriters; James Lee, one of the central figures in the rise of Goldcrest Films and Television, was brought up there as was the actor Richard Wilson.

On screen, Greenock turns up in many documentaries about the Clyde. In features it was the destination of a sailing ship at the beginning of *Rulers of the Sea* (1939), directed by Frank Lloyd (1888?-1960). The film tells the story of the first steamship crossing of the Atlantic and Greenock is actually represented by San Francisco.

Judging by the number of Academy awards and nominations he received, Frank Lloyd was the most successful Scottish film director ever. He received three Academy nominations in 1928 (for *Drag*, *Weary River* and *The Divine Lady*), winning an Oscar for the last one. *Cavalcade* won him another Oscar in 1932 and he received a further nomination, in 1935, for perhaps his best known film, the Charles Laughton version of *Mutiny on the Bounty*.

Born in Glasgow, Lloyd was the son of a shipbuilding engineer and the youngest of seven brothers and sisters. The Lloyd family emigrated to Canada where Frank became involved in a theatrical troupe in Winnipeg. He arrived in Hollywood in 1914 as an actor but was directing a year later. He directed more than a hundred films of which the most successful seem to have been to do with the sea. Geraldine Farrar, quoted in Kevin Brownlow's book, *The Parade's Gone By*, said he had, 'better luck with ships than with people'.

The list of Lloyd's films reads like a cross-section of early Hollywood adventure movies. *When a Man Sees Red* (1917); *Pitfalls of the Big City* (1919); *Roads of Destiny* (1921); *The Man from Lost River* (1921); *The Sea Hawk* (1924); *The Wise Guy* (1926); *The Lash* (1930); *A Passport to Hell* (1932) with Donald Crisp; *Wells Fargo* (1937); and *Blood on the Sun* (1945), with James Cagney, are just a few of the better-known ones. Lloyd also directed screen adaptations of several classics, including *A Tale of Two Cities* (1917) and *Oliver Twist* (1922). He said it was 'a privilege to bring the works of Dickens before sixty people', but with the movies, 'what a marvellous opportunity to bring them before sixty million'.

Mutiny on the Bounty was remarkable not only for Laughton's and Gable's performances but for the strength-in-depth of the whole cast, among whom were the Scots Donald Crisp (see **Aberfeldy**), David Torrence (see **Edinburgh**) and Mary Gordon (see **Glasgow**). The extras included the young David Niven.

Lloyd, a highly respected member of the Hollywood community, was President of the Academy of Motion Pictures in 1934-35.

● *Rulers of the Sea*
US, 1939, Paramount, 96 mins. Directed by Frank Lloyd. With Douglas Fairbanks Jnr, Margaret Lockwood, Will Fyffe, Montagu Love, Alan Ladd and Mary Gordon.

H*h*

HELENSBURGH: stars

The douce town, twenty five miles along the north shore of the Firth of Clyde from Glasgow, has glamorous connections with the movies. Jack Buchanan (1890-1957) was born there. Deborah Kerr (born 1921) is also closely associated with Helensburgh, the family home in her early years being in West King Street though she was actually born in a nursing home in the West End of Glasgow.

Jack Buchanan was the personification of screen elegance. Talent-spotted by Ivor Novello, Buchanan played in Broadway musicals and appeared in several silent films before his first major part, in *Goodnight Vienna* (1932). In Hollywood, Buchanan and Fred Astaire were friends as well as rivals; they starred together in *The Band Wagon* (1953) and Astaire wrote the introduction to Buchanan's biography *Top Hat and Tails*.

Kerr, like Buchanan, found her way into movies via the stage and dance. Her film career, which began in 1941, has many highlights. Almost fifty screen roles have earned her six Oscar nominations for Best Actress and an award for career achievement in 1993.

Less well known than these two, but popular with millions of cinema-goers throughout the world, was the appropriately named Andy Clyde (1892-1967). Clyde was born into a very enterprising show-business family and brought up in Helensburgh. Andy's father, John Clyde, played Rob Roy on the Scottish stage and starred in the earliest *Rob Roy* film made in 1911 (see **Aberfoyle** and **Blairgowrie**). Andy himself went on to play, amongst many other roles, *Hopalong Cassidy's* faithful side-kick. His brother, David, and sister, Jean, also had successful stage and screen careers.

Jack Buchanan

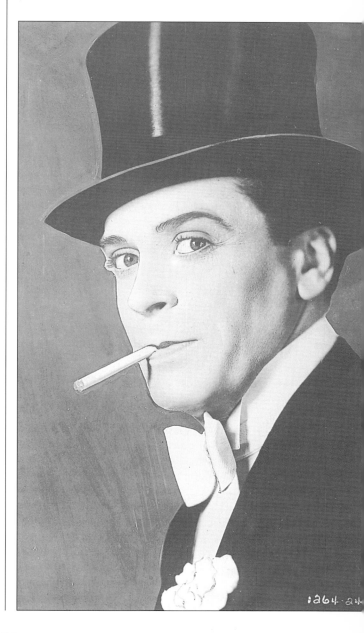

– 175 –

Andy Clyde

David MacDonald, the director, was born in Helensburgh in May 1905. Among the fifty or so feature films to MacDonald's credit, there are some notable works including the Gainsborough Pictures version of *Christopher Columbus* (1949) with Frederic March in the title role and, importantly, *The Brothers* (1947) (see **Skye**). Others of his productions enjoy colourful titles such as *Death Croons the Blues* (1937), *Bad Lord Byron* (1949), *Devil Girl From Mars* (1954), in which the Devil Girl tries to capture Scottish males for breeding purposes, and *A Lady Mislaid* (1958). MacDonald died in 1983.

Helensburgh's greatest contribution to the development of the moving image was as the birthplace of John Logie Baird (1888-1946) the 'Inventor of Television', as the signs welcoming you to the town announce. More recent local encounters with the medium include providing locations for *Take the High Road* (see **Luss**) and *Dr Finlay*.

Neil Munro, author of the Para Handy tales, and George Blake, whose novel *Floodtide* was filmed in 1949 (see **Clydebank**) both lived in Helensburgh. So, briefly, did W H Auden when he was an English master at what is now Lomond School (see **Beattock**).

All Helensburgh's cinemas are long gone. The saddest loss is the Scala Picture House in James Street, a very early (1913) purpose-built hall with an unusual layout including semi-raised boxes around the stalls. Neither bingo nor gaming machines have sustained the building which now lies empty.

HOLLYWOOD

Depending on how you view it, the Los Angeles suburb of Hollywood, founded in 1912, may stand for anything from Mecca to the very embodiment of cultural imperialism. For Scots it has been both; for some, both at the same time. The power that Hollywood and its image exert throughout the world is awesome.

Even before Hollywood and the American film industry had become synonymous, there were Scots on their way across the Atlantic to try their luck in the new business of motion pictures. The 'Hollywood Scots' (worth a book in their own right) included many who made it and plenty whose names are scarcely remembered and deserve better. Colin Campbell, Colin T Campbell, Eric Campbell, Andy Clyde, Donald Crisp, James Finlayson, Mary Garden, Mary Gordon, Frank Lloyd, David and Ernest Torrence and William Shea had all appeared in (and Crisp and Lloyd had directed) Hollywood movies before 1920. Traffic continues to this day but with a better prospect that the ticket is not just one way.

Over the last twenty years, the best known 'Hollywood' Scot – probably the best known Scot – has been Sean Connery (see **Edinburgh**,

Deborah Kerr

Fountainbridge) but there have been others working behind the camera with considerable success, such as the director Michael Caton-Jones (see **Bathgate**).

Allan Shiach has been a key figure in the development of film in Scotland since 1990. Chairman of the Scottish Film Council and the Scottish Film Production Fund from 1992 (see **Glasgow, Dowanhill**), his efforts were crucial in giving credibility to the idea that film in Scotland had to be taken seriously by Government. In April 1996, he was appointed by the Secretary of State for Scotland to preside over the new all-purpose agency, Scottish Screen. The case was greatly assisted by his unique position as both the chairman of a highly successful business, MacAllan-Glenlivet Whisky, and, under the name 'Allan Scott', as a Hollywood screenwriter living part of each year in Beverly Hills. As a writer he is frequently associated with the director Nicholas Roeg in movies such as *Don't Look Now* (1973), *Castaway* (1986), *The Witches* (1989), and *Cold Heaven* (1992). Nearer home, he was executive producer on *Shallow Grave* (1994).

Whatever the view of Hollywood from Scotland, whether as a career destination or simply the greatest dream factory, Hollywood's view of Scotland is problematic. It is a test of our maturity as a nation, not to mention our sense of humour, to be able to cope with the fact that our strongly identifiable culture can lay us open to such a variety of fascinating, charming, alarming, degrading, ludicrous, insulting, patronising and flattering versions of ourselves. At least it is better than being ignored (see **Introduction**).

When it comes to accolades, the awards given by the American Academy of Motion Picture Arts and Sciences, the 'Oscars' (allegedly so called because the statuette resembled somebody's uncle of that name) are in a league of their own. If definitions are not too rigorously applied, it is possible to identify at least a few Scots (together with some Scottish films, or films on Scottish subjects), who have had their moment of glory.

'Scots Oscars'

(Note: dates for films relate to the year they were released rather than the date of the award. So, for example, *Braveheart* was Best Picture of 1995 but the ceremony was in 1996.)

1928-29 Frank Lloyd. Best Director. *The Divine Lady*.

1932-33 Frank Lloyd. Best Director. Best Picture. *Cavalcade*.

1935 *Mutiny on the Bounty*. Best Picture. Directed by Frank Lloyd.

1941 Donald Crisp. Best Supporting Actor. *How Green was my Valley*.

1952 Norman McLaren. Best Documentary (Short Subject). *Neighbours*.

1954 Jon Whiteley and Vincent Winter. Special Juvenile Awards (miniature statuettes). *The Kidnappers*.

1958 David Niven. Best Actor. *Separate Tables*.

1959 Neil Paterson. Best Adapted Screenplay. *Room at the Top*.

1961 *Seawards the Great Ships*. Best Short Subject (live action).

1980 *The Dollar Bottom*. Best Short Film (dramatic live action).

1987 Sean Connery. Best Supporting Actor. *The Untouchables*.

1993 Deborah Kerr. Career Achievement.

1994 *Franz Kafka's It's a Wonderful Life*. Best Short Film (live action).

1995 *Braveheart*. Five awards, including Best Picture and Best Director (Mel Gibson).

I*i*

INVERARAY: Thomasina and Finlay Currie

With its eighteenth century civic buildings and whitewashed houses on the water this Loch Fyne village is so photogenic that it has inevitably attracted film-makers. It was a location for Disney's *The Three Lives of Thomasina* (1963), a children's fantasy centring on the adventures of a cat. The director was Don Chaffey who had previously been in Scotland working for Disney on the dog-centred *Greyfriars Bobby* (see **Edinburgh, Greyfriars Churchyard**).

According to Forsyth Hardy in his book *Scotland in Film*, Inverary shares with Culross, Braemar, Dunkeld, and Comrie the distinction of having been turned down as the possible setting of *Brigadoon* (1954) (see **Brigadoon**). None of these were sufficiently 'Scottish' so the movie was made in a Hollywood studio instead.

Coincidentally, Finlay Currie (1896-1968), who played in *The Three Lives of Thomasina*, was brought up in Inveraray, the son of a soldier in the Seaforth Highlanders. Currie chose a musical career, becoming a professional organist and choirmaster. At some point, he became a member of a vaudeville troop with whom he toured Africa and America.

After the First World War he returned to the stage and in 1932 found his way into films. He was 54 when he began his screen career and yet has over sixty film credits. In 1946 he was memorable as Magwitch in David Lean's *Great Expectations*. In 1950, he played Captain Billy Bones in *Treasure Island*; 1951, the Apostle Peter in *Quo Vadis*; 1959, King David in *Solomon and Sheba*; 1961, Pope Innocent III in *Francis of Assisi*: as well as appearing in significant roles in films such as *Saint Joan* (1957), *Ben Hur* (1959), *Billy Liar* and *Cleopatra* (both 1963).

Currie appeared in several films with Scottish subjects including *The Edge of the World* (1937), *The Shipbuilders* (1943), *I Know Where I'm Going* (1945), *The Brothers* (1947), *Bonnie Prince Charlie* (1948), *Rob Roy* (1954) and *Kidnapped* (1960). In *The Mudlark* (1950), he made one of his most successful screen appearances, as John Brown to Irene Dunne's Queen Victoria.

The expression 'caper' tends to be used to describe light adventure films that have not been as successful as they might. Michael Winner's *Bullseye* (1990) about scientists and mistaken identities seems to fit that description. It was filmed in Inveraray and at the nearby castle of Dunderave.

● *The Three Lives of Thomasina*
GB, 1963, Disney, 97 mins. Directed by Don Chaffey. With Susan Hampshire, Patrick McGoohan, Karen Dotrice, Vincent Winter, Laurence Naismith, Finlay Currie and Wilfrid Brambell.

● *Bullseye*
US, 1990, 21st Century Films, 92 mins. Directed by Michael Winner. With Sally Kirkland, Michael Caine, Roger Moore and John Cleese.

INVERKEITHING: Viz Films

The contribution to film in Scotland made by Murray Grigor and his wife Barbara (who died in 1994) goes well beyond the work of their independent production company, Viz Films, based in Inverkeithing in Fife. Murray Grigor was a film editor for the BBC in Glasgow before becoming assistant to Forsyth Hardy at Films of Scotland. He was Director of the Edinburgh International Film Festival during the late sixties, a time when the event was attempting

Finlay Currie as Magwitch with Anthony Wager as Pip in
Great Expectations (1946).

to redefine itself. More than twenty years later, he served as the Festival's Chairman.

An intense commitment to all aspects of Scottish culture is reflected not only in the choice of subject matter for the Grigors' films but in their work for exhibitions and publications, for example the memorable (and controversial) 'Scotch Myths' exhibition, presented in St Andrews and then at the Edinburgh Festival of 1981. Simultaneously a celebration of, and blast against, the corruption of Scottish culture by 'tartanry', it confronted Scots with the awfulness and degradation of a largely imposed vision of our past. Based on the exhibition, the film *Scotch Myths*, featuring such figures as Byron and McGonagall, and a splendid Harry Lauder played by Bill Paterson, appeared the following year.

An unusual degree of understanding of the potential of film to explore other visual arts was evident in the first film Murray Grigor made after leaving the BBC. Produced by IFA (Scotland) with Eddie McConnell as cameraman and Bill Forsyth as editor, *Mackintosh* (1968) remains easily the best account to date of the life and work of Charles Rennie Mackintosh. The film played a large part in bringing about Macintosh's overdue recognition in his own country.

A US Bicentennial Fellowship in 1977 developed Grigor's long-standing interest in American architecture, and to several films including one on the work of Frank Lloyd Wright.

Murray Grigor's interest in his subjects was often enduring (*Maltamour* (1972), *E.P. Sculptor* – which won the Rodin Prize at the Paris Biennale in 1987 – and *Top Casting* – made for Scottish Television in 1993 – are all about Eduardo

Paolozzi) and International awards have come the way of many of his films.

Viz's choice of subjects for its biographical films is nothing if not eclectic. In addition to those mentioned above, Robert Adam, Billy Connolly, Richard Demarco, Sean Connery, Henry Moore, George Wyllie and Bud Neill have all received Viz's attention.

Barbara Grigor's capacity to connect people across different arts, disciplines and media produced wonderful collaborations. Her work with Paolozzi was both film and exhibition and she produced George Wyllie's *Day Down a Gold Mine* for the stage then turned it into a film for Channel Four, paper boat and all. In 1992, Barbara Grigor produced her only full-scale feature film, *Blue Black Permanent* (see **Edinburgh, Rose Street** and **Orkney**). Not the least remarkable aspect of that project was her persuasion of the veteran film maker and writer Margaret Tait to direct her first major feature. Scotland may never have enough energetic and intelligent producers; the loss of Barbara Grigor was a major blow to the film-making community and to the wider Scottish arts world.

INVERNESS: James Nairn; Highlands and Islands Film Guild

Inverness was the final posting for one of Scotland's most formidable and imaginative cinema showmen. James Nairn (1900-82) came to the town in 1941 to manage The Playhouse Cinema and to supervise La Scala and the Empire, all three belonging to Scotland's most enduring native circuit, Caledonian Associated Cinemas. CAC, unusually for a national organisation, have their registered offices in Inverness. Although in due course Nairn became Controller of CAC's Northern Area, it was as a front-of-house man that he built his remarkable reputation. His earlier managerial charges had included two Edinburgh cinemas, the Savoy at Stockbridge and the Ritz, at Rodney Street, whose building he supervised and filmed as a record of cinema construction. The Ritz (1929), whose architect, W R Glen

(1884-1950), later became staff architect for ABC, was one of the first cinemas to be built specifically to accommodate sound films.

Throughout his long career, Nairn devoted huge amounts of energy to publicising and marketing his cinemas. Elaborate front-of-house decorations and a succession of devices and gimmicks to attract the public earned him a reputation as one of the best managers in the business. At a time when cinemas at the upper end of the market were installing organs, Nairn surprised his patrons and shocked his head office by appearing in his more down-market picture-house at the console of a 'Burleta' organ . The name, and the sight of a small boy pumping a pair of bellows, surprisingly failed to alert customers and bosses to the fact that the organ was a cardboard mock-up and the sound was from records.

Jimmy Nairn at the 'Burleta'.

Commercial cinema in Inverness is now confined to La Scala. However, the regional film theatre at Eden Court extends the local diet of movies beyond the mainstream. Together these two serve a huge area and have the most widely spread 'local' cinema audience in Britain. Fortunately, the Highlands are in line to get the first modern mobile cinema in the UK with the establishment of a 'Cinemobile' circuit in 1997. In this, history will be repeating itself.

In 1946, a conference held by the Scottish Agricultural Organisation Society in Inverness decided to improve the educational, cultural, and recreational amenities available to rural communities in the Highlands and Islands of Scotland by exhibiting films on a non-profit-making basis. The resulting Highlands and Islands Film Guild began operations in 1947 with two units equipped with portable 16mm projectors, one in Shetland and the other covering Caithness and North Sutherland. Less than ten years later there were fourteen mobile units, sixteen static units and a total annual

A rural audience in Orkney in the 1950s.

audience of a quarter of a million. The geographical spread was from the Northern and Western Isles to Argyll. In due course, attendances declined and the number of units reduced until, by 1970, there was only one. A little later the Guild ceased to be, leaving a gap which hopefully will be bridged by more sophisticated technology and better communications.

The proximity of the famous Loch Ness (see **Loch Ness**) was one of the main reasons most of the key people in European animation chose Inverness for their annual 'Cartoon Forum' in September 1993. Animation is a form of film-making in which Scotland ought to, and occasionally does, shine. Animation is not weather-dependent and we have the stories and the graphic skills. In Norman McLaren (see **Glasgow, Glasgow School of Art**) Scotland produced one of the most successful and famous creative people in the field. In the seventies two new talents emerged, Donald Holwill in Edinburgh and in Glasgow Lesley Keen, who trained in Prague and recently became a producer of CD-Roms.

The 1993 event in Inverness brought Scottish animators together in a European context for the first time. It also highlighted the variety of applications of contemporary animation in Scotland - work in education by, for example, Jessica Langford and Leslie Mackenzie, and the growth of a younger generation of Scottish animators including Claire Armstrong, John Colin, Sarah Crawford, Edward O'Donnelly and Walter McCrorie.

Major international film events are relatively rare in Scotland but with its excellent facilities, Eden Court has also twice, in 1987 and 1991, attracted the Celtic Film and Television Festival.

INVERURIE: The Victoria

In 1996, the Donald family, for decades the North East's most significant cinema exhibitors, had only one regularly functioning cinema left. Opened in 1934, the 464 seat Victoria in West High Street, Inverurie, is unusual in that it remains almost exactly as it was when it was built. The Victoria shows films three days a week and is one of the last surviving rural cinemas in Scotland.

The Victoria Cinema, Inverurie, opened 1934.

IONA

Among the many documentaries, travelogues and educational films which have told the story of Iona one of the best was directed by Mike Alexander. *Iona - The Dove across the Water* (1982) used music by the band Ossian to evoke the spirit of the place. One of Iona's most celebrated visitors, Dr Samuel Johnson, was not inclined to praise much of what he found in Scotland, but he made an exception of Iona. His famous dictum, 'That man is little to be envied .... whose piety would not grow warmer among the ruins of Iona' set the tone for all subsequent visitors and pilgrims.

Ironically, the best-known contemporary portrayal of the quintessential English metropolitan was by a Scot, Robbie Coltrane, born in Rutherglen in 1950. Although Coltrane's first realisation of the good Doctor was in a one-man stage show, he portrayed the great man very successfully on screen in *Boswell and Johnson's Tour to the Western Isles* (1993). John Byrne's entertaining, if historically and geographically liberal, account of 'The Jaunt' gave Coltrane, and John Sessions as Boswell, ample scope for fun but was also a reminder of the extraordinary enterprise required by the pair to accomplish their journey in a country still suffering the aftermath of the failed Jacobite Rising of 1745.

Although at first sight Robbie Coltrane's large physical presence would suggest the natural comic, his ability to express a wide range of emotion and his skills in mimicry, particularly with accents, gives him great versatility as his very different television performances in *Tutti Frutti* and *Cracker* demonstrate. In cinema, too, he appears in a wide range of work: for example in a Disney, *The Adventures of Huck Finn* (1993), in Branagh's *Henry V* (1989), disguised as a nun in *Nuns on the Run* (1990), as a cardinal in *Caravaggio* (1986) and as the Pope in *The Pope Must Die* (1991).

● *Boswell and Johnson's Tour to the Western Isles*
GB, 1993, Paravision Production. Written and directed by John Byrne. With Robbie Coltrane, John Sessions, Leo Sho-Silva, Celia Imrie, Tony Halfpenny and Alan David.

ISLAY: *The Maggie*

The island of Islay and the mainland around Crinan were the pricipal locations for *The Maggie* (1953), Alexander Mackendrick's fourth feature film, following *Whisky Galore!* (1949) (see **Barra**), *The Man in the White Suit* (1951) and *Mandy* (1952). Mackendrick was to make only one other film for Ealing, *The Ladykillers* (1955), before returning to America which he had left at the age of six to be brought up in Glasgow.

The Maggie is even more the archetypal post-war Scottish film than *Whisky Galore!* as it charts the decline into humiliation of the outsider faced with the innocent cunning of charming but lethal natives. Calvin B Marshall (a name loaded with symbolism) only wants to get his goods to the island of 'Kiltarra' but fate has placed him in the hands of the crew of *The*

Maggie. His reasonable American expectations that contracts will be honoured and delivery made on time are inevitably overwhelmed by behaviour that is impossibly alien to him. The conflict of cultures provides the tension and the humour but, unlike *Whisky Galore!*, something dark lurks not far below the surface.

The public and critical reception of *The Maggie* was mixed. It was not a great success at the box office. Comparisons were made with other light offerings of the period and many reviewers dismissed it as a charming 'regional' comedy. It was left to later generations of writers, particularly in Scotland, to examine the entrails and find the movie to be not so much gently amusing but (in their view) seriously flawed, the main charge being against its sentimental 'kailyard' representation of Scottish life.

Mackendrick himself considered it his least successful Ealing film but nonetheless thought of it as a very personal work, and liked it. He was right to do so. Only the thin-skinned would take offence at its portrayal of the 'puffer culture'. The fun works on several levels. Marshall's agent, Pusey, the unfortunate stereotype Englishman with bowler hat and rolled umbrella, lands in jail for poaching. Piers are wrecked, authority outmanoeuvred, and the American succumbs to a combination of double-dealing, blackmail and cultural subversion which undermines his position so comprehensively that he ends up losing his cargo and yet paying for the repair of the boat.

The virtues of *The Maggie* are not confined to the story, which was by Mackendrick himself and arose from his experiences on *Whisky Galore!*. As in the earlier film, Mackendrick used a mixture of professional and amateur actors to produce first class ensemble playing. The inter-relationship (sometimes verging on the internecine) of the four members of the crew, played by Alex Mackenzie, James Copeland, Abe Barker and Tommy Kearins, was beautifully conceived. The performance of Kearins as the boy Dougie was outstanding, no doubt owing

The Maggie (1953). Shooting at sea.

The Maggie(1953). The Boy (Tommy Kearins) supplies change for Marshall (Paul Douglas).

much to Mackendrick's extraordinary ability to bring the best out of child actors (as in *Mandy* and *Sammy Going South)*. As Calvin B Marshall the Hollywood actor Paul Douglas had a difficult task to grade his conversion from hard businessman to willing sucker, but with a couple of wobbles, particularly when the sentiment really did get out of hand at the ceilidh, he gave a fine performance.

Mackendrick's directorial technique had certainly changed in the years since *Whisky Galore! The Maggie* is extremely well crafted. Anyone in doubt should look at the scene in which The Boy and Marshall meet after the former has almost killed the latter. Their relationship is subtly expressed through lighting in counterpoint to dialogue. The other develop-

ment, seen more clearly in *The Man in the White Suit*, and again in *The Ladykillers*, is the introduction of a dark thread into the superficially bright texture. It comes as no surprise to learn (from Philip Kemp's book *Lethal Innocence, The Cinema of Alexander Mackendrick*) that, however briefly, the possibility of an ending in death by drowning was contemplated for *The Maggie*. That would have foreshadowed the corpses tumbling into railway trucks in *The Ladykillers*, but at least in that case the crooks were professionals.

● *The Maggie*
GB, 1953, Ealing, 93 mins. Story and direction by Alexander Mackendrick. Script by William Rose. With Paul Douglas, Alex Mackenzie, James Copeland, Abe Barker, Tommy Kearins, Hubert Gregg, Geoffrey Keen, Andrew Keir, Meg Buchanan and Jameson Clark.

K*k*

THE KAILYARD

Not a location or a reference to rural agriculture, but a state of mind similar to that induced by tartanry (see **Brigadoon**). Used, often inaccurately, as a short-hand for a kind of mawkish sentimentality and thought, mistakenly, to be peculiar to Lowland Scotland, the expression 'Kailyard' is part of the armoury of those who damn parts of our culture which lack intellectual rigour.

Film does not have the monopoly on this perceived affliction. Other media promoted kitsch before cinema was invented, but certain movies have contributed substantially to the image of Scotland as a country suffering from bouts of terminal couthiness. Our best excuse is that most of the worst screen perpetrations have been made by outsiders.

KINLOCHLEVEN: *Rob Roy*

The opening shot of *Rob Roy* (1995) says it all according to producer, Peter Broughan. 'These are the men; this is the landscape. Look, this is it; nothing up our sleeves'. Although most of the filming was done elsewhere in Lochaber, the image (which owes more to Western movies than to Sir Walter Scott) of MacGregor's small band moving towards the camera up the hill above Lochleven is one of the strongest in recent Scottish cinema (see **Aberfoyle**).

KIRKINTILLOCH: *Tutti Frutti*

Television programmes can be so influential that they impinge on the whole audiovisual culture. Few television dramas have so effectively gripped the Scottish national consciousness as *Tutti Frutti* (1987). The story of The Majestics' eventful jubilee (and last) tour touched on parts of Scottish geography and psyche hardly visited by moving pictures before. The key scene involving the band's first gig at the Kirkintilloch Miners Welfare is a good case in point. Missing an episode was just not on and, for a few weeks, life, or at least all intelligent conversation, revolved around the antics of Coltrane and company.

Tutti Frutti was great television. John Byrne's writing and design and Tony Smith's directing were brilliant, and the performance of several members of the cast ensured their future stardom. Yet much of the programme's style and effects came from its use of images and conventions shared and understood by an audience reared largely on American movies.

● *Tutti Frutti*
1987. BBC Scotland. 6 Episodes. Directed by Tony Smith. Written by John Byrne. Produced by Andy Park. With Robbie Coltrane, Emma Thompson, Maurice Roeves, Stuart McGugan, Richard Wilson, Katy Murphy and Jake D'Arcy.

KIRRIEMUIR: Barrie

Sir James Matthew Barrie (1860-1937), the son of a weaver, was Kirriemuir's most famous native. Novelist turned playwright, his work has provided a rich seam of stories for the movies.

Nearest to home, *The Little Minister*, set in 'Thrums' (Barrie's fictional name for Kirriemuir), and concerned with illicit romance and the plight of the weavers, generated at least six film versions: in 1912 by Vitagraph (US); in 1915 by Neptune (GB) and also, under the title *The Little Gypsy*, by Fox (US); in 1921 by Paramount (US); and once again by Vitagraph in 1922. A 1934 version from RKO starred Katherine

Hepburn as the aristocrat masquerading as a gypsy and John Beal as the minister. Three Hollywood Scots were prominent in the cast. Donald Crisp, Andy Clyde and Mary Gordon.

Katherine Hepburn also led in *Quality Street* (RKO, 1937) directed by George Stevens, though Barrie's regency romance had already been made into a film by MGM in 1927 with Marion Davies starring.

There are at least three screen realisations of *The Admirable Crichton*. The best known was directed by Lewis Gilbert in 1957 and starred Kenneth More, Diane Cilento and Cecil Parker, but there were silent versions made in 1918 by Samuelson and in 1919, under the title *Male and Female*, by Cecil B De Mille with Gloria Swanson and Thomas Meighan.

There was a *Twelve Pound Look* in 1920, directed by Jack Denton for the Ideal Film Company (GB) and William De Mille made *What Every Woman Knows* in 1921. RKO made their version of *What Every Woman Knows*, directed by Gregory La Cava, in 1934. Helen Hayes starred and Donald Crisp was among the main supports. So also was the Edinburgh born actor David Torrence.

David Torrence's brother, Ernest, played Captain Hook in the Herbert Brenon production of *Peter Pan* for Famous Players-Lasky Corporation (US) in 1924 but the most famous *Peter Pan* is the full length animation by Disney (1952). The story of the boy who never grew up spawned various movie derivatives and updated versions including *Second To The Right And Straight On Until Morning*, directed by Paul Annett for Mimo Productions (GB, 1980), with Petula Clark and Harry Andrews, and the 1991 Spielberg spectacular *Hook* with Dustin Hoffman, Robin Williams, Julia Roberts, Bob Hoskins and Maggie Smith.

The translation of Barrie from Kailyard novel or play to big screen has not always been an unqualified success and critics (and some audiences) have been known to squirm at the

– Mary Gordon in **The Little Minister** (1934, RKO).

sentimentality. Expressions such as 'cloyingly whimsical' are not uncommon among descriptions of the films and even those inclined to stand by the originals did not necessarily like the screen versions. C A Lejeune, for example, found the Disney *Peter Pan* 'a painful travesty' (quoted in *Halliwell's Film Guide*). These strictures, however, have to be set against the obvious popularity of the films. It would seem a reasonable bet that

Tutti Frutti (1987, BBC Scotland). 'The Majestics': Coltrane and company.

The Little Minister (1934).

Katherine Hepburn with director Richard Wallace.

we have not seen the last of the man from Kirriemuir's work on the big screen.

Kirriemuir was also the birthplace of David Niven (1910-83), though some accounts claim he was born in London. What is not in dispute is that during the Second World War he served with the Highland Light Iinfantry and became a major in the Commandos. In Niven's almost eighty films the only significant Scottish connections amount to the lead role in *Bonnie Prince Charlie* (1948) and an appearance in the tartan fantasy *Happy Go Lovely* (1951). Niven won an Oscar for his role in *Separate Tables* (1958).

● *The Little Minister*
US, 1934, RKO, 110 mins. Directed by Richard Wallace. Original novel and play by J M Barrie. With Katherine Hepburn, John Beal, Alan Hale, Donald Crisp, Andy Clyde, Mary Gordon and Lumsden Hare.

● *Quality Street*
US, 1937, RKO, 83 mins. Directed by George Stevens. from the play by J M Barrie. With Katherine Hepburn, Franchot, Fay Bainter and Joan Fontaine.

● *Peter Pan*
US, 1952, Disney, 76 mins. Directed by Wilfred Jackson.

KNOCKSHINNOCH: *The Brave Don't Cry*

The rescue of 116 out of 128 miners after an underground collapse at Knockshinnoch colliery in Ayrshire in September 1950 was the basis for one of the most successful films produced by John Grierson's Group 3 (see **Cambusbarron**). In fact, *The Brave Don't Cry* (1952) was Grierson's own personal favourite. Despite being reduced to a second feature by the cinema trade, who were against Group 3 because it was a Government-backed scheme, the film was well received, particularly at the Edinburgh Film Festival which it was chosen to open the year it appeared.

Grierson's own upbringing in a mining community in Stirlingshire clearly attracted him to the story and ensured a very genuine feeling for the subject. Mining disaster films were not a new genre. The greatest antecedent was Pabst's *Kameradschaft* (1931) which carried a political message; cross-border co-operation between

The Brave Don't Cry (1952). The pit-head.

French and German miners effects the rescue. *The Brave Don't Cry* was more to do with the will to survive and the sense of community peculiar to mining villages.

The Brave Don't Cry was shot in a London studio but most of the players were drawn from the Citizens Theatre in Glasgow and the casting made it one of the most authentically Scottish films in decades.

● *The Brave Don't Cry*
GB, 1952, Group 3, 90 mins. Directed by Philip Leacock. Executive Producer John Grierson. Written by Montagu Slater. With John Gregson, Meg Buchanan, John Rae, Fulton Mackay, Andrew Keir, Wendy Noel, Russell Waters, Jameson Clark, Eric Woodburn, Jean Anderson, Archie Duncan, Anne Butchart and Jack Stewart.

L*l*

LANGHOLM: MacDiarmid

Christopher Murray Grieve (1892-1978) was born in Langholm. In the persona of Hugh MacDiarmid, Grieve was one of the most important figures in twentieth century Scottish culture, as much because of the huge volume and influence of his cultural propaganda as his poetry. MacDiarmid took a view on almost every aspect of Scottish cultural life so it it would not be unreasonable to expect him to have film connections. In fact he seems to have had very little to do with film.

One of his very few utterances on the cinema is characteristically blunt. In *VOX - The Radio Critic and Broadcast Review* (a short-lived periodical for which he worked, under Compton Mackenzie's editorship, in November 1929), MacDiarmid reviewed *The Film Finds its Tongue*, a book about the coming of the talkies by one Fitzhugh Green. Writing under the name 'Stentor', MacDiarmid's opening shot is unequivocal: 'The book is written in an American fashion which I do not like'. He goes on to assert that 'good literature' and 'good art' appeal only to small fractions of the population while 'the Cinema has a virtual monopoly of the remainder.' However, he was at least right in being convinced that the 'talkies' had come to stay.

In February 1947, MacDiarmid appeared on the BBC radio programme 'Arts Review'. Ostensibly he was reviewing *The Green Years* (1946) (see **Dumbarton**), the film realisation of A J Cronin's novel of the same title, but he

used the occasion to attack Cronin's work in general. 'As to film,' he declared, 'I am very far from being a movie fan. If I see a couple of films a year that's about all I want of the silver screen...I find more to interest me in really bad films than in the general averge.'

MacDiarmid's disapproval of the Cronin film centred on the lack of Scottishness of the cast, which included Beverly Tyler and Gladys Cooper. 'I do not know the nationality of these players. But not one of them looks Scottish.' He went on to castigate every aspect of the enterprise – the accents, the lack of authenticity of the settings, the attitude to Scotland of the film-makers and what he saw as being wrong with the majority of Scottish novelists – their distortion of Scottish life – in which 'Mr Cronin is perhaps the worst of them all'.

As to signs of MacDiarmid on the screen, there is not a great deal beyond television interviews and a few documentaries. Honourable mention, therefore, must be made of *Hugh MacDiarmid: A Portrait* (1964) by Margaret Tait, which used the poet reading his own work and the music of his old teacher, the composer Francis George Scott; of *Hugh MacDiarmid: No Fellow Travellers* (1972) directed by Oscar Marzaroli from a treatment by Douglas Eadie and edited by Brian Crumlish; and for Murray Grigor's *Hammer and Thistle* (1977).

LINLITHGOW: Mary, Queen of Scots

Mary, Queen of Scots was born at Linlithgow Palace in 1542. From the very beginnings of cinema, there have been numerous film versions of her romantic and tragic story, all with one thing in common – they are not by Scots. Pathé produced what was probably the first in 1908 and another in 1910. Gaumont's appeared in 1911. In the USA in 1913, Edison made a film based on Schiller's play and a stage performance of the play given in Vienna in 1959 was filmed. A British version appeared in 1922 followed by another, *The Loves of Mary, Queen of Scots*

Katherine Hepburn in **Mary of Scotland** (1936, RKO).

Vanessa Redgrave in **Mary Queen of Scots** (1971, Universal).

(with Fay Compton and Gerald Ames) in 1923. In 1927 a German 'Mary' movie was released, and there are no doubt more.

The two significant English-language versions were *Mary of Scotland* (1936) directed by John Ford, and *Mary, Queen of Scots* (1971), directed by Charles Jarrott. Both of these were very substantial productions with star leads – Katherine Hepburn and Vanessa Redgrave, respectively, but neither was an unqualified success. While films based on historical events can be great to look at, the complex politics some of them try to deal with may be virtually impenetrable. Moreover, for obvious reasons, any serious rendering of Mary's story is bound to end in disaster and gloom. The danger is that the film-maker resorts to basic costume intrigue, with heavy rhetoric and stagey acting to compensate for the inability to do justice to the

nuances. In the case of the John Ford version Hepburn was accused by the critics of using 'exalted speech'. In the other, Redgrave was described as bringing a 'tremulous, romantic-goddess quality to Mary'. In the latter even the sets and settings were described as unconvincing and the accents wayward in the extreme.

If a film about Scottish history is going to work the greater the Scottish input the better. *Rob Roy* (1995) may not be perfect history, or even perfect Walter Scott, but there is a credibility about it stemming from the depiction of the landscape and the provenance of the cast, which immediately places it above other screen portrayals of Scotland's past.

The Scottish contribution to *Mary of Scotland* was largely confined to the presence of Donald Crisp and Mary Gordon. The cast list of the 1971 *Mary, Queen of Scots* was long and distinguished, but only two were Scots, Andrew Keir and Tom Fleming (who, ironically, played an Englishman). On the other hand,

Scots inclined to be snooty about this particular version should note that, despite its shortcomings, the film was successful at the box office and received two Oscar nominations - for Redgrave, and for John Barry who wrote the music.

One of the little known minor tragedies surrounding Mary, Queen of Scots involved a film about her which was never made. For most of his life, Alexander Mackendrick (1912-1993) harboured the idea of making a film about her. It was the one project above all that he wished to see realised. Even at the beginning of his career, when he was directing comedies at Ealing in the early 1950s, he had proposed such a film to Michael Balcon, and been turned down. Ten years later Mackendrick teamed up with James Kennaway and the project was developed further only to be set aside when Balcon offered Mackendrick *Sammy Going South*. Five or six years after that it seemed the film might at last get off the ground, courtesy of Universal's London office. With further redrafts by Kennaway and the participation of Gore Vidal, with sets being constructed and the storyboarding done, everything finally looked set fair for the film to be made in 1968. Then the whole thing collapsed as American companies which had invested heavily in British-based film-making for most of the sixties decided it was time to return home. All of the six projects Universal had in active preparation by their London office were abandoned. To make matters much worse, Kennaway died suddenly in December. All hope of the project ever reaching fruition disappeared for good. Fate put in an extra twist when it was Universal who released the Vanessa Redgrave version just four years later.

If the reasons for the final abandonment are clear enough (the quality of the project was never in doubt), the explanation of the earlier failures must be in part attributable to the intriguing approach Mackendrick and Kennaway took to their subject. They were of one mind that this would be no conventional costume drama. To begin with, the film would deal only with the short period of Mary's life from the murder of Rizzio to her wedding to Bothwell. Several of the usual set-pieces – return from France, flight to England, confrontation with Elizabeth (the fact that it never happened didn't stop it featuring in most of the movies) – would be missing, and, of course, there would be no grand climax in the execution of the Queen of Scots. Almost as bad, from a producer's point of view, the language would be sparse and direct and definitely not high-flown in the manner usually associated with historical epics. It was not a recipe designed to win friends among the money-men.

Instead, this would be a film of the most intensely political nature, about the Queen-outsider dropped from France into the mire (to put it politely) of a Scotland 'like a Mexican frontier town with bandits'. The dirt would be everywhere and literal. The people would be odious. She would, said Mackendrick, be 'up to her armpits in nasty wee Scotsmen'. Much of the focus would be on Maitland, the scheming, lying, and cheating Secretary of State. Rizzio's murder would be squalid. And so on.

Such a film would surely have been marvellous to behold. Casting ideas for Mary included (ironically) Vanessa Redgrave, as well as Leslie Caron, Jeanne Moreau, and Catherine Deneuve. With an approach to the subject so much at variance with the conventions of filmed period drama, it is not surprising, just deeply disappointing, that backers failed to materialise and we have been deprived of one of the potentially great movies.

● *Mary of Scotland*
US, 1936, RKO, 123 mins. Directed by John Ford. From the play by Maxwell Anderson. With Katherine Hepburn, Frederic March, Florence Eldridge, Douglas Walton, John Carradine, Ian Keith and Donald Crisp.

● *Mary, Queen of Scots*
GB, 1971, Universal Pictures, 128 mins. Directed by Charles Jarrott. Written by John Hale. Music by John Barry. With Vanessa Redgrave, Glenda Jackson, Patrick McGoohan, Timothy Dalton, Nigel Davenport, Trevor Howard, Ian Holm, Tom Fleming and Andrew Keir.

LOCH HOURN: *Ring of Bright Water*

Sandaig in Knoydart (where Loch Hourn meets the Sound of Sleat) was the real location for the Gavin Maxwell otter story *Ring of Bright Water* (1969), as opposed to the film location on Loch Melfort south of Oban. Knoydart is one of the most remote places on the west coast. Scotland as a setting for animal stories is better endowed than most places. Apart from the usual tourist benefits, *Ring of Bright Water* provided work for a number of actors and actresses who provided local colour. The cinematographer, incidentally, was Wolfgang Suschitzky who, in a very different context, captured some striking images for *Children of the City* (1944) (see **Dundee**).

● *Ring of Bright Water*
GB, 1969, Brightwater/Palomar, 107 mins. Directed by Jack Couffer. Script by Jack Couffer and Bill Travers. From the book by Gavin Maxwell. Photography by Wolfgang Suschitzky. With Bill Travers, Virginia McKenna, Peter Jeffrey, Roddy McMillan, Jameson Clark, Jean Taylor Smith, Helena Gloag, Willie Joss, Archie Duncan, Kevin Collins, John Young and James Gibson.

LOCH LAGGAN

The Year of the Comet (1992) was one of those films in which Scotland equals a castle and some highland backdrops (in this case several locations including Loch Laggan). Given that it was the work of Peter Yates, the director of *Bullitt* (1968), and William Goldman, the doyen of screenwriters perhaps best known for his work on *Butch Cassidy and the Sundance Kid* (1969), it is hard to understand why the result was so unmemorable. The story of an incredibly valuable bottle of wine found in a Scottish castle, and the resulting chase, should have been great fun.

 ● *The Year of the Comet*
US, 1992, Castle Rock, 89 mins. Directed by Peter Yates. Script by William Goldman. With Penelope Ann Miller, Louis Jourdan, Ian Richardson and Art Malik.

LOCH NESS

According to a 1992 article in *The South China Morning Post*, the average Chinese citizen knows only three things about Britain. The first is that we have a Queen whose name is 'Margaret Thatcher'; the second is that the capital of the country in permanently enveloped in a thick fog; and the third is that in the mountains in the north there is a lake inhabited by a monster.

This last piece of intelligence is of particular interest to the Chinese because they too have a monster in a northern lake, but it does rather raise the question: is the Loch Ness Monster the only thing most of the rest of the world knows about Scotland? If that is the case, we owe it to ourselves not to deny the beast but to seek every opportunity to promote it. Without the Loch Ness monster we may be nothing at all.

In this cause, cinema has been a willing accomplice. Loch Ness – probably never without reference to the monster – has cropped up on the world's screens fairly regularly. One of the earliest instances purported to be serious in intent. *Things that Happen* (1936) was the first edition of a magazine film produced by Scottish Film Productions (see **Glasgow, India Street**). It presented what claimed to be footage of the beast and a slightly cautious assessment of the chances of its existence by the zoologist Eric Foxon. Foxon, who became chairman of the British Universities Film Council, later admitted privately that his involvement had not exactly furthered his academic career (prefiguring the utterly fictional plot of *Loch Ness* – see below). In fact, the controversial footage was shot on Loch Lomond.

The Loch Ness monster surfaced for the first time in a feature film, *The Secret of the Loch* (1934), in which a diver believes he has found an aquatic dinosaur in the depths. Since then there have been a number of film sightings of variable distinction and clarity. *What a Whopper!* (1961) had Sidney James, Charles Hawtrey and several other 'Carry On' team members in pursuit.

The great Hollywood director Billy Wilder, on unfamiliar territory, made the under-rated

Private Life of Sherlock Holmes (1970), the only known instance of Conan Doyle's heroes venturing into Scotland to find strange happenings by the famous loch. This very enjoyable entertainment had no connection with the author's work beyond the main characters.

In the last few years, Scotland has become increasingly successful at attracting film-makers, particularly through the work of Scottish Screen Locations (see **Glasgow, Dowanhill**) so it was probably inevitable that sooner or later another Loch Ness film would be made. *Loch Ness* (1996) came with a good pedigree and with signs of potential commercial success. It starred Ted Danson, of *Cheers* fame, and was made by Working Title whose previous venture, *Four Weddings and a Funeral* (1994), was one of the major British film-making successes of the nineties.

Loch Ness is the undemanding story of a scientist with a suspect academic reputation in the field of unusual phenomena who comes to disprove and disapprove. Predictably, he is eventually overwhelmend by the landscape, the people and the myth; not the first American to whom this has happened in the movies.

Loch Ness was shot mainly in its true location but with the help of the village of Lower Diabaig on Loch Torridon and with Eilean Donan Castle as stand-in for Urquhart Castle which was deemed insufficiently complete.

● *The Secret of the Loch*
GB, 1934, Wyndham Productions, 78 mins. Directed by Milton Rosmer. With Seymour Hicks and Nancy O'Neil.

● *What a Whopper!*
GB, 1961, Viscount Films, 89 mins. Directed by Gilbert Gunn. Written by Terry Nation. With Adam Faith, Sidney James, Carole Lesley, Terence Longdon, Clive Dunn, Charles Hawtrey, Spike Milligan, Ewan Roberts, Archie Duncan and Molly Weir.

The Caledonian Account (1975). Walter Scott and Thomas Telford (John Bett and Bertie Scott) in imaginary conversation on Loch Ness (see **Abbotsford**).

Loch Ness (1996, Working Title). Ted Danson.

● *The Private Life of Sherlock Holmes*
GB, 1970, Phalanx/Mirisch/Sir Nigel Films, 125 mins. Directed and produced by Billy Wilder. Written by Billy Wilder and I A L Diamond. Original characters by Arthur Conan Doyle. Music by Miklos Rozsa. With Robert Stephens, Colin Blakely, Irene Handl, Christopher Lee, Tamara Toumanova, Genevieve Page, Stanley Holloway, James Copeland and Alex McCrindle.

● *Loch Ness*
GB, 1996, Working Title, 101 mins. Directed by John Henderson. Produced by Tim Bevan. Written by John Fusco. With Ted Danson, Joely Richardson, Ian Holm, Harris Yulin, James Frain and Kirsty Graham.

LONDON

The geographical location of the metropolis would seem to put it beyond the scope of this book. The fact is that no Scottish film is ever made without some London connection, if only in having to be submitted to the British Board of Film Classification in Soho Square. So no survey of film in Scotland can be complete without reference to what the poet William Dunbar called the 'flour of cities all'.

London, or south-east England, is where the studios and the processing laboratories are. Most major Scottish actors have their base or at least their agents there. Companies like Figment, who made *Shallow Grave* and *Trainspotting*, have their offices there. It is the location of the National Film and Television School, where much of Scotland's best new creative film talent was trained. It is where much of the British money is to be found, at Channel Four and British Screen, and where the deals are done with distributors. It is, most conspicuously, where Government resides and where ultimately the arguments about tax breaks and virtually anything`else, have to prevail if the Scottish film scene is to progress to become an industry.

According to the *Encyclopaedia Britannica*, one of the interesting effects of the 1707 Union between Scotland and England was that whereas Scotland retained many of its institutions

England lost most of its own, in the sense that they ceased to be English and became British. The 'Britishness' of the film institutions has been a touchy subject since their inception.

The British Film Institute (whose Director, Wilf Stevenson is a Scot) is financed by the Department of National Heritage, and has a Royal Charter that gives it a remit for the whole of Britain and Northern Ireland. In practice, film culture in Scotland is promoted and serviced by the Scottish Film Council (see **Glasgow, Dowanhill**) for which it is funded by the Scottish Office (see **Edinburgh, Waterloo Place**). 'National' initiatives, for example the founding of the (crucial) regional film theatre movement, were heavily dependent on the expertise and capital provided by the BFI though the energy and revenue funding required to get the schemes off the ground and keep them going has been SFC's, in partnership with local authorities and others.

The BFI is in a difficult situation. It is regarded with suspicion when it takes an interest in what is going on in Scotland and with even more when it does not. A recent reduction in BFI funding for the Edinburgh Film Festival has an interesting precedent. It was the desire of the Edinburgh film enthusiasts to run their own event (in its early years it was largely organised from London) that led to the BFI setting up the London Film Festival in the fifties. Similarly, there have been periods when the BFI has been belaboured for failing to support Scottish film production, particularly at times when there was no public finance for such activity in Scotland. On the other hand, the BFI has been very supportive of some Scottish ventures, notably the founding of the Scottish Film Archive, the financing of films by Bill Douglas (if not those by Bill Forsyth), and promoting Scotland internationally. All in all, the relationship is probably no better or worse than many other situations in which London's power and money seem to produce less than sensitive behaviour towards what it calls 'the regions'. One need look no further than the BBC in London, which, almost without being aware of it, has a crucial influence on the whole of Scotland's audio visual culture.

Whatever the complaints the Scottish film business is unlikely ever to become so self sufficient that London support and opinion is of no consequence. There will always be the need to look to London for some form of validation (particularly to see how well Scottish films perform at the London box office). Besides, not everyone Scots film-makers deal with in London is unaware of Scottish problems. Many of them are themselves Scots!

LOWER LARGO

There are fifty or more films with *Robinson Crusoe* in the title. Since the early days of the cinema Crusoe movies have come from many countries. They include one of Bunuel's masterpieces and some of Laurel and Hardy's foolery. Since Alexander Selkirk, the original of Defoe's tropically abandoned hero, came from this part of Fife all these films have a Scottish connection. But maybe that's pushing it....

LUSS: *Take the High Road*

The epitome of Loch Lomond picturesque, the village of Luss has retained more homogeneity of appearance than almost any other Scottish community of its size, even allowing for the intrusion of a couple of very out of key tourist shops.

Luss has a good reason for avoiding change and development. As 'Glendarroch' it has appeared on the the world's television screens as the delightful locus of a most successful soap opera. Scottish Television's *Take The High Road* (later known as simply *High Road*) was first transmitted in February 1980. Its relevance to cinema in Scotland is not least in its importance as a continuing source of employment for Scottish writers, actors and technicians.

Eileen McCallum has been with *High Road* since the first episode. Her big-screen credits include *Mauro the Gypsy* (see **Arbroath**) and *Just Another Saturday*.

Mm

MACHRIHANISH

The airbase near the end of the Mull of Kintyre provided the location for the spectacular crash crucial to the plot of *White Nights* (1985), a late Cold War thriller with ballet in the subplot. The unusual cast list included stars of screen and dance as well as the distinguished Polish director Jerzy Skolimowski in an acting role.

● *White Nights*
US, 1985, Columbia, 135 mins. Directed and produced by Taylor Hackford. With Mikhail Baryshnikov, Gregory Hines, Jerzy Skolimowski, Helen Mirren, Geraldine Page and Isabella Rossellini.

MAXWELLTOWN: Annie Laurie

Famed in song, Annie Laurie has lent her name to at least three movies, none of which have much connection with the famous braes near Dumfries where she was wont to wander. The earliest *Annie Laurie* movie was made in 1916, directed by Cecil Hepworth.

In 1927, MGM used this 'Highland' romance as a vehicle for Lillian Gish. The Director was John Stuart Robertson, a Canadian of Scots ancestry (and an important film-maker), and the cast included Edinburgh-born David Torrence as Annie's father.

There was also an *Annie Laurie* released in 1936. Directed by Walter Tennyson and starring Will Fyffe, it was described as being about 'a

couple who adopt a baby girl'. Fyffe had over twenty films to his credit including several in which he took the lead. Although some were no more than an excuse to present the music hall talents for which he was famous others, including *Rulers of the Sea* (1939), directed by Frank Lloyd (see **Greenock**), and *The Brothers* (1947) (see **Skye**), involved substantial characterisation.

● *Annie Laurie*
US, 1927, MGM, 89 mins. Directed by John S Robertson. Story and script by Josephine Lovett. With Lillian Gish, Norman Kerry, Creighton Hale, Joseph Striker, Hobart Bosworth, Patricia Avery, Russell Simpson and David Torrence.

● *Annie Laurie*
GB, 1936, Mondover Film Productions, 82mins. Directed by Walter Tennyson. With Will Fyffe, Polly Ward and Bruce Seton.

THE MEARNS

Although there have been fine BBC television adaptations of Lewis Grassic Gibbon's *A Scots Quair* (*Sunset Song* was produced by Pharic McLaren in 1971; *Cloud Howe* (in four episodes) and *Grey Granite* (in three) by Rod Graham in 1982 and 1983) so far there has been no cinema version. The Kincardineshire landscape plays a central role in *A Scots Quair* and the saga has great big screen potential.

MORAR: *Local Hero*

The beaches to the south of Morar share with the village of Pennan on the Moray coast, the distinction of being locations for *Local Hero* (1983), Bill Forsyth's tale of capitalism, the environment and rabbit stew. Three years after *Gregory's Girl* (see **Cumbernauld**), Forsyth was given the opportunity by David Puttnam to make a film with a £3m budget, a chance to prove what he could do when freed from the technical and other constraints that had confined him up to that point.

Lillian Gish in **Annie Laurie** (1927, MGM).

Annie Laurie (1927, MGM).

An outline of the plot (the idea was Puttnam's and the script was by Forsyth) would not upset the most conscientious followers of the Ealing light comedy tradition or devotees of the image of Scotland as a picturesque place peopled by quaint and canny souls with strange accents. An ambitious young American oil executive is sent to Scotland to acquire territory to build an oil terminal but he and his boss are so overwhelmed by the magic of the place and its inhabitants that rather than spoil the landscape the company agrees to set up a marine research station instead.

Forsyth's film antecedents and models were clear enough, as he himself acknowledged. Alexander Mackendrick's *Whisky Galore!* (see **Barra**), the films of Powell and Pressburger, even *Brigadoon* could be quoted. Interestingly, since Forsyth had not seen it before making his film, the most obvious parallel was with *The Maggie* (see **Islay**) in which an American is corruptly enlisted into the cause of preserving the unpreservable way of life of his tormentors.

Forsyth's vision contrasts markedly with that of most of his forerunners in one vital respect. The stereotypes, situations as well as characters, are there to be subverted; beneath the apparently conventional humour there is another, and in some ways even funnier, agenda. One that perhaps only Mackendrick in *The Maggie* had examined before. So, for instance, Happer the great American tycoon, played by Burt Lancaster, may be won over by the view of the sky from the beach at Ferness, but unlike the unfortunate Marshall in *The Maggie* he is dangerously (probably certifiably) off his head. The idyllic landscape is shattered by the noise of jet fighters. The company hack (Peter Reigert), sent because he has apparently a Scottish name, turns out to be Hungarian by origin. The villagers, far from resisting the offer of big money for their land out of loyalty to the past, can't wait to get their hands on it. The parish minister is scarcely a fixture from times immemorial – he is black. The cuddly rabbit, rescued on the road at a point where the mists of *Brigadoon* prevail, ends up being eaten. The community's negotiator (Denis

Lawson) is no Joseph Macroon from *Whisky Galore!* but an accountant. All the usual assumptions are undermined by Forsyth's curiously unnostalgic humour. In the end, it falls to the hermit (Fulton Mackay), living on his beach in an upturned boat and, in his own way, as daft as Happer – he is certainly the only other person on the Happer's wavelength – to ensure the happy ending.

Sentiment, even romance, are not entirely absent. The joke about the scientist and her webbed feet, the hotel proprietor's enthusiasm for his wife, the Russian seaman who visits for economic as much as social reasons, and so on, would not be totally out of place in some earlier films. But the overall feel of the piece is quite different from anything that had gone before, not only in indigenous production – such as it was – but in anything made by incomers.

Like *Gregory's Girl*, *Local Hero* (Forsyth is terrific at picking titles) was very successful with the public well beyond these shores. The tremendous appeal of Mark Knopfler's score, which itself received international acclaim, was a bonus. American critics, particularly, made extremely approving noises: a 'nearly perfect' movie, a 'gem', 'charmingly whimsical', 'a small film to treasure', a 'magical comedy' and so on. In fairness, one found it boring and much preferred *Brigadoon*. Some had misgivings about (ironically) the scenes in Houston. But the majority thought it was wonderful and probably failed to notice that there was anything odd in the representation of Scotland, choosing instead to regard the anomalies as Forsyth's 'quirky sense of humour'.

Even with hindsight it is not entirely clear how important *Local Hero* was to the progress of film in Scotland. The suspicion is that it was very important indeed; even more of a breakthrough than *Gregory's Girl*. *Gregory's Girl* had shown that 'our' stories, made into movies, could command significant audiences at home and abroad (though not necessarily in that order). *Local Hero* showed that a film vision of Scotland could, in the hands of a Scottish director, be something that not only entertained but stimulated.

Local Hero (1983, Enigma). Happer's helicopter arrives from the West.

There was no doubt that the look of the film, as much as its content, had a lot to do with its success. After all the carefully crafted Films of Scotland documentaries, the use in a fictional context of the beaches of the west with the mountains of Skye, Rhum and Eigg beyond was hard to resist. Happer's helicopter arriving as a star in the western sky was pure movie magic. Most of all, *Local Hero* gave a degree more credibility to the idea that a big film with a broad canvas and a Hollywood star was legitimately part of our culture.

● *Local Hero*
GB, 1983, Enigma/Goldcrest, 111 mins. Written and directed by Bill Forsyth. Produced by David Puttnam. Associate producer Iain Smith. Cinematography Chris Menges. Music Mark Knopfler. With Burt Lancaster, Peter Reigert, Denis Lawson, Peter Capaldi, Fulton Mackay, Christopher Rozycki, Jenny Seagrove, Jennifer Black, Rikki Fulton, Gyearbuor Asante, Alex Norton, David Anderson, Willie Joss and John Gordon Sinclair.

MULL: *I Know Where I'm Going*

The partnership of Michael Powell (1905-90) and Emeric Pressburger (1902-88) was one of the most creative in the history of British cinema. Between 1943 and 1956 they produced fourteen films under the banner of their company The Archers, giving themselves joint credits as director, producer and writer.

Although Powell was brought up in Kent, he became very interested in Scotland. His first film north of the border, the twelfth of his career, was *Red Ensign* (1934) about Clyde shipbuilding (see **Clydebank**), but it was *The Edge of the World* (1936), the story of the last days of St.Kilda, shot on Foula (see **Foula**), that he said changed his life. In 1939 he joined with Pressburger to make *The Spy in Black* (see **Orkney**) and in 1943 they produced *The Silver Fleet* partly made in Dundee (see **Dundee**).

Local Hero. Fulton Mackay considers the value of a handful of sand.

Clearly one of the best products of the Powell-Pressburger collaboration was *I Know Where I'm Going!* Shot mainly on Mull, using Carsaig as a base, with scenes at Duart Castle and Calgary, the film was released in October 1945. The timing of its appearance was important. Although set during wartime it was concerned with changes in society at that crucial and unsettling period and therefore with the clash of values between the traditions of an island community and those of more mercenary incomers. In this it was another manifestation of The Archers' ethos in which spiritual values must win out over materialism. Superficially, the plot resembles that of many of the 'incomer' films made in Scotland over the years. The central character, this time a woman, is wilful, headstrong and arrogant. She despises the natives and their outmoded culture but falls under the spell of the landscape and the sound of Gaelic spoken and sung, eventually finding love, happiness and her true self.

I Know Where I'm Going! is far more interesting in its approach than most in its genre. The woman, Joan Webster (Wendy Hiller), sets off from Manchester where her father is a bank manager, single-mindedly determined to marry her rich businessman fiancé who, she believes, owns an island called 'Kiloran' where he waits to marry her. Everybody else knows that this is a bad idea and much of the interest of the film is in waiting to see when the truth will dawn on her. Overlaying this, is the story of a journey frustrated by West Highland weather so that, although the heroine makes it to Mull, she cannot get to 'Kiloran'/Colonsay (see **Colonsay**) until fog and gales give way. The handsome naval officer on leave, with whom she is forced to share her impatience, turns out to be the real owner of the island, Torquil MacNeil (Roger Livesey). He saves her from drowning in the Corryvreckan whirlpool and from herself, ensuring a happy ending.

What makes the difference between this film and most of its successors is its visual conception and the obvious effort on the part of the film-makers to engage sympathetically with the indigenous culture as far as they possibly can. There are the conventional markers of 'Hebrideanism', kilts, the Glasgow Orpheus Choir and small flurries of Gaelic (actually, rather more Gaelic, better deployed, than usual, including remarkably credible place names). Nonetheless there is a greater sense of place about it than in any incoming film for forty years (with the possible exception of the two Mackendrick films, *Whisky Galore* (1949) and *The Maggie* (1954)).

I Know Where I'm Going! is arguably more complex than either of Mackendrick's films. Its sense of humour is very visual – the top hat that emits steam as it dissolves into the funnel of a railway engine or the telephone box (just as good as the one in *Local Hero*) sited so near the water-fall that conversation is impossible. The tale of the stranger subverted by myth and purified by ordeal, is certainly not unusual in cinema but it is rarely presented with such redeeming wit.

The film itself is surrounded by a sea of anecdotal detail. Much admired by Martin Scorsese, it has been compared to Mozart's 'Magic Flute'. It was made at short notice while Powell and Pressburger waited for Technicolour stock to start *A Matter of Life and Death* (1946). Roger Livesey, unlike the rest of the cast, never set foot on Mull because of West End engagements and a double stood in for him in the (extensive) scenes on the island, a deception of which Powell was very proud as it did no damage to the performances on screen. The ceilidh scene (obligatory in Highland movies) features John Laurie and Finlay Currie, seen briefly conducting the assembled singers and thereby relating to his past as a professional choirmaster. The improbable household full of wolfhounds was based on a real establishment on Mull. And no doubt there is much more.

On location for **I Know Where I am Going** (1945). Michael Powell is on the right.

Mull was the location for a very different kind of adventure a quarter of a century later. *When Eight Bells Toll* (1971) was full of action, gold bullion, and secret agents and as such was not untypical of most films based on the works of Alistair MacLean (1922-87). In terms of novels translated to the screen MacLean was one of the most successful Scottish authors. The films his work gave rise to were on a big scale, very exciting, and usually excellent box office if not much favoured by the critics. Among more than a dozen titles, the best, such as *the Guns of Navarone* (1961), *Ice Station Zebra* (1968), *Where Eagles Dare* (1968) and *Puppet on a Chain* (1970) could fill a cinema and give good value entertainment anywhere.

The unlikelihood of a link between Mull and Bette Davis is confounded by *Madame Sin* (1972) in which she plays an evil genius scientist whose 'Thought Factory' is located on the island, and who plans the hijacking of a Polaris submarine. Mull also provided locations for part of *The Year of the Comet* (1992) (see **Loch Laggan**) and Bill Anderson's National Film and Television School feature *Creatures of Light* (also 1992). Just off the west coast of Mull, Inch Kenneth was one of the locations for the Tim Neat international

Madame Sin (1972, Cecil). Bette Davies on Mull.

co-production with Dutch and German companies, *Walk Me Home* (1993).

I Know Where I'm Going!
GB, 1945, The Archers, 92 mins. Written directed and produced by Michael Powell and Emeric Pressburger. With Wendy Hiller, Roger Livesey, Pamela Brown, Finlay Currie, George Carney, Nancy Price, Catherine Lacey, Jean Cadell, John Laurie, Valentine Dyall and Duncan McIntyre.

When Eight Bells Toll ✓
GB, 1971, Winkast Films, 94 mins. Directed by Etienne Périer. Produced by Elliott Kastner. Orignal novel and screenplay by Alistair MacLean. With Anthony Hopkins, Robert Morley, Nathalie Delon, Jack Hawkins, Corin Redgrave and Maurice Roeves.

Creatures of Light
GB, 1992, National Film and Television School, 76 mins. Written and directed by Bill Anderson. With Robin McCaffrey, Paul Higgins and Jenny Lee.

NAIRN: Chaplin

The golfing resort east of Inverness was for many years a holiday retreat for one of the most famous cinema figures of them all, Charlie Chaplin. In the early 1970s, Chaplin, along with his wife, secretary, chauffeur, nanny and children, took over the whole back wing of the Newton Hotel for three or four weeks every year. Then in his eighties, Chaplin enjoyed a fair amount of privacy in Nairn as the locals tended to keep their distance. However, his children joined in community activities and took part in plays performed at the hotel.

NEWCRAIGHALL: Bill Douglas

It may still be too early to make a definitive assessment of the importance of Bill Douglas (1943-91) to film-making in Scotland. If that seems a strange statement, given that his contribution to all film-making amounts to no more than a trilogy of relatively short films and one conventional feature film, it has to be understood that Douglas was a very special film-maker (and film teacher). Douglas's concerns were at some distance from the mainstream of commercial film production and his vision was of a very personal kind. Lindsay Anderson (*Bill Douglas – A Lanternist's Account*, BFI Publications, 1993) said that he was, 'A poetic film-maker whose feeling for moment and the intensity of the image makes him unique'. Film-making was, 'a kind of agony for Bill because,

particularly at the start, his films were torn out of himself'.

Bill Douglas was born in the mining village of Newcraighall and it is there that his largely autobiographical trilogy, *My Childhood* (1972), *My Ain Folk* (1973) and *My Way Home* (1978), begins. These are films of an uncompromising nature, an evocation of childhood poverty and the pain of growing up in circumstances of the most discouraging kind. There is no attempt in them to shrink from the hardships of life in such a community and no attempt at all to sidle up to the viewer to gain cheap sympathy.

Not surprisingly, the trilogy is greatly admired by film-makers throughout the world. *My Childhood* won the Silver Lion at the 1972 Venice Film Festival (and many other international awards) but failed to gain popular recognition at home. Even those with a vested interest in the promotion of film in Scotland found his work difficult to come to terms with, so it was possible for 'Scotch Reels', the conference on Scotland's image on film at the 1982 Edinburgh Film Festival, to ignore Bill Douglas almost entirely. Simply, his films did not fit the perceived idea of 'Scottish' film.

The story of Jamie and his desperate circumstances is told with a harsh clarity that at times is difficult to bear but which emanates from undeniable reality of a kind recognised and utilised by Scottish writers for centuries. Scottish film-makers to date have rarely attempted to explore their history or themselves in such a way. (Arguably, *Small Faces* (1996 - see **Glasgow**) is a very recent example but it relies as much on wit as on confrontation with the facts).

The Bill Douglas Trilogy is not easy viewing. Its picture of Scotland could hardly be more remote from that delivered in features and documentaries at the time he was working, but that is to his everlasting credit. His one conventional feature film, *Comrades* (1987), the story of the Tolpuddle martyrs, is imbued with great passion for the characters' cause and is a most skilful piece of film-making, but it is

My Childhood (1972, BFI).

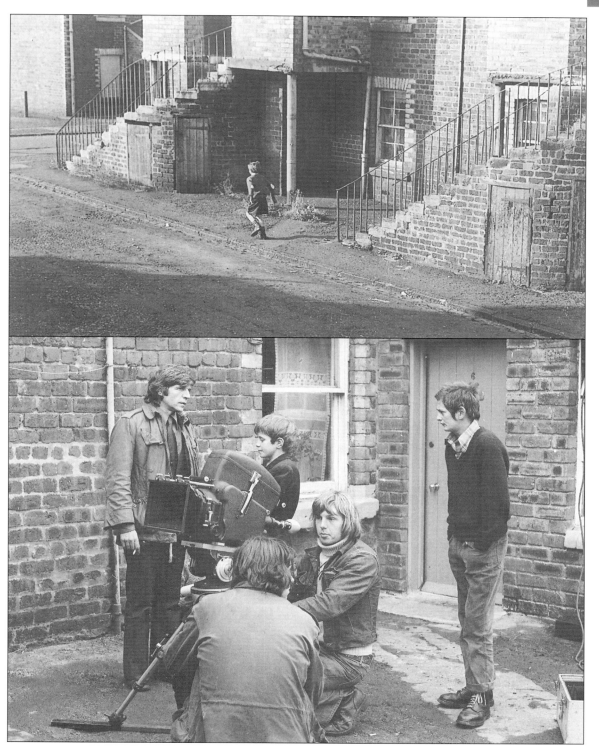

the trilogy that makes Bill Douglas one of the indisputably great film-makers Scotland has produced.

In 1995, a grant from the new National Lottery enabled the realisation of one of Bill Douglas's un-filmed scripts. *Ring of Truth* was filmed in the Necropolis in Glasgow (see **Glasgow**). A much more important piece of unfinished business, however, was his script for James Hogg's *Private Memoirs and Confessions of a Justified Sinner* (see **Ettrick**), whose filming has yet to be achieved.

● *My Childhood*
● *My Ain Folk*
1972, 48 mins/ 1973, 55 mins, BFI Production Board. Written and directed by Bill Douglas. With Stephen Archibald, Hughie Restorick, Jean Taylor Smith.
● *My Way Home* 1978, BFI Production Board, 72 mins. Written and directed by Bill Douglas. With Stephen Archibald, Paul Kermack, Jessie Combe and Lennox Milne.

Mairi, Romance of a Highland Maiden (1912).

● *Comrades*
1987, Skreba, in association with the National Film Finance Corporation and Film Four International, 182 mins. Written and directed by Bill Douglas. With Alex Norton, Robin Soans, William Gammara, Stephen Bateman, Philip Davies, Jeremy Flynn, Keith Allen and James Fox.

NEWTONGRANGE: miners

An unusual instance of Scotland substituting for somewhere else occurred in *Margaret's Museum* (1995). The supposed setting was the coal mines not of the Lothians but of Nova Scotia. There were no longer any working mines of the necessary kind in Nova Scotia but, thanks to the Scottish Mining Museum, a Victorian mine was filmable at Newtongrange. Later, mock-ups of the Lady Victoria Mine surface installations were constructed in Canada to fit in with the setting of the movie.

Skyline Films of Edinburgh were partners with a Canadian consortium including Telefilm Canada and the Nova Scotia Film Development Corporation in making *Margaret's Museum*, which won the Concha D'Ora at the 1995 San Sebastian Film Festival.

● *Margaret's Museum*
Canada 1995 114 mins, Directed by Mort Ransen. With Helena Bonham-Carter, Clive Russell, Craig Olejnik, Kate Nelligan, Kenneth Walsh and Andrea Morris.

NORTH KESSOCK: *Mairi*

The shore of the Beauly Firth opposite Inverness was the location for what was quite possibly the first indigenous fiction film to be made in Scotland. *Mairi, Romance of a Highland Maiden* was made by an Inverness photographer, Andrew Paterson, in 1912, and told a brief tale (about 12 minutes) of love and smuggling.

One of the Scotland's greatest twentieth century writers, Neil Gunn (1891-1974) (see **Dunbeath**), spent his last years in North Kessock. Shortly before his death Gunn was interviewed at his home by the poet George Bruce for the documentary *Light in the North*, directed by Mike Alexander for The Scottish Arts Council and The Scottish Film Council.

ORKNEY

Following the success of *The Edge of the World* (1937) (see **Foula**), Michael Powell, now working for Alexander Korda and in partnership for the first time with Emeric Pressburger, returned to the Northern Isles. This time the location was less inaccessible – Scapa Flow, where he filmed the J S Clouston espionage story *The Spy in Black* (1939). The plot (an unfortunate anticipation of a real event) involved a U-Boat Commander determined to enter Scapa Flow and sink the British fleet. The fact that it was set during the First World War, more than twenty years previously, must have made it seem sufficiently distant from reality. Unlike *The Edge of the World*, however, there was no question of making the entire film on location. This was a much more conventional affair with location shots for atmosphere and the main action filmed at Denham Studios.

A very different Orkney film was *Andrina* (1981), made primarily for television. Based on a story by George Mackay Brown (1921-96), it was adapted and directed by Bill Forsyth, his first production after *Gregory's Girl* (see **Cumbernauld**). Two years later another George Mackay Brown story, *The Privilege* (1983), a horrifying tale of feudal rights invoked on a wedding night, was made into a short film by Ian Knox.

Venus Peter (1989) was a more important film, certainly in historical terms. It was significant as the first feature collaboration between the director Ian Sellar and the producer Christopher Young (who went on to make *Prague* (1992)) but also because it became a crucial model for the involvement of a local authority in film funding. The argument was that the money required to attract the production to the islands would be repaid many times by the money spent in the course of making the film. Thanks to the film-makers' persuasive powers, the reasoning was accepted and vindicated by the outcome. The investment of £60,000 by Orkney Islands Council brought a return many times that amount in expenditure on accommodation, services, wages and ancillaries. The other part of the argument involves the potential tourism gains to a community resulting from hosting a successful film, as in the case of *Local Hero* (see **Pennan**). However, it was the precedent of direct investment at community level that made *Venus Peter* something new.

Ironically, the film might not have come to Orkney at all. It was based on Christopher Rush's semi-autobiographical *Twelve Months and a Day*, set in St Monans (see **St Monans**) in Fife. Present day Fife could not be made to look like itself forty years before and Stromness was chosen as substitute. So the engaging story of a boy growing up in a small Scottish fishing community became universal as it became an Orkney story.

Orkney was also a major location for *Blue Black Permanent* (1992) which was remarkable for several reasons, none more so than the fact that it was the feature film debut of its Orcadian director Margaret Tait, then in her seventies. Set in Edinburgh as well as Orkney and at three periods of time, it told of a daughter in search of her mother's past (see **Edinburgh, Rose Street**).

The Film Society Movement in Scotland has played a very significant role in the development of film culture. It was largely instrumental in the formation of national institutions such as the Scottish Film Council and British Film

Spy in Black (1939). Conrad Veidt.

Venus Peter (1989, Channel Four). Ray MacAnally and Gordon R Strachan.

Institute. It also had an important part to play in establishing the Edinburgh Film Festival (see **Edinburgh**) and in the setting up of regional film theatres through the country. In this, the Scottish Group of the British Federation of Film Societies had a prominent place. Its main function, however, is to help make movies accessible to communities by encouraging the formation of film societies and sustaining them once they are in being. Societies come together for a wide variety of reasons – common interest in a particular sort of film, for example, or the wish to provide a regular social activity for the staff in a large organisation. But perhaps the best reason is to bring a community together in enjoying film, particularly if there is no other easy access to cinema. A spectacular example of the last category occurred on the Orkney island of Rousay where virtually the entire population of about 200 people formed a film society. It was so successful that in 1977 the British Federation of Film Societies gave it the national award for UK Film Society of the Year.

● *The Spy in Black*
GB, 1939, Harefield Productions, 82 mins. Directed by Michael Powell. Written by Emeric Pressburger from an original story by J Storer Clouston. With Conrad Veidt, Sebastian Shaw, Valerie Hobson, Marius Goring, June Duprez, Athole Stewart and Grant Sutherland.

● *Venus Peter*
GB, 1989, Channel Four, Orkney Islands Council, British Film Institute, British Screen, Scottish Film Production Fund. Directed by Ian Sellar. Produced by Christopher Young. Screenplay by Ian Sellar and Christopher Rush. With Ray McAnally, Caroline Paterson, Peter Caffrey, Sinead Cusack, Gordon R Strachan, David Hayman and Alex McAvoy.

PAISLEY: the Glen Cinema tragedy

Although this book, like the Centenary of Cinema with which it is associated, is primarily about the celebration of our cinema heritage, it should not be forgotten that cinema has had its tragedies. One such was the disaster which occurred at the Glen Cinema in Paisley on the afternoon of 31 December 1929, when seventy out of about seven hundred children attending a matinee were killed in a panic to escape from smoke in the auditorium.

The immediate cause of the disaster was a piece of extraordinary bad luck, the freak circumstance of a closed can of nitrate film igniting through being laid on top of a piece of electrical equipment in the rewinding room. James McVey, the fifteen year old assistant, was 'a very small boy for his age but gave a very intelligent account of what happened', according to the official Report to the Secretary of State for Scotland by Major T H Crozier, HM Chief Inspector of Explosives.

McVey had noticed a 'hissing' from a can of film in a corner of the rewinding room. 'Knowing that if he left it in the room fire might spread to the other films there, he picked it up and ran to a door in the passage just opposite the rewinding room'. He could not open it and ran to tell the projectionist, Alexander Rosie, aged twenty. He told Rosie to fetch the Manager while he continued to run the film on screen.

The manager did in fact succeed in removing the can from the building, but by that time the children, already excited by a cowboy film, *Desperado Dude*, had become aware of the emergency and were rushing towards exits which were inadequate in number and too stiff for them to open. Of sixteen children from one Paisley street, only one (who had illegally sneaked into the balcony) survived.

Terrible as the event was, it had a lasting positive effect on the progress of cinema operation in Britain. As a direct result of the tragedy, new legislation was introduced to tighten up safety measures in cinemas throughout the country.

Nitrate film stock continued to be a potential menace to cinema safety even after it began to be phased out in the 1950s. Its propensity for self combustion and the extraordinary amount of dense poisonous fumes even a small amount could generate continued to make it a rightly feared substance. In the early days of the Scottish Film Archive (see **Glasgow, Dowanhill**) the highest priority was given to finding nitrate stock, much of which was in private hands. Only 35mm professional gauge film was nitrate based but that still meant that it could be found stored or forgotten in all sorts of places.

In the 1930s, some film companies made presentation copies on nitrate film of, for example, Royal weddings or visits, and gifted them in special shiny cans to local authorities and other public bodies. One such was given to Aberdeen Town Council where it was reputedly kept amongst the City's treasures including their medieval manuscripts. It took some persuasion by the Scottish Film Archive to extract it from there. When it was, it was found to be wrapped in brown paper on which was written, 'Not to be opened for one hundred years'.

In fact, nitrate film in a sealed tin is more likely to crumble to a fine brown dust than to explode. Either way, a century later there would be nothing left to view. This is the fate of all nitrate stock and the cause of archivists' anxiety to find it before it and its precious images are beyond recall.

Paisley was the birthplace of Tom Conti (born 1941) whose long list of screen credits include *The Duellists* (1977), *American Dreamer*

(1984), *Merry Christmas, Mr Lawrence* (1982), *Reuben, Reuben* (1982), *Heavenly Pursuits* (1986) (see **Glasgow**), and *Shirley Valentine* (1989).

Phyllis Logan (born 1956) also came from Paisley. Her films include *Another Time, Another Place* (1983) (see **The Black Isle**), *Nineteen Eighty-Four* (1984), *The Doctor and the Devils* (1985), *The Kitchen Toto* (1987), *Soft Top, Hard Shoulder* (1992) and the Oscar-winning short, *Franz Kafka's It's a Wonderful Life* (1994) (see **Glasgow, Queen Margaret Drive**).

PEEBLES: films for children

Peebles and the surrounding area provided the locations for *Flash the Sheepdog* (1967) which despite its modest budget and target audience was actually quite important in the development of film production in Scotland. It had its origins in that great cinema institution, the Saturday morning children's matinee.

The Children's Film Foundation (CFF) was set up in 1951 following the demise of the Children's Entertainment Division of the Rank Organisation. Funded originally by the film trade, it was guaranteed an unspecified annual

Flash the Sheepdog (1967).

amount from the new British Film Production Fund under the Cinematograph Films Act 1957. Its purpose was to ensure a supply of good quality, moral (but not moralising) films for young people to see, mainly in their local cinemas on a Saturday morning.

Special (low) rates of pay were set out for all those involved in making CFF films and there were strict rules about how and where the films could be shown, excluding, for example, television or ordinary commercial screenings. The virtue of the system was that it allowed relatively inexperienced actors and film-makers the opportunity to develop their skills within the context of genuine feature film-making for the cinema, albeit on a small scale.

During the 1960s, the Director of the CFF was Henry Geddes, a Dundonian by birth. Aware that the Foundation's films were biased towards the south-east of England, which was where virtually all the fiction film making capacity was based, he approached Forsyth Hardy, Director of the Films of Scotland Committee, to ask if there was a Scottish outfit which could be entrusted with a CFF film. The result was a commission for IFA (Scotland), the Glasgow-based company formed by Laurence Henson and Eddie McConnell.

Flash the Sheepdog was about a young London boy who comes to stay on a farm in the Borders and learns local ways, particularly with regard to the rearing and training of sheepdogs. The film was very successful and led to further commissions for IFA including *The Big Catch* (1968) (see **Ullapool**) and *Mauro the Gypsy* (1973) (see **Arbroath**). Just as important, these led to other kinds of fiction work and provided first drama experience for several key figures in Scottish film-making.

● *Flash the Sheepdog*
GB, 1967, IFA (Scotland), 58 mins. written and directed by Laurence Henson from the novel by Kathleen Fidler. Produced by John B Holmes. Cinematography by Eddie McConnell. With Earl Younger, Ross Campbell, Alex Allan and Victor Carin.

PENICUIK

Nine Mile Burn, on the Biggar Road near Penicuik, is the home of Edinburgh Film and Video Productions, one of the longest running independent companies in Scotland. Founded in the 1960s by Robin and Trish Crichton it is unusual in at least two respects. They started in 1961, like several contemporaries, with an office and a cutting room and by 1969 had built a small but effective studio, the basis of much of their work since. From as early as 1964, they collaborated with European partners in co-producing a wide range of material, which put them in a good position more than twenty years later to benefit from the EU MEDIA initiatives with their strange acronyms such as BABEL, GRECO, and 16:9 (see **Edinburgh, Alva Street**).

The bulk of the company's work, particularly in recent years, has been for television, with Channel Four an important customer. However, *The Curious Case of Santa Claus*, with John Pertwee and James Coco, was made in co-production with a Czechoslovakian partner for the American ABC, while *Moonacre* and *Sara* had input from Grampian Television and the CTG (Comataidh Telebhisein Gaidhlig).

Edinburgh Film and Video Production's output for cinema has been slight in comparison to the quantity of their work for television but they have provided second unit effort on a number of projects including *Ring of Bright Water* (1969, see **Loch Hourn**). In 1975, the company produced the second story film to be commissioned by Films of Scotland (see **Edinburgh, Randolph Crescent**) when Robin Crichton directed *The Great Mill Race*. A successful cross between a comedy chase and a documentary, it told how within one day wool taken from a sheep was spun, woven and delivered as a suit. Notably, the writers of the screenplay were Alasdair Gray and Cliff Hanley.

● *The Great Mill Race*
GB, 1975, Edinburgh Film and Video Productions, 32 mins. Directed by Robin Crichton. Screenplay, Alasdair Gray and Cliff Hanley. Cinematography, David MacDonald, David Peat and Peter Warrilow. Music by Frank Spedding. With John Cairney, Russell Hunter, John Grieve, Leonard Maguire, Ros Drinkwater, Walter Carr, Michael Elder and John Young.

PENNAN: local connections

Pennan is a very small village at the foot of steep cliffs on the Moray coast, half way between Fraserburgh and Macduff, and approximately one hundred and forty seven miles from the sands of Morar (see **Morar**). For the purposes of *Local Hero* (1983), however, the village and the sands were alleged to be next to each other – such is the mendacity of the movies. Despite this, the beach and the village gave every impression of being part of a coherent landscape.

Pennan's most famous landmark is the telephone box which appeared in the film. Thousands of visitors come each year to admire it, though it too is a bit of a cheat; the one in the film was some yards from the real thing.

PERTH: Scott and Soutar

Sir Walter Scott's novel, *The Fair Maid of Perth*, was published in 1828. Nearly a century later, two films with that title were produced. In 1923, Edwin Greenwood directed Russell Thorndyke and Sylvia Caine in the highland romance and in 1926 DeForest Phonofilms offered Louise Maurel as the heroine (see **Abbotsford**).

The Perth poet William Soutar (1893-1943) spent the last dozen years of his life bed-ridden in a house in Wilson Street. Soutar is mainly remembered for his poems, his 'Whigmaleeries', in Scots. *The Garden Beyond* (1977) was written and produced by Douglas Eadie based on Soutar's *Diaries of a Dying Man* which were published in 1954. Directed by Brian Crumlish, *The Garden Beyond* presented a dramatic reconstruction of Soutar's last years and ran for nearly an hour. As such it had a claim to be one of the earliest of the modern indigenous Scottish features, contemporaneous with Children's Film

Local Hero (1983, Enigma). The phone box and the village street, Pennan.

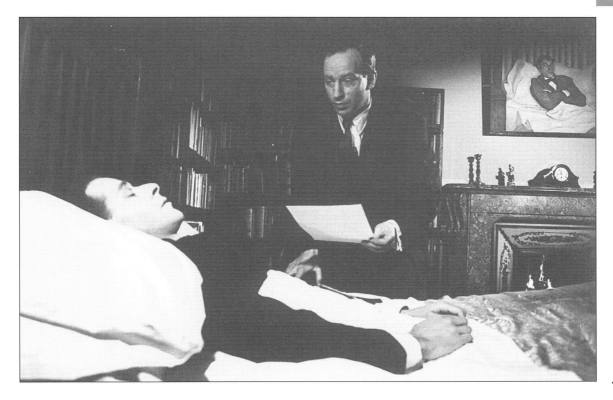

Foundation projects such as *Nosey Dobson* and *That Sinking Feeling*. In that context it was a challenging project, the more so given the physical limitations of the subject matter.

Perth had a stake in *Rob Roy* (1995) as some of the interiors were filmed at an equestrian centre in the town.

● *The Garden Beyond*

GB, 1977, Breck Films, 55 mins. Directed by Brian Crumlish. Written and produced by Douglas Eadie. With Bertie Scott, Henry Stamper, Bill Paterson, Gerry Slevin, John Sheddon and John Young.

PERTHSHIRE: Orson Welles in the glen

There are some occasions when even the most determined effort to suspend disbelief is of no avail. Faced with the sight of Orson Welles as a Perthshire Laird resplendent in kilt even the most dedicated audience was liable to collapse in

The Garden Beyond (1977). Bertie Scott and Bill Paterson.

laughter. Forsyth Hardy reported John Grierson saying he never laughed at anything so much in his life as he did at *Trouble in the Glen* (1954). However, this sentimental comedy, about an expatriate (Welles) who has made his fortune in South America and returns to treat his rural tenants (delightful but cunning) as though they were mere peasants, was a miserable failure which Hardy described as the nadir of film-making in Scotland.

Trouble in the Glen was made at a time when Scottish subjects, particularly of a lighter nature, were fashionable - a situation which would recur in the wake of Bill Forsyth some thirty years later. In the preceeding few years *Whisky Galore!* (1949), *Happy-Go-Lovely* (1951), *You're Only Young Twice* (1952) and *Laxdale Hall* (1953) all appeared. 1954 saw the release of *The Maggie* and *Brigadoon,* and *Geordie* dates from 1955.

Trouble in the Glen (1954, Republic). Orson Welles and Margaret Lockwood.

● *Trouble in the Glen*
GB, 1954, Republic Studios, 91 mins. Directed and produced by Herbert Wilcox. From the novel by Maurice Walsh. With Orson Welles, Margaret Lockwood, Forrest Tucker, Victor McLaglen, Ann Gudrun, Moultrie Kelsall, Alex McCrindle, Duncan McIntyre and Jack Stewart.

PETERHEAD

The North East corner of Scotland, associated mainly with fishing documentaries or television references to the prison at Peterhead, provided the Scottish element in an international co-production, *Salt on Our Skin*, (1992), a romance starring Greta Scacchi. The plot concerned a girl called George who is at school in Paris but spends her summers in Scotland where she falls in love.

● *Salt on Our Skin*
Germany/France/Canada/GB, 1992, Constantin /RTL/Canal Plus/, 110 mins. Directed by Andrew Birkin. Written by Andrew Birkin and Bee Gilbert from an original work by Groult Benoite. With Greta Scacchi, Vincent D'Onofrio, Claudine Auger and Hanns Zischler.

PLOCKTON: policemen

Plockton's popularity as a tourist destination increased exponentially with the transmission of the BBC Scotland's first series of *Hamish Macbeth* in 1995. However, the village had already appeared on screen, in a much more sinister context at the beginning of *The Wicker Man* (1974) (see **Wigtown**) when the doomed Sergeant Howie arrives on what is supposed to be a Hebridean island.

Plockton has also come close to film fame of an entirely different sort. On two occasions within the past twenty years there have been proposals to establish a film school at Duncraig Castle, across the bay from the village. The idea was that a large mansion surrounded by beautiful scenery and plenty of peace and quiet would make an ideal retreat for aspiring film-makers. However, nothing has been realised as yet.

PORTPATRICK: kidnapping

The picturesque fishing port on Scotland's extreme south-west corner has served as a location in at least two films which might be rated as curios rather than blockbusters but deserve attention nonetheless. The more recent was *Double X: The Name of the Game* (1992).

Also known as *Run Rabbit Run*, it saw the return to the screen after many years of Norman Wisdom. *Double X* was a suspense story involving a kidnapping.

The same, coincidentally, could also describe *Hunted* (1952) (known in the US as *The Stranger in Between*) except that the central relationship in the latter is rather more ambiguous than that. More than forty years later *Hunted* is still a very engaging film. It was directed by Charles Crichton whose better known 'Scottish' film was *The Battle of the Sexes* (1960) which was set in Edinburgh and starred Peter Sellers.

Happy-Go-Lovely (1951, ABPC). Vera-Ellen.

Hunted (1952). Dirk Bogarde and Jon Whiteley.

Hunted tells the story of a small boy who finds himself on the run from London with a murderer. The man, played chillingly by Dirk Bogarde, at first uses the boy as convenient cover. By the time they have travelled through the whole of England and into Scotland, he has developed such strong ties to him that, even as they escape on a stolen fishing boat, he decides to sacrifice his freedom to save the boy when he becomes ill.

The boy, Robbie, the adopted son of a Scottish couple living in London, is played by Jon Whiteley, better known for his part in *The Kidnappers* (1953) (see **Glen Affric**).

● *Hunted*
GB, 1952, Independent Artists, 84 mins. Directed by Charles Crichton. Written by Jack Whittingham. With Dirk Bogarde, Jon Whiteley, Kay Walsh, Elizabeth Sellars, Frederick Piper and Geoffrey Keen.

● *Double X: The Name of the Game*
GB, 1992, String of Pearls, 96 mins. Directed by Shani S Grewal. With Norman Wisdom, William Katt, Gemma Craven, Simon Ward and Bernard Hill.

Rr

RANNOCH MOOR: Boggy Scotland

As all-purpose wilderness, parts of Scotland have much to recommend them. Film-makers, from Hitchcock to the Monty Python team have recognised that places such as Rannoch Moor afford the perfect backdrop for fight and flight on a grand scale. Not only the boggy parts of the Highlands but also the rocky coastline serve to supply 'second unit' footage (the bits that do not need to be shot by the main crew), for example in *From Russia with Love* (1963) and *The Land That Time Forgot* (1974). The most spectacular use of the Scottish landscape in this way, implying (but surely not deliberately) that we live on a different planet, was in Stanley Kubrick's masterpiece, *2001: A Space Odyssey*. At the climax, the rocks of the Outer Hebrides, suitably tinted, stood in for the surface of Jupiter.

A less fleeting view of desert Scotland than that extraordinary fly-by was afforded in Jean-Jacques Annaud's epic, *La Guerre du Feu (The Quest for Fire)* (1981) in which the stone age tribe of Ulams, who know how to keep fire going, but not how to ignite it, lose their fire and have to set out across Rannoch to find some more.

● *Quest For Fire*
Canada/France, 1981, 100 mins. Directed by Jean-Jacques Annaud. Special language created by Anthony Burgess. Body language/gestures

The Quest for Fire (1981).

created by Desmond Morris. With Everett McGill, Ron Perlman, Rae Dawn Chong, Nameer El Kadi and Gary Schwartz.

ROTHESAY: The Gillespies

The two James Gillespies, father and son, occupy a notable place in the story of film in Scotland. The senior Gillespie was the manager of The Palace Cinema in Rothesay. He had previously worked in cinema in Aberdeen where he had been a manager and a 'describer' – someone employed to provide commentaries for silent films. In Rothesay, he also made 'local topical' films (anticipating Hitchcock by making small personal appearances in them) and contributed to *Scottish Moving Picture News* (which later became *British Moving Picture News*), a cinema newsreel produced from about 1918 by Greens of Glasgow (see **Glasgow, Renfield Street**).

James Gillespie junior, working with the Elder-Dalrymple company in the late thirties, wrote a unique chapter in the history of film as an educational medium. Commissioned by the Glasgow Education Committee, Blake Dalrymple and Gillespie drove from Cape Town to Cairo making educational films along the way. Their expedition began in 1936 and took two years. The results were distributed by Educational and General Films, Golden Square, London, and provided countless children with their first sight of Africa.

In August 1939 Dalrymple and Gillespie set off by yacht for the Amazon but, calling in Portugal, discovered that war had broken out and returned home. By the end of the war, Gillespie was devoting himself full time to painting and there were no more epic filming expeditions for him. Forty years later, a Scottish film crew *did* make it to the Amazon. *The Legend of Los Tayos* was Bill Forsyth's last documentary before he turned to fiction. It is about caves in the Ecuadorian jungle believed to contain proof that earth had been visited by aliens. The remarkable thing was that the film got made at all and that the unit – Forsyth, Charlie Gormley, David Peat and Ian Leslie – lived to tell the tale.

Rothesay no longer has the Palace, but films are still shown, in the refurbished Winter Gardens.

Gillespie and Dalrymple on safari (1936).

S s

ST ANDREWS: *Chariots of Fire*

It is ironic that the most famous film image of the ancient university town is of it not as itself but masquerading as Broadstairs in Kent. As the group of athletes runs across the West Sands in *Chariots of Fire* (1981), they do so against one of the most famous skylines in the land. But movies depend on the suspension of disbelief and when the story is strong enough it is quite remarkable what we will accept without question.

Chariots of Fire was so successful that it achieved almost mythic status in the history of British film. It attracted large audiences at home and abroad and collected numerous awards including four Oscars. It occasioned British hearts to swell with pride because it was about winning in that best of all contests, the Olympic Games, and the victory of morality over the appetite for personal glory. It had real heroes in Eric Liddell (played by Ian Charleson) and Harold Abrahams (Ben Cross). Liddell, the Scottish divinity student, driven by his faith to excel, was to forfeit the chance of a gold medal because he would not run on the Sabbath. Abrahams, the Jew, ran against the evil of anti-Semitism.

It was the ideal film for the times. Pride in nation was being actively promoted under Mrs Thatcher and a film about British excellence which was itself an excellent British film was just what was required. It also reinvigorated the perennial debate about Government support for British film-making. The usual vicious little circular argument applied: sure, we have the talent to make great films, and the Government loudly applauds the efforts of all concerned, but since the triumph was achieved without Government funding, there clearly is no need for it.

Chariots had benefits beyond the promotion of one of our heroes and the use of several Scottish locations. It demonstrated the possibilities for modern film-making in Scotland, not on an epic scale, not tartan bedecked or whimsical, but in a relatively mainstream form and at reasonable cost. It also provided experience for Scottish cast and crew, including the location manager Iain Smith who went on to work with *Chariot's* producer, David Puttnam, on several major films including *The Killing Fields* and *The Mission*.

One of the smaller roles in *Chariots* was played by Patrick Doyle (born 1953) from Uddingston, who later was to fill supporting parts in films by Kenneth Branagh including *Henry V* (1989) and *Much Ado About Nothing* (1993), in which he played Balthasar. But Doyle's acting career is overshadowed by his work as a highly successful composer for film (and other media). A graduate of the Royal Scottish Academy of Music and Drama, he joined Branagh's Renaissance Theatre Company in 1987 and his music credits include not only the Branagh films *Henry V, Much Ado About Nothing, Dead Again* (1991) and *Mary Shelley's Frankenstein* (1994), but also *Indochine* (1992), *Exit to Eden* (1994), *Une Femme Française* (1995), *Sense and Sensibility* (1995), for which he received an Oscar nomination, and *The Little Princess* (1996).

In charge of music at St. Andrews University from 1945 until 1978, Cedric Thorpe Davie (1913-83) composed at least a dozen film scores. Although he wrote for a variety of titles, features and documentaries, he is mainly associated with films on Scottish subjects. His non-Scottish work included *The Dark Avenger* (1955), an Erroll Flynn swashbuckler about the Black Prince (with two Scots in the cast -

Chariots of Fire (1981, Enigma). On the beach.

Moultrie Kelsall and Robert Urquhart); *The Green Man* (1956), with Alastair Sim; *The Bad Lord Byron* (1951) directed by David MacDonald (see **Helensburgh**); and *A Terrible Beauty* (1960), an IRA drama set in 1940, starring Robert Mitchum. (The music for these last two films and for hundreds of others was directed by Muir Mathieson (see **Stirling**)).

Davie's 'Scottish' film scores included *The Brothers* (1947) (see **Skye**), *The Bridal Path* (1959) (see **Trossachs**), *Rockets Galore* (1958) (see **Barra**), and *Kidnapped* (1960) (see **Appin**).

● *Chariots of Fire*
GB, 1981, Enigma Productions, 123 mins. Directed by Hugh Hudson. Produced by David Puttnam. Screenplay by Colin Welland. Music by Vangelis Papathanassiou. With Ian Charleson, Ben Cross, Nigel Havers, Daniel Gerroll, Cheryl Campbell, John Gielguid, Lindsay Anderson, Nigel Davenport, Ian Holm, Patrick Magee, John Young, Gerald Slevin and Wallace Campbell.

ST KILDA

The island group of St Kilda, furthest west of the Hebrides, would be fascinating enough on account of its remoteness, its outstanding scenery and its natural history, but given the drama of its human history and particularly its evacuation in August 1930, it is in a league of its own. St Kilda under human habitation was recorded on film several times. As early as 1908, Oliver Pike made *St Kilda: Its People and Birds* for the Williamson Kinematograph Company. In 1917 (or possibly earlier), Pathé produced *The Island of St Kilda*.

The best known film of St Kilda while still inhabited was made in 1923 by Topical Productions (Paul Robello and Bobbie Mann) for John McCallum and Company who operated steam services to the Western Isles. *St Kilda – Britain's Loneliest Isle* was essentially a tourist film. The remarkable details of the way of life, including bird catching on the cliffs, is partly compromised by the attitudes displayed towards the inhabitants by the smartly dressed

St Kildans and a movie projector, 1923.

tourists, and by the film itself. A joke about how busy the village street is compared to Sauchiehall Street (quick shot of trams) is no worse than heavy-handed, but the portrayal of the islanders as objects of curiosity is on a par with the most patronising footage of 'primitive' cultures. Pleasure is expressed that 'they never saw a movie camera before' (which was certainly not the case) and that 'the natives have a sweet tooth', as bob-bons are distributed.

In 1925, Ronald Jay, of Jay's Screen Service, made *A Cruise to St Kilda and the Western Isles*. He was probably the last professional film-maker to observe St Kilda as a living community before its terminal decline. Among the many amateurs who found their way to the islands was one Frank Lowe who shot a ten minute film in 1929.

The evacuation of St Kilda was voluntary, in the sense that the islanders had requested it, but their circumstances really left little option. Disease and emigration had left the population below the viable minimum for self-sustenance. The manner of the removal of the people from St Kilda, however, was not to the credit of those concerned. Indeed The Scottish Office, who were generally criticised for their handling of the whole affair, tried to cloak the operation in secrecy and prohibited any photographic or film record being made. In 1979, however, footage turned up that had been shot in the days immediately before the evacuation by John P Ritchie, an ornithologist who had been visiting the islands in August 1930. This unique material, showing preparations for the islanders' removal, had been kept secret for almost fifty years.

Since 1930, factual film coverage of St Kilda has remained largely the province of the naturalists. In 1967, Christopher Mylne, in collaboration with the National Trust for Scotland (the permanent owners) and Films of Scotland, produced a memorable study of the wildlife and the remaining traces of habitation but for the full strength of the story it fell to fiction film to recreate the realities in a way that documentary could not.

Michael Powell, who some modern critics would argue was the best film director Britain ever produced, was fascinated by the St Kilda story from the time he heard about it in 1931. At that time he had scarcely embarked on his career but with admirable determination he was able, in 1936, to realise his ambition to make a film about the island. *The Edge of the World* (1937) could not, unfortunately, be made on the island itself (see **Foula**).

The other dramatised account of the last days of St Kilda had also to be made at some distance from the island group. Bill Bryden's *Ill Fares the Land* (1983) was shot on the mainland at Applecross (see **Applecross**) and was less geographically faithful than Powell's version but more accurate in other ways.

This raises the vexed question about how important it is that a movie dealing with historical events should be shot in the actual places where the events took place. In the case of St Kilda, the topography and weather were essential elements in the story. The physical context was clearly of great significance. The same might be said for some other subjects but not many. That is probably just as well given that the modern appearance of a large number of our key historical sites (including several of the great battlefields) makes them quite unsuitable as locations for film realisation of what took place there.

● *Ill Fares the Land*
GB, 1982, Portman Films for Scottish and Global TV Enterprises and Channel Four, 102 mins. Written and directed by Bill Bryden. Produced by Robert Love. With Joseph Brady, James Copeland, J G Devlin, Morag Hood, Robert Stevens, Fulton Mackay and David Hayman.

ST MONANS

St. Monans was the setting for Christopher Rush's book, *A Twelvemonth and a Day*, the original work on which the film *Venus Peter* (1989) was based. The film was made in Orkney (see **Orkney**) as Stromness had an atmosphere and appearance more in common with the St Monans of forty years before than the St. Monans of today did.

SCOURIE: humans

Scourie, on the west coast of Sutherland, was the location for the bronze age sequence in Bill Forsyth's saga, *Being Human* (1994). It was the first film-making Forsyth had done in Scotland since *Comfort and Joy* almost ten years before.

In those ten years Forsyth made two North American movies, both successful to some degree. *Housekeeping* (1987) was set in British Columbia in the fifties. Based on the novel by Marilynne Robinson about two sisters brought up by relatives, latterly by a strange free spirit of an aunt, in a remote community. Forsyth brought to it his instinct for character, situation, and his skill in handling young actors. The result had a mixed reception. Some made the case that it was his best film to date; others found it too long and not particularly interesting. Certainly some American reviewers found it strange that a film coming from the 'light', 'droll', 'quaint' Forsyth could have such a dark overlay. (Obviously they had not looked closely enough at *Local Hero* or *Comfort and Joy*.) Getting on for ten years after its release, *Housekeeping* remains striking for its warmth, its feeling for period, its character development, and for the way it places credible people in a tremendous landscape.

Breaking In (1989) was much more conventional. An insufficiently subverted 'buddy movie' about an older burglar (Burt Reynolds) who has to pass on his skills to a youngster (Casey Siemaszko), it nonetheless had enough of Forsyth's human observation to be enjoyable without being outstanding. Perhaps significantly, the script was not written by Forsyth. Forsyth's own view, was that, ironically, the film needed less of a star – a more anonymous central character in keeping with the part – but the producers wanted a 'name' and Reynolds' fame could hardly be denied.

Bill Forsyth directing Casey Siemaszko and Burt Reynolds in **Breaking In** (1989, Goldwyn).
Being Human (1994, Enigma). Robin Williams and offspring.

Housekeeping (1987, Columbia). Christine Lahti (centre) with Sara Walker and Andrea Burchill.

In going to America to make movies Forsyth was following a well-worn trail, but in the American film business he was, by his own account, dealing with an entirely different culture from anything he was used to. For some people, the style and methods of the Hollywood studios, or of independent producers who were as demanding on their £5m budgets as studios on their £20m, could be very congenial. This was not so for Forsyth who became determined to return to film-making as near to home as possible. In fact, his experience was probably not so very different from those who had gone before. The parallels with Mackendrick, for example, are interesting, though the eventual outcome for the latter was to cease production and become a great teacher, to the profession's gain and the audience's loss.

For Forsyth, *Being Human* was, therefore, a chance to break with the conventional flow and to return (at least in part) to his roots. The result was an epic story in five segments which told of the striving for happiness of Hector, the universal man (Robin Williams), from the bronze age to contemporary New York, by way of ancient Rome, the Middle Ages and an African shore in the sixteenth century. With only a limited release, it was not a film that readily found a public and most debate about it tried to diagnose its 'failure' rather than attempting to assess its merits.

Certainly it had embarrassing moments, perhaps the worst element was the narration. But it also had plenty of humour and, by Forsyth's standards, a good quota of dramatic action, which made the time journey worthwhile. Maybe the problem was that whereas in all his previous films Forsyth's plea for humanity had been implicit, by bringing it up front something important had been lost. His technical expertise, however, had clearly continued to develop through his American experience. The question of what would come next from Forsyth remains as exciting as ever.

● *Housekeeping*
US, 1987, Columbia Pictures Corporation, 116 mins. Directed by Bill Forsyth. Script by Bill Forsyth from the novel by Marilynne Robinson. Produced by Robert F Colesberry. Cinematography by Michael Coulter. Music by Michael Gibbs. With Christine Lahti, Sara Walker, Andrea Burchill, Anne Pitoniak, Barbara Reese and Margot Pinvidic.

● *Breaking In*
US, 1989, Samuel Goldwyn Company, 94 mins. Directed by Bill Forsyth. Produced by Harry Gittes. Written by John Sayles. With Burt Reynolds, Casey Siemaszko, Harry Carey Jnr and Sheila Kelly.

● *Being Human*
GB, 1994, Enigma Film and Television/ Fujisankei Communications Group/British Sky Broadcasting/NatWest Ventures, 125 mins. Directed and written by Bill Forsyth. Produced by David Puttnam. Cinematography by Michael Coulter. Music by Michael Gibbs. With Robin Williams, John Turturro, Vincent D'Onofrio, Anna Galiena, Kelly Hunter, Maudy Johnson, Robert Carlyle and Hector Elizondo.

SHETLAND: Jenny Gilbertson

The Shetland Islands' most notable contribution to film culture was in providing the setting for Michael Powell's *The Edge of the World* (1937). Apart from two scenes shot among the boats in Lerwick Harbour, almost all of the film was made during an extraordinary five months in 1936 on the most westerly of the islands, Foula (see **Foula**).

Somewhat earlier Lerwick gained a place in film history when the port was the point of departure for Grierson's *Drifters* (1929), the film that defined the idea of cinema documentary by bringing ordinary hard-working lives before the camera in a 'creative treatment' that was a new way of engaging the viewer.

Grierson had another Shetland connection. Jenny Gilbertson (neé Brown) (1902-90) was born in Glasgow and trained as a teacher. Only by chance, after seeing a friend's amateur holiday film of Loch Lomond and realising that the medium could be used effectively in teaching, did she turn to film-making. Having made *A Crofter's Life in Shetland* (1931), on 16mm, she asked Grierson to look at the film and was amazed at his enthusiasm.

Grierson insisted she make more films, but on 35mm, and helped her greatly by giving her space in the Soho Square cutting room and buying her first batch of five films (including *Seabirds of Shetland,* and *Da Makkin' o' a Keshie)* for the GPO Film Library. In 1934 she made *Rugged Island* (and married the hero) which ran in cinemas throughout Britain over the next five years.

Thirty years later, Gilbertson, by now a widow, began filming again – in the High Arctic. At an age when practically nobody else would think of doing such a thing, she refreshed and developed her skills as a solo film-maker in one of the most remote and hostile environments on the planet. Her direct, patient and humane style of film-making, which had served her so well in documenting the life around her in the Shetland Isles, worked just as well among the Inuit and her films of the seventies are as valuable and enjoyable as those of the thirties.

The role of women in Shetland society was the subject of a more recent documentary, *The Work They Say is Mine* (1986), directed by Rosie Gibson. In its subject matter it was in direct descent from Jenny Gilbertson's films and indeed employed some of her archive footage, but with a contemporary message.

The ancient links between Shetland and Norway found dramatic expression during the Second World War when the islands became the base for the 'Shetland Bus', the clandestine operation run by Norwegians to supply the resistance in their occupied country by fishing boat. *Shetlandsgjengen* (1954) (literally 'The

(top) **Drifters** (1929). (bottom) **Rugged Island** (1934).

Shetland Gang') starred Leif Larsen, the leader of the venture, as himself. A version was also made with an English language commentary.

Cinema-going in Shetland has had a somewhat uneven history, due to dependence on sea and air transport to deliver films to the islands. For many years The North Star (an excellent name for the nearest British cinema to the Arctic Circle) sustained the public in Lerwick. It was opened in September 1913 and through much of its long history was in local ownership. From about the mid 1980s, it has had periods of closure but still gives occasional film performances.

After the Second World War, The Highlands and Islands Film Guild (see **Inverness**) provided rural screenings in Shetland until its demise in the 1970s. Its successor, in effect, is the Shetland Film Club which was formed in 1980. The club's activities have gone well beyond those of a normal film society. It established a mobile facility and by the early 1990s could claim that over a four year period it had mounted 94 screenings in 28 venues to audiences totalling 7000 people.

● *Drifters*
GB, 1929, Empire Marketing Board, 40 mins. Directed, produced, written and edited by John Grierson. Cinematography, Basil Emmott.

● *Shetlandsgjengen*
Norway, 1954, Nordsjo Film, 69 mins. Directed and produced by Michael Forlong. From the book, *The Shetland Bus*, by David Howarth. With Leif Larsen, Per Christensen, Oscar Egede Nissen, Atle Larsen and Michael Aldridge.

● *The Work They Say is Mine*
GB, 1986, Edinburgh Film Workshop Trust, 50mins. Written and directed by Rosie Gibson. Produced by Penny Thomson. Cinematography, Dianne Tammes. Edited by Fiona Macdonald.

SKERRAY: *The Duna Bull*

On the north coast of Scotland, to the west of Bettyhill there is a small place called Skerray

which once stood in for an island. The story of *The Duna Bull* (1972) had the apparent characteristics of several sentimental Highland tales – island community loses only bull, bureaucracy stands in the way of replacement, native ingenuity solves the problem with outsiders made to look ridiculous or be won over by the local attractions. In fact it was derived not from such as *Whisky Galore!* but from a real incident affecting the islanders on Foula (see **Foula**).

The film was made by Films of Scotland as one of their, disappointingly few, excursions into fiction. The director was Laurence Henson who by that time had made two films for the Childrens' Film Foundation. It was not without difficulty for the film makers (swimming in the sea not being part of regular bull behaviour) but the result was an agreeable film which annoyed some critics and pleased cinema audiences.

● *The Duna Bull*
GB, 1972, IFA for Films of Scotland, 33 mins. Directed by Laurence Henson. Written by Cliff Hanley from an idea by Forsyth Hardy. Cinematography, Eddie McConnell. Music by Frank Spedding. With Juliet Cadzow, Richard Harbord, Victor Carin, Willie Joss, Tom Watson, Mary Riggins, James Cosmo, James Mackenzie, Jean Taylor-Smith and Alex McCrindle.

SKYE

With its marvellous scenery and romantic associations, real and imaginary, the Isle of Skye has been one of the most favoured locations for films in Scotland. What might be called the 'indigenous' material includes work by Douglas Mackinnon (born on Skye) including *Ashes* (1990), his graduation film from the National Film and Television School.

The life and poetry of Sorley Maclean (born in 1911, on the neighbouring island of Raasay and now living in Skye) was beautifully conveyed in Timothy Neat's *Hallaig* (1984) which related landscape to the story of a people whose Gaelic language and culture seemed always to be under threat. The same theme, but presented in feature form, sustained *Mairi Mhor: Her Life and Songs* (1994) the true story of Mary McPherson, a widow from Skye wrongly imprisoned for stealing, whose response to the injustice she suffered was to write some of the finest songs in the Gaelic language.

Less 'indigenous' features (a great deal so in some cases) shot in Skye, or purporting to have been, included parts of *Boswell and Johnson's Tour of the Western Isles* (1993) (see **Iona**) and *The Ghost of St. Michael's* (1941) in which a school is evacuated to Skye where the headmaster is murdered and the games master (Will Hay) suspected of doing the deadly deed.

(below and right) **The Brothers** (1947). The rowing contest.

Probably the most significant film associated with the island was the 1947 production, *The Brothers*. The original story by L A G Strong is set in Morar but was relocated to Skye for the film. It concerns a young girl who, in 1900, is sent to live with relatives on the island. The effect of her arrival is to bring to a dramatic head the tensions between two crofting families and particularly between the brothers of the title. It is an extremely dark tale of murder and ritual. Early on one of the characters is floated helplessly out to sea with a herring tied to his cap in the sure expectation that a gannet will dive on him and split his skull.

The Brothers was described by Dilys Powell as 'a grim poetic tragedy'. Others saw it as merely melodramatic. But there is no doubting

the powerful impact of its striking black and white photography. The director was David MacDonald (see **Helensburgh**) and the cast, apart from Patricia Roc as an unlikely refugee from Glasgow, which included Will Fyffe, Finlay Currie, John Laurie and Duncan Macrae, was unusually Scottish. Macrae's performance in the film is widely believed to have been his best (it is certainly his most sinister) on screen. While all around him were exaggerating for effect (Laurie had some grand eye-rolling moments) Macrae was a study in controlled menace.

Almost fifty years later, Skye and Mallaig were once again the setting for a film about domestic tensions. *Breaking the Waves* (1996) was the story of an incomer, an oil worker, who marries a local girl but is crippled in an accident with grave consequences for the relationship. It was by the Danish director Lars von Trier and was a prize winner at the Cannes Film Festival in 1996.

● *The Brothers*
GB, 1947, Triton Films, 98 mins. Directed by David MacDonald. Produced by Sydney Box. Script by Muriel and Sydney Box from the novel by L A G Strong. Music by Cedric Thorpe Davie conducted by Muir Mathieson. With Patricia Roc, Duncan Macrae, Will Fyffe, Maxwell Reed, Finlay Currie, John Laurie, Andrew Crawford, James Woodburn, Morland Graham, Megs Jenkins, Donald McAllister and David Keir.

The Brothers (1947, Triton). Patricia Roc, Maxwell Reed, Finlay Currie and Duncan Macrae.

● *Hallaig*
GB, 1984, Island House Film and Video
Workshop, 72 mins. Directed by Timothy
Neat. Produced by Murray and Barbara
Grigor. Cinematography, Mark Littlewood.

● *Ashes*
GB, 1990, National Film and Television School,
39 mins. Directed and written by Douglas
Mackinnon. Produced by Kate Swan. With ❜
Willie Blair, Paul Young, Alec Heggie, Lloret
Mackenna, Mairead Ross and Domnhaill Ruadh.

● *Mhairi Mhor*
GB, 1994, Freeway Films, 63 mins. Directed
by Mike Alexander. Produced and Screenplay

Chariots of Fire (1981, Enigma). Struan Rodger and
Cheryl Campbell in the Sma' Glen.

by John McGrath. Cinematography, Mark
Littlewood. With Alyxis Daly, Ceit Kearney,
Sim MacCoinnich, Andrew Stanson and
Pauline Lockhart.

● *Breaking the Waves*
Denmark, 1996, Zentropa, 159 mins. Directed
and screenplay by Lars von Trier. With Emily
Watson, Stellan Skarsgard, Katrin Cartlidge,
Jean-Marc Barr, Adrian Rawlins and Udo Kier.

SMA' GLEN

The glen to the north of Crieff has been used
several times for filming. It is probably best known
as the location for the Highland Games scene in
Chariots of Fire (1981) (see **St Andrews**) in which
Eric Liddell is persuaded to participate in a race
and demonstrate his world class as an athlete.

A much less celebrated use of the Sma' Glen landscape was for *The Crystal Case* (1938), made over a three year period by the amateur film-maker George D Brown. Scotland's amateur tradition in film-making is a fine one, not only measured by those who progressed to the professional ranks. George D Brown's science fiction story was premiered in a church hall in Perth. It ran for a week.

STIRLING

Stirling Castle was the intended location for *Tunes of Glory* (1960). James Kennaway (see **Strathearn** and **Linlithgow**) wrote the screenplay based on his own novel, with the castle – the headquarters of the Argyll and Sutherland Highlanders – very much in mind. However, when the Army learned that the script was about conflict within the Officers' Mess, the Regiment, perhaps understandably, declined to be associated with the project, even asking that the exterior shots of the castle be modified to avoid recognition. 'Stirling Castle' was therefore constructed on the back lot at Shepperton Studios.

For all its relocation, *Tunes of Glory* was a very strong and successful film. The core struggle, ending in suicide and madness, between the two Colonels, played by Alec Guinness and John Mills, was hypnotic (despite a less than convincing Scots accent from Guinness) and the supporting roles were all of a very high calibre. The director was Ronald Neame whose other celebrated film on a Scottish subject was *The Prime of Miss Jean Brodie* (1968) (see **Edinburgh**). Kennaway's achievement was recognised in an Oscar nomination for Best Script Adaptation from another medium (namely his own work). It acknowledged his exceptional talent and potential which was only beginning to be fulfilled when he died in a car accident in 1968.

The town of Stirling has several other movie connections. John Grierson, 'the father of the documentary' was born and brought up nearby (see **Cambusbarron**) and the University of Stirling hosts the John Grierson Archive in partnership with McGill University in Montreal.

The University also houses the MacRobert Arts Centre one of whose functions is to provide the regional film theatre for central Scotland. It also boasts one of the most successful academic departments dealing with film and the media.

Stirling was the birthplace of Muir Mathieson (1911-75), the musical director whose conducting, arranging and composing, contributed outstandingly to hundreds of British films from the 1930s onwards. His credits include *Things to Come* (1936), *Brief Encounter* (1946), *Henry V* (1944), *A Diary for Timothy* (1944), *Odd Man Out* (1944), *The Brothers* (1947), *Oliver Twist* (1948), *The Wooden Horse* (1950), *The Beggar's Opera* (1953), *Vertigo* (1958), and *Kidnapped* (1960).

Grierson's protegé, Norman Maclaren, one of the greatest animators in world cinema was also a native of Stirling (see **Glasgow, School of Art**).

● *Tunes of Glory*
GB, 1960, Knightsbridge Films, 107 mins. Directed by Ronald Neame. Screenplay and original novel by James Kennaway. Music by Malcolm Arnold. With Alec Guinness, John Mills, Dennis Price, Gordon Jackson, Duncan Macrae, Kay Walsh, Susannah York, John Fraser and Alan Cuthbertson.

STORNOWAY: Comataidh Telebhisein Gaidhlig

The capital of the Outer Hebrides houses a unique media agency. Comataidh Telebhisein Gaidhlig (CTG). The Gaelic Television Committee, was formed in 1991 in response to a cleverly organised campaign led by CNAG (Comunn na Gaidhlig), based largely on the precedent of the public funding of the Welsh Channel Four, S4C. CTG began to fulfil its function as a funder of Gaelic language programmes in 1993, in which year it received £9.5 million from the Scottish Office. As a boost to the indigenous culture of the western Highlands and Islands it was one of the most significant developments in many years, enabling major expansion of the then very limited

Tunes of Glory (1960, Knightsbridge). Alec Guiness and fellow officers.

Gaelic language output by the established broad-casters, BBC Scotland, Grampian Television and Scottish Television.

Although CTG's Government funding has not been sustained at the original level (in 1995-96 it was £8.7m), it has continued to be a key player not only in its own immediate heartland but in Scottish broadcasting as a whole. Cinema does not fall within its remit but, as with all the broadcasters, the effect of creating a healthy production sector for television inevitably has an knock-on effect on big screen film in terms of resources, skills and employment.

So far two feature films, *As an Eilean* (1993) (see **Aultbea**) and *Mairi Mhor* (1994) (see **Skye**) have benefited from CTG support and some short films with cinema potential have also gained from it. In 1995 a new scheme, 'Geur Ghearr' was announced under which the Scottish Film Production Fund with support from CTG and BBC Scotland will produce at least two short films in Gaelic per year.

STRATHEARN

Country Dance (1969) was made partly in Strathearn, where the story was set, but mainly at the Ardmore Studios in Ireland. The screenplay, based on his own novel (and play), *Household Ghosts* was by James Kennaway, (1928-68) whose personal experience of the Perthshire upper classes (he was born in Auchterarder) lent veracity to what would otherwise have seemed a highly implausible tale in which the drunken Sir Charles (Peter O'Toole) heads towards madness via incest.

Country Dance (1969, Windward). Susannah York and Peter O'Toole.

The film made relatively little impact with the public or the critics, certainly compared with *Tunes of Glory* (1960) (see **Stirling**), the only other feature film based on a work by Kennaway (his other screenwritings being adaptations). Tragically, before *Country Dance* was produced, Kennaway was killed in a car crash.

Kennaway's talent had been obvious to the film industry for some time. He had already been used as a script writer for *Violent Playground* (1957), *The Mind Benders* (1963), *Shoes of the Fisherman* (1968) and *The Battle of Britain* (1969). His work on *Tunes of Glory* had been nominated for an Oscar. Ironically, in 1981, one of his stories realised as a short film, *The Dollar Bottom*, did actually win an Academy Award (see **Glenalmond**).

Shortly before his death, Kennaway had teamed up with Alexander Mackendrick to devise a screenplay for a film of Mary Queen of Scots (see **Linlithgow**). The incalculable loss of Kennaway is somehow made worse by speculating about what sort of monument to him that film might have been had it been made.

● *Country Dance*
GB, 1969, Windward/MGM, 112 mins. Directed by J Lee Thompson. Screenplay, play and original novel by James Kennaway. With Peter O'Toole, Susannah York, Michael Craig, Harry Andrews, Cyril Cusack, Judy Cornwell, Brian Blessed, Robert Urquhart, Lennox Milne, Jean Anderson, Marjorie Dalziel, Helena Gloag, Madeleine Christie and Leonard Maguire.

STRICHEN: Lorna Moon

Helen Low (1886-1930) was born in the Buchan village of Strichen. She was a remarkable character. Under the name Lorna Moon she published a book of short stories, *Doorways of Drumorty* (1926), about her native area and a novel, *Dark Star* (1929). Some years before that she had established herself as a writer in Hollywood where she was closely involved with the De Milles, Cecil B and his brother William, by whom she had a son.

Her credits show that she was working at the highest level of the business. She provided original stories and screenplays, for example, *Don't Tell Everything* (1921) directed by Sam Wood for Famous Players-Lasky Corporation and *After Midnight* (1927) for MGM. Her own *Dark Star* became *Min and Bill* (1930) for which Marie Dressler received an Oscar. She was a writer on *Love* (1927), starring Greta Garbo, the first film based on *Anna Karenina*, and *Mr Wu* (1927) with Lon Chaney.

Helen Low died of tuberculosis in Alberquerque, New Mexico, but her ashes were returned to Aberdeenshire and scattered on the summit of Mormond Hill.

Lorna Moon

T*t*

THE TROSSACHS: *Geordie* and *The Bridal Path*

Early photographers and tour operators such as George Washington Wilson and Thomas Cook were the first to note the commercial potential of the beauty of the Trossachs. They took their cue from the approval of the area expressed by Walter Scott, Keats, Wordsworth and Queen Victoria. The admiration, and the capitalising, has continued ever since.

Among the movies to benefit from the picturesque nature of this landscape was *Geordie* (1955). Directed by Frank Launder and filmed in the Trossachs, this sentimental tale of a gamekeeper's son (played by ten year old Paul Young) who takes a correspondence course to improve his physique and ends up as an Olympic hammer thrower (Bill Travers), had charm and some nice jokes. Alastair Sim as the local Laird and Molly Urquhart and Jameson Clark as Geordie's parents provided a degree of authenticity and local scenery and

Geordie (1955, Argonaut). Bill Travers and Norah Gorsen.

customs were exploited in an entertaining way. In Norah Gorsen as Geordie's inspirational sweetheart, the film had a contender for the most memorably bad Scottish accent on film, a fiercely competitive category.

The Bridal Path (1959), directed by Frank Launder was another of a number of post-Second World War British films that found Scotland attractive not only for the pleasing appearance of the countryside but also for the quaintness of the natives. The novel on which it was based was by Nigel Tranter and related the adventures of a Hebridean islander, a widower with two small children, sent to the mainland to find a new wife, the stock of women on the island being very limited since they were all interrelated.

Films of this nature (*Trouble in the Glen*, (1954) (see **Perthshire**) was another example of the genre) did little or nothing for film-making in Scotland and maybe not even much for tourism in such an obviously benighted country. Their principal saving grace was that they gave welcome employment to a few Scots, behind as well as in front of the camera.

● *Geordie*
GB, 1955, Argonaut Films, 99 mins. Directed by Frank Launder. Produced by Sidney Gilliat. Screenplay by Frank Launder and Sidney Gilliat from an original novel by David Walker. Music, William Alwyn. With Alastair Sim, Bill Travers, Paul Young, Norah Gorsen, Miles Malleson, Molly Urquhart, Jameson Clark and Jack Radcliffe.

● *The Bridal Path*
GB, 1959, Vale Film Productions, 95 mins. Directed by Frank Launder. Produced by Sidney Gilliat. Screenplay by Frank Launder and Geoffrey Willans from an original novel by Nigel Tranter. Music, Cedric Thorpe Davie and the Campbeltown Gaelic Choir. With Bill Travers, Fiona Clyne, George Cole, Gordon Jackson, Duncan Macrae and Alex MacKenzie.

U u

the Children's Film Foundation production, *The Big Catch* (1968).

The Big Catch was significant in the progress of wholly indigenous film. It was the second CFF film made by Laurence Henson and Eddie McConnell. The writer was Charlie Gormley, later the director of *Living Apart Together* (1983) (see **Glasgow**) and the story involved a boy, a pony on a deserted island, and a great shoal of fish.

● *The Big Catch*
GB, 1968, International Film Associates, 55 mins. Directed by Laurence Henson. Written by Charles Gormley. Cinematography, Eddie McConnell. With David Gallacher, Ronald Sinclair, Andrew Byatt, James Copeland, Michael O'Halloran, Willie Joss and Callum Mill.

Filming **The Big Catch** (1968). Director Laurence Henson and cameraman Eddie McConnell.

ULLAPOOL: *The Big Catch*

The village and the spectacular hinterland of Assynt form another of Scotland's great under-used feature locations. Although a number of shorts, documentaries and feature inserts, including Bill Forsyth's *Being Human* (1994) (see **Scourie**), have been shot in the area there seems to have been only one film based in Ullapool;

WIGTOWN: *The Wicker Man*

The county at the extreme south-west of Scotland, together with parts of the nearby town of Kirkcudbright and some highland locations, contributed substantially to the making of one of the strangest films ever to come out of Scotland. *The Wicker Man* (1974) is commonly referred to as a 'cult' movie, which is probably a fair enough description of both its content and its status.

The story involves bizarre events on a Hebridean island and the fate of the islanders and the policeman sent to investigate. It would probably never have risen above the 'B-movie' level of a hundred other horror films had it not been done with such obvious style and relish by all who participated in it, from stars to extras. Twenty years after it was made it is regarded as a minor classic. Human sacrifice by fire in the monumental 'wicker man', filmed on Burrow Head, certainly provided the most spectacular and grisly ending to a film made in Scotland. In the following years when Scottish film was mainly concerned with gentle comedy or gritty realism, it was maybe a pity that we failed to develop a companion strain of horror. It is surely in the blood.

The Wicker Man was very much an import into Scottish film-making. Few Scots were involved. Walter Carr, playing the uncharacteristically sinister role of the schoolmaster, was an exception. Much more true to type was Christopher Lee who, years later, and despite one of the most extensive careers in the screen horror business, declared in an interview with Brian Pendreigh (*On Location – the Film Fan's guide to Britain and Ireland*) that *The Wicker Man* was his best film.

Wigtown was the birthplace of an actor of great distinction who became one of the most unmistakable, and mostly amiable, screen presences with a huge list of films to his credit. James Robertson Justice (1905-1975) was, ironically, famous for a kind of eccentric Englishness, for example as the pompous Sir Lancelot Spratt of the *Doctor* series beginning with *Doctor in the House* (1954).

In over sixty screen appearances he played in a wide range of films including several major dramas such as *Scott of the Antarctic* (1948), *Les Miserables* (1952), *Above us the Waves* (1955), *Land of the Pharaohs* (1955), *Campbell's Kingdom* (1957), *The Guns of Navarone* (1961) and *Mayerling* (1968). But it was as a comic character that he was known best, always good for a scene-steal in films such as *An Alligator Named Daisy* (1955), *Very Important Person* (1961), *A Pair of Briefs* (1961), *The Fast Lady* (1962) and *Chitty Chitty Bang Bang* (1968).

Although he retained connections with his roots (he served two terms as Rector of Edinburgh University 1957-60 and 1963-66), his Scottish screen appearances were relatively few. In *Rob Roy - The Highland Rogue* (1953) he played the Duke of Argyll, and in *Two Weeks in September (A Coeur Joie)* (1967) he was McLintock, providing straw bedding for Brigitte Bardot. Perhaps he should be best remembered as Dr Maclaren, the island GP in *Whisky Galore!* (1949).

● *The Wicker Man*
GB, 1973, British Lion, 86 mins. Directed by Robin Hardy. Written by Anthony Shaffer. With Edward Woodward, Britt Ekland, Diane Cilento, Christopher Lee, Ingrid Pitt, Lesley Mackie, Walter Carr and Lindsay Kemp.

Christopher Lee in **The Wicker Man** (1973, British Lion).

WMS 93

XYZ

XYZ: THE AFTERWORD

At the end of this *tour d'horizon* or stravaig on the lookout for film, is there any conclusion to offer? There certainly seems to be a lot more evidence of film activity, past and present, than might have been expected, and that is good in itself.

As a nation, we still like the movies and after the great decline in the sixties we now go to them in increasing numbers. We appreciate them even more when they are well made and relate to our own culture. Given that most do not, we still like them well enough for there to be ten million admissions to cinemas in Scotland each year, an average of two visits per head of population per annum. Cinema may not be so community based as it used to be (at least in the city centres) but the experience of the dark hall full of moving pictures and sound retains its pull.

Historically, there is a great deal more to investigate and maybe the time has come for a proper academic history of Scots and Scotland in film. It is extraordinary how many Scots found their way to America and Hollywood in the very beginnings of cinema (at least a hundred), many of them extremely interesting but, particularly those behind the camera, hardly known to us today. There were people like John Urie who was associated with Edison and is said to have *retired* from the film business in 1903, or George Gibson, the designer who painted the yellow brick road in *The Wizard of Oz*. Moreover, there are many of Scots extraction who contributed significantly to the development of the movies – William Cameron Menzies (whose family were from Aberfeldy), John Stuart Robertson, Donald Mackenzie and others – whose origins may well have influenced their work. We should know more about them.

Domestically, too, there are plenty more riches to explore. The contribution of the exhibitors to the shaping of our experience of cinema deserves more attention than it has yet had. There are sagas to be told of the families, Green, Poole, Singleton, Clarke, Donald, and the like.

Then there are the reminders that really nothing is new. It seems there have been Scots anxious to create a truly indigenous industry as long as there has been cinema. But the fact remains that when the world sees Scotland on the screen it is seldom because we put it there ourselves. Hollywood, although it has been here many times over the years, rarely helps in any way to further our own moving picture aspirations. The toe-curling versions of our culture will probably always have to be endured.Our ability to influence the screen represention of Scotland by outsiders conditioned by two hundred years of myth is minimal.

But there is good news as well. There is now a great amount of Scottish talent, based here and abroad, to deploy at all stages of the film-making process, as we have seen in several recent movies. In addition to those who have achieved major success in the last couple of years, there are several young Scottish film-makers likely to produce important work in the near future. For example, Jim Gillespie (following the success of his short film *Joy Ride*) is under contract to make a film for Twentieth Century Fox; Angus Lamont, who produced *Joy Ride* ; Peter Mullan, whose short film *Fridge*, made under the Tartan Shorts scheme, has won several international prizes; Mullan's producer on *Fridge* and two other films, Frances Higson; and Lynne Ramsay, a student at the National Film and Television School, who won the Best Short Film category at the Cannes Film Festival in 1996 for *Small Deaths*.

On the political front, there have been constitutional and economic developments in the 1990s which will allow film in Scotland a higher profile and greater resources than before (though the motives of politicians should be examined with care). If the opportunities are taken the prospects for Scotland at last achieving its potential as a small but mature and complete film culture are better than they have ever been.

BIBLIOGRAPHY

Barnes, John *The Rise of the Cinema in Great Britain*
Bishopgate Press, London, 1983
Bawden, Liz-Anne (ed.)*The Oxford Companion to Film*
Oxford University Press, Oxford, 1976
Bold, Alan (ed.) *The Letters of Hugh MacDiarmid*
Hamish Hamilton, London, 1984
Bold, Alan *Scotland: A Literary Guide* Routledge,
London, 1989
Brownlow, Kevin *Hollywood - The Pioneers*
Collins, London, 1979
Brownlow, Kevin *The Parade's Gone By...*
Secker Warburg, London, 1968
Brownlow, Kevin *Behind the Mask of Innocence*
Knopf, New York, 1995
Cinemania 95 (CD ROM) Microsoft, 1995
Cloy, David *Campbell Harper* unpublished dissertation
Daiches, David (ed.) *The New Companion to Scottish Culture*
Polygon 1993
Dick, E; Noble, A; Petrie D (eds.) *Bill Douglas: A Lanternist's
Account* BFI/Scottish Film Council, London, 1993
Dick, Eddie (ed.) *From Limelight to Satellite*
Scottish Film Council/BFI, 1990
Dickinson, Thorold *A Discovery of Cinema*
Oxford University Press, Oxford, 1971
Donaldson and Morpeth (ed.) *A Dictionary of Scottish History*
John Donald, Edinburgh, 1977
Dyja, Eddie (ed) *BFI Film and Television Handbook 1996*
British Film Institute, London 1995
Eyles, Allen *ABC - The First Name in Entertainment*
Cinema Theatre Association/BFI, London, 1993
Film Bang - Scotland's Film and Video Directory
Film Bang Core Group, Glasgow, 1995
Film Index International 1995 (CD ROM)
British Film Institute, London, 1995
Grierson, John (ed. Lockerbie) *Eyes of Democracy*
John Grierson Archive, Stirling, 1990
Hardy, Forsyth (ed.) *Grierson on Documentary*
Faber & Faber, London, 1966
Hardy, Forsyth (ed.) *John Grierson - A Documentary
Biography* Faber & Faber, London, 1979
Hardy, Forsyth (ed.) *John Grierson's Scotland*
Ramsay Head Press, Edinburgh, 1979
Hardy, Forsyth (ed.) *Grierson on the Movies*
Faber & Faber, London, 1981
Hardy, Forsyth *Scotland in Film*
Edinburgh University Press, Edinburgh, 1990
Hardy, Forsyth *Slightly Mad and Full of Dangers*
Ramsay Head Press, Edinburgh, 1992
Hunter, Allan (ed.) *Chambers Film and Television Handbook*
Chambers, Edinburgh, 1991
Kelly, Gordon E *Sherlock Holmes - Screen and Sound Guide*
Scarecrow, USA, 1994
Kemp, Philip *Lethal Innocence: The Cinema of Alexander
Mackendrick* Methuen, London, 1991
Lambert, R S (ed.) *For Filmgoers Only: The Intelligent
Filmgoers Guide to Film* Faber & Faber, London, 1934

Lindsay, Maurice and Bruce, David *Edinburgh Past and
Present* Robert Hale, London, 1990
Lindsay, Maurice (ed.) *As I Remember*
Robert Hale, London, 1979
Lowden, T *The Cinemas of Cinema City* Glasgow, 1983
Macgregor, Forbes *Greyfriars Bobby*
Gordon Wright, Edinburgh, 1990
Mackenzie, Compton (ed.) *VOX - The Radio Critic and
Broadcast Review,* Vol 1, No 3, London, 1929
McArthur, Colin (ed.) *Scotch Reels - Scotland in Cinema
and Television* British Film Institue, London, 1982
McBain, Janet *Pictures Past - Scottish Cinemas Remembered*
Moorfoot, Edinburgh, 1985
McLaren, Moray *The Shell Guide to Scotland*
Ebury Press, London, 1965
Mega Movie Guide (CD ROM) Infobusiness, USA, 1995
Oakley, C A *Fifty Years at the Pictures*
Scottish Film Council, Glasgow, 1946
Oakley, C A *Where We Came In*
George Allen & Unwin, London, 1964
Oakley, C A (et.al.) *21 Years of the Scottish Film Council*
Scottish Film Council, Glasgow 1955
Oakley, C A (et.al.) *Men With Bees in their Bonnets*
Scottish Film Council, Glasgow, 1963
Pendreigh, Brian *On Location - The Film Fan's Guide to
Britain and Ireland* Mainstream, Edinburgh, 1995
Perry, George *The Great British Picture Show*
Hart-Davis MacGibbon, London, 1974
Peter, Bruce *100 Years of Glasgow's Amazing Cinemas*
Polygon, Edinburgh, 1996
Powell, Michael *The Edge of the World*
Faber & Faber, London, 1990
Rotha, Paul and Griffith, Richard *The Film Till Now - A
Survey of World Cinema* Hamlyn, Feltham, 1967
Schickel, Richard *D W Griffith and the Birth of Film*
Pavilion, London, 1984
Scotland On Screen Study Commissioned by Scottish Enterprise
and Highlands and Islands Enterprise, SE/HIE, 1996
Scottish Screen Data 95 Scottish Film Council, Glasgow, 1995
Sherington, Jo *'To Speak Its Pride' - The Films of Scotland
Committee* Scottish Film Council, Glasgow, 1996
Stott, William *Documentary Expression and Thirties
America* University of Chicago Press, Chicago, 1986
Taylor, Walton and Liddell *A Night at the Pictures*
Dumbarton District Libraries, Dumbarton, 1992
Thomas, Brendon *The Last Picture Shows Edinburgh*
Moorfoot, Edinburgh, 1984
Thomson, David *A Biographical Dictionary of Film*
Andre Deutsch, London, 1994
Thomson, Michael *Silver Screen in the Silver City*
Aberdeen University Press, Aberdeen, 1988
Vazzana, Eugene Michael *Silent Film Necrology*
McFarland & Co, North Carolina, 1995
Walker, John (ed) *Halliwell's Filmgoer's Companion*
Harper Collins, London, 1995
Walker, John (ed) *Halliwell's Film Guide*
Harper Collins, London, 1995
Warren, Patricia *British Film Studios*
Batsford, London, 1995

FILM INDEX

GENERAL INDEX